African-American Christianity

African-American Christianity

Essays in History

Paul E. Johnson

UNIVERSITY OF CALIFORNIA PRESS
Berkeley   Los Angeles   London

University of California Press
Berkeley and Los Angeles, California
University of California Press, Ltd.
London, England
© 1994 by
The Regents of the University of California

Library of Congress Cataloging-in-Publication Data
African-American Christianity : essays in history / edited by Paul E.
  Johnson.
      p. cm.
    Includes bibliographical references and index.
    ISBN 0-520-07593-5 (alk. paper).—ISBN 0-520-07594-3 (pbk. :
  alk. paper)
        1. Afro-Americans—Religion. 2. Afro-American churches—
  History.
      3. United States—Religion.   I. Johnson, Paul E., 1942–
  BR563.N4A354   1994
  277.3′0089′96073—dc20   93-3895

                                                                  CIP

Printed in the United States of America
9 8 7 6 5 4 3 2
The paper used in this publication meets the minimum requirements
of American National Standard for Information Sciences—Permanence of Paper
for Printed Library Materials, ANSI Z39.48-1984.

CONTENTS

FOREWORD

Early in the unfolding of this valuable series of cross-disciplinary essays on African-American religion, Charles Joyner establishes one of the central themes of the collective work. Focusing on the early American experiences of the enslaved peoples of Africa in the lowcountry areas of South Carolina and Georgia, he writes, "The originality of African-American Christianity . . . lies neither in its African elements nor in its Christian elements, but in its unique and creative synthesis of both."

Joyner's emphasis on the creative and interfacing processes which produced the extraordinary gift of Black American Christian faith is echoed throughout these pages. The testimony is enriched by Albert Raboteau's thoughtful presentation of the African-American uses of the biblical story of the Exodus. Raboteau (author of the seminal study *Slave Religion*) reminds us that "slaves did not simply become Christians; they fashioned Christianity to fit their own peculiar experience of enslavement in America." Essential to that Black "experience of enslavement" was the participation of Black people in the quintessential human struggle for freedom and integrity, both internal and external.

The essays by Joyner and Raboteau, which both focus on the pre-Civil War development of African-American Christianity, open for us several other major themes and issues which pervade the entire volume. These include the crucial nature of African roots and continuities; the traumatic discontinuities imposed by the experience of slavery in the new American nation; and the struggle for freedom and humanity in the midst of and against the institution of slavery—and its successors. Throughout, the authors of the book portray the remarkable creativity that was, and continues to be, at work in the development of a Christian faith and practice which engages and encompasses not only the critical realities of Africa but also American slavery and racism, as well as the deep human hunger for freedom and integrity.

Reflecting on the continuing product of this harrowing and magnificent blend of experiences, Charles Long, one of our most wide-ranging and provocative historians of religions (whose wise voice I miss here), once said, "If we Black folk in America are Christians, then we're certainly unlike any other Christians I've met around here." For Long, this difference was cause for affirmative celebration, not complaint. A similar sense of celebration is conveyed by Margaret Washington's study of Gullah folk religion and its early development of what she calls "an autonomous Christianity." Indeed, this term describes much of African-American Christian faith. One of the continuing themes in these pages is the recognition of the powerful gifts that this non-mainstream (often "countercultural" in the richest sense of that term), energizing religious force has brought to the life of the American nation. As Washington describes, it is a force based historically at least as much on African continuities as on Christian faith, and especially on the profound experience of African-based community and the humanizing rites of initiation into that community's inner life.

Lest we are tempted to forget the weaknesses which are also part of this extraordinary African-American Christianity, Cheryl Townsend Gilkes takes a clear look at the struggle of women within the Black household of faith and ancestry. In her essay on the politics of silence, Gilkes, a sociologist of religion and a Baptist pastor, explores what she calls the "dual-sex political systems and women's traditions of conflict in African-American religion." Throughout her stimulating essay run the dual themes of Africanity and creativity. In addressing the abiding reality of the struggle for liberation in America, Gilkes focuses on the contesting dynamics of male and female life within the African-American church community. Gilkes calls on sociological and anthropological explorations of female creativity and women's institutions of autonomy within African society to help explain "the prominence (not dominance) of women in a context of patriarchy" so familiar to African life. Against that background of creative tension she makes the case that "women's roles in the African-American tradition have been constructed largely through the assertiveness and enterprise of women within a system of contested gender relations."

Of course, the fact that Gilkes's essay on women stands alone in this collection is another testimony to the disadvantages with which women have too often been forced to contend within the African-American Christian community—and within the guild of scholars who study it. Both aspects of the problem are powerfully, though inadvertently, reinforced in these pages by the work of the literary critic and historian

William L. Andrews, whose essay "is based on a reading of approximately thirty-five male-authored ministerial autobiographies published between 1875 and 1925." Why this genre—and the institutional ministry that it describes—was (and is) almost entirely dominated by males is another part of the continuing story of "contested gender relations." Here, as within so many other aspects of Black Christianity, both the presence and the absence of women serve as reminders that both faith and practice have often been shaped by all too familiar internal (as Gilkes reminds us) and external (as Andrews so eloquently brings out) struggles over the right to name, to ordain, to legitimize, and to tell the story.

Moving into the present century, Randall Burkett returns us to the dynamics of the larger context while continuing to focus within the Black family of faith, as he examines the life and ministry of the legendary Chicago pastor and national church leader Rev. Junius C. Austin (1887–1968). Here was a life indelibly marked by all the Africanity, creativity, and autonomous Americanness which were still throbbing at the heart of the Black church and its people well into the twentieth century, a long way from its original home. Insistently building a new place of pilgrimage and settlement, re-visioning and recreating the meaning of "home" in the decades leading to the 1950s, Austin and the women and men of his generation were grappling with all the insidious institutional and personal successors to American slavery, while laying the foundations for the many who would follow them. The flood of liberating faith and work which roiled through the Black churches and into the life of the nation after 1954 cannot be fully understood without considering the complex and often frustrating vitality of pioneers like this great preacher-politician and his fellow Baptist keepers of the faith.

From these reflections on J. C. Austin, we move appropriately to the work with which the volume closes: Clay Carson's sensitive clarification of the religious evolution of Martin Luther King, Jr. Continually absorbing the nurturing heritage of family, church, school, and community into the capacious center of his being, King was, in every literal and figurative sense of the term, a child of African-American Christianity. Creatively utilizing his access to the King Papers, Carson urges us to avoid the current scholarly temptation to focus exclusively on the African-American Christian core of King's life.

For although the preacher's son emerged from the complex richness of Atlanta's African-American community, he was not immediately fully engaged by what he later came to call an "undying urge to serve God and humanity through the ministry." Only after much searching of soul and intellect did he become convinced "that God had placed a responsibility upon my shoulders and the more I tried to escape it the more frustrated I would become." Rather than continue to try to escape, he entered more deeply into the house that had shaped him, the home that had been in creation ever since his foreparents in the lowcountry of Georgia brought the genius of African religious faith into a deep and abiding encounter with Christianity and with the tragically flawed greatness of America. Like Howard Thurman and Mary McCleod Bethune, like Diane Nash, Malcolm X, and Fannie Lou Hamer, like John Lewis, Bob Moses, Prathia Hall Wynn, and a host of others, King was a product of this spiritually grounded encounter. All his magnificent strengths and disappointing weaknesses are best viewed through the prism of African-American Christianity, most fully appreciated when we begin to understand what it must have meant for a God-obsessed, socially conscious young Black man to believe in the 1940s, in the South, that "the Lord had laid his hands on me."

Taken together, in their variegated richness, these essays provide a liberating way of seeing not only King but all of us, of every faith and ancestry, who have been engaged over the centuries in the beautiful and terrifying embrace known as America. Bound together as we are in the historically mandated quest for "a more perfect union" on behalf of our posterity and ourselves, we may avoid the familiar but cruelly destructive repetitions of our national racial dance only as we make use of such honest mirrors and clarifying points of view as these essays provide for us. They are essential not only for our teaching and learning, but also for the development of our lives as compassionate citizens of hope, always bringing into being a nation that does not yet exist, a nation profoundly informed by the unparalleled resources of African-American Christianity.

Vincent G. Harding
Denver, Colorado

ACKNOWLEDGMENTS

These essays began as public lectures presented at the University of Utah in autumn 1987 and spring 1989. The series was funded by a generous grant from the Quinney Foundation of Salt Lake City; it also benefited from the assistance of the Departments of History and Ethnic Studies and the Humanities Center at the University of Utah. Special thanks are due to Larry R. Gerlach, then chair of the History Department, and Ronald Coleman of Ethnic Studies. The Humanities Center provided the editor with time off from other duties, and with the valuable administrative assistance of Laurie Spetsas.

In December 1989 we presented the essays as a "Symposium on the History of African-American Christianity" at Harvard Divinity School, under the joint sponsorship of the W. E. B. Du Bois Institute for Afro-American Research at Harvard University, the Harvard Divinity School, and the University of Utah Humanities Center. Randall K. Burkett and the Du Bois Institute organized the Symposium; its success was very largely a result of their efforts. Thanks are also due to Ronald Thiemann and Preston N. Williams of the Divinity School, and to the late Nathan I. Huggins of the Du Bois Institute. David W. Wills, Evelyn Brooks Higginbotham, Robert L. Hill, and James M. Washington served as commentators, and contributed both to the symposium and to the final writing of the essays. At the University of California Press, editors Lynne Withey and Erika Büky have been skillful and patient, as has our copyeditor, Liz Gold.

CHAPTER ONE

African-Americans, Exodus, and the American Israel

Albert J. Raboteau

> *Canaan land is the land for me,*
> *And let God's saints come in.*
> *There was a wicked man,*
> *He kept them children in Egypt land.*
> *Canaan land is the land for me,*
> *And let God's saints come in.*
> *God did say to Moses one day,*
> *Say, Moses, go to Egypt land,*
> *And tell him to let my people go.*
> *Canaan land is the land for me,*
> *And let God's saints come in.*
> —SLAVE SPIRITUAL

In the encounter with European Christianity in its Protestant form in North America, enslaved Africans and their descendants encountered something new: a fully articulated ritual relationship with the Supreme Being, who was pictured in the book that the Christians called the Bible not just as the Creator and Ruler of the Cosmos, but also as the God of History, a God who lifted up and cast down nations and peoples, a God whose sovereign will was directing all things toward an ultimate end, drawing good out of evil. As the transplanted Africans reflected upon the evil that had befallen them and their parents, they increasingly turned to the language, symbols, and worldview of the Christian holy book. There they found a theology of history that helped them to make sense of their enslavement. One story in particular caught their attention and fascinated them with its implications and potential applications to their own situation: the story of Exodus. What they did with that ancient story of the Near East is the topic of this essay. I begin by surveying the history of evangelization among the slaves in order to situate and define the Christianity that confronted them in North America. Then I describe what slaves and free blacks made of Christianity by focusing on

1

their interpretation of the Exodus story, an interpretation which dif-
fered drastically, as we shall see, from that of white Americans.

CONVERSION

From the beginning of the Atlantic slave trade, Europeans claimed that
the conversion of slaves to Christianity justified the enslavement of Africans. Yet the conversion of slaves was not a high priority for colonial
planters. British colonists in North America proved especially indifferent, if not downright hostile, to the conversion of their slaves. At first,
opposition was based on the suspicion that English law forbade the enslavement of Christians and so would require slaveholders to emanci-
pate any slave who received baptism. Masters suspected that slaves
would therefore seek to be baptized in order to gain freedom. These
fears were quickly allayed by colonial legislation declaring that baptism
did not alter slave status.

With the legal obstacles aside, slaveowners for the most part still demonstrated scant interest in converting their slaves. According to the common wisdom, Christianity spoiled slaves. Christian slaves thought too
highly of themselves, became impudent, and even turned rebellious.
Moreover, Anglo-Americans were troubled by a deep-seated uneasiness
at the prospect that slaves would claim Christian fellowship with white
people. Africans were foreign; to convert them was to make them more
like the English and therefore deserving of better treatment. In fact religion, like language and skin color, constituted the colonists' identity. To
Christianize black-skinned Africans, therefore, would confuse the distinctiveness of the races and threaten the social order based upon that
distinctiveness. Finally, the labor, not the souls of the slaves, concerned
most slaveholders. Peter Kalm, a Swedish traveler in America from 1748
to 1750, perceptively described the colonists' objections to religious instruction for slaves:

> It is . . . to be pitied, that the masters of these negroes in most of the En-
> glish colonies take little care of their spiritual welfare, and let them live on
> in their Pagan darkness. There are even some, who would be very ill
> pleased at, and would by all means hinder their negroes from being in-
> structed in the doctrines of Christianity; to this they are partly led by the
> conceit of its being shameful, to have a spiritual brother or sister among
> so despicable a people; partly by thinking that they should not be able to
> keep their negroes so meanly afterwards; and partly through fear of the
> negroes growing too proud, on seeing themselves upon a level with their
> masters in religious matters.[1]

A concerted attack on these obstacles to slave conversion was
mounted by the Church of England in 1701 when it established the Soci-

ety for the Propagation of the Gospel in Foreign Parts to support missionaries to the colonies. The first task was to convince masters that they had a duty to instruct their slaves in the truths of the gospel. In tract after tract, widely distributed in the colonies, officers of the Society stressed the compatibility of Christianity with slavery. Masters need not fear that religion would ruin their slaves. On the contrary, Christianity would make them better slaves by convincing them to obey their owners out of a sense of moral duty instead of out of fear. After all, Society pamphlets explained, Christianity does not upset the social order, but supports it: "Scripture, far from making an alteration in Civil Rights, expressly directs that every man abide in the condition wherein he is called, with great indifference of mind concerning outward circumstances."[2] To prove the point, they reiterated ad nauseam the verse from Ephesians (6:5): "Slaves be obedient to your masters." The missionaries thus denied that spiritual equality implied worldly equality; they restricted the egalitarian impulse of Christianity to the realm of the spirit. So, in effect, they built a religious foundation to support slavery. As the historian Winthrop Jordan aptly put it, "These clergymen had been forced by the circumstance of racial slavery in America into propagating the Gospel by presenting it as an attractive device for slave control."[3]

The success of missions to the slaves depended largely on circumstances beyond the missionaries' control: the proportion of African-born to Creole slaves, the geographic location and work patterns of the slaves, and the ratio of blacks to whites in a given locale. Blacks in the North and in the Chesapeake region of Maryland and Virginia, for example, experienced more frequent and closer contact with whites than did those of the lowland coasts of South Carolina and Georgia, where large gangs of African slaves toiled on isolated rice plantations with only limited and infrequent exposure to whites or their religion. Even if a missionary gained regular access to slaves, the slaves did not invariably accept the Christian gospel. Some rejected it, according to missionary accounts, because of "the Fondness they have for their old Heathenish Rites, and the strong Prejudice they must have against Teachers from among those, whom they serve so unwillingly."[4] Others accepted Christianity because they hoped—colonial legislation and missionary pronouncements notwithstanding—that baptism would raise their status and ensure eventual freedom for their children, if not for themselves. One missionary in South Carolina required slaves seeking baptism to swear an oath that they did not request the sacrament out of a desire for freedom.[5] (Apparently he missed the irony.) Missionaries complained that, even after instruction and baptism, slaves still mixed Christian beliefs with the traditional practices of their African homelands.

Discouraging though the prospects were, colonial clergymen had established a few successful missions among the slaves by the early eighteenth century. When the Bishop of London distributed a list of questions in 1724 requiring ministers to describe their work among the slaves, several respondents reported impressive numbers of baptisms. The great majority, however, stated vague intentions instead of concrete achievements. During the first 120 years of black slavery in British North America, Christianity made little headway in the slave population.

Slaves were first converted in large numbers in the wake of the religious revivals that periodically swept parts of the colonies beginning in the 1740s. Accounts by George Whitefield, Gilbert Tennent, Jonathan Edwards, and other revivalists made special mention of the fact that blacks were flocking to hear the message of salvation in hitherto unseen numbers. Not only were free blacks and slaves attending revivals, but they were also taking active part in the services as exhorters and preachers. For a variety of reasons Evangelical revivalists succeeded where Anglican missionaries had failed. Whereas the Anglicans had depended upon a slow process of indoctrination, the evangelicals preached the immediate experience of conversion as the primary requirement for baptism, thereby making Christianity more quickly accessible. Because of the centrality of the conversion experience in their piety, evangelicals also tended to de-emphasize instruction and downplay learning as prerequisites of Christian life. As a result, all classes of society were welcome to participate actively in prayer meetings and revival services, in which the poor, the illiterate, and even the enslaved prayed, exhorted, and preached.

After the Revolution, revival fervor continued to flare up sporadically in the South. More and more slaves converted to Christianity under the dramatic preaching of evangelical revivalists, especially Methodists and Baptists. The emotionalism of the revivals encouraged the outward expression of religious feeling, and the sight of black and white converts weeping, shouting, fainting, and moving in ecstatic trance became a familiar, if sensationalized, feature of the sacramental and camp meeting seasons. In this heated atmosphere slaves found a form of Christian worship that resembled the religious celebrations of their African heritage. The analogy between African and evangelical styles of worship enabled the slaves to reinterpret the new religion by reference to the old, and so made this brand of Christianity seem less foreign than that of the more liturgically sedate Church of England.

The rise of the evangelical denominations, particularly the Methodists and the Baptists, threatened the established Anglican church in the South. Because they appealed to the "lower sort," the evangelicals suffered persecution at the hands of the Anglican authorities. Baptist preachers were jailed, their services were disrupted, and they were even roughed up by rowdies such as those in Virginia who thought it humorous to immerse the Baptists in mud. They were thought of as different in an unsettling sort of way. "There was a company of them in the back part of our town, and an outlandish set of people they certainly were," remarked one woman to the early Baptist historian David Benedict. "You yourself would say so if you had seen them. . . . You could hardly find one among them but was deformed in some way or other."[6] The evangelicals seemed to threaten the social as well as the religious order by accepting slaves into their societies. An anti-Baptist petition warned the Virginia assembly in 1777 that "there have been nightly meetings of slaves to receive the instruction of these teachers without the consent of their masters, which have produced very bad consequences."[7]

In the 1780s the evangelicals' implied challenge to the social order became explicit. Methodist conferences in 1780, in 1783, and again in 1784 strongly condemned slavery and tried "to extirpate this abomination," first from the ministry and then from the membership as a whole, by passing increasingly stringent regulations against slave-owning, slave-buying, and slave-selling.[8] Several Baptist leaders freed their slaves, and in 1789 the General Committee of Virginia Baptists condemned slavery as "a violent deprivation of the rights of nature."[9] In the South, these antislavery moves met with strong, immediate, and, as the leadership quickly realized, irreversible opposition. In 1785, the Baltimore Conference of the Methodist Church suspended the rules passed in 1784 by the Methodist General Conference. Methodist leader Thomas Coke explained, "We thought it prudent to suspend the minute concerning slavery, on account of the great opposition that had been given it, our work being in too infantile a state to push things to extremity." Local Baptist associations in Virginia responded to the General Committee's attack on slavery by declaring that the subject was "so abstruse" that no religious society had the right to concern itself with the issue; instead, each individual should be left "to act at discretion in order to keep a good conscience before God, as far as the laws of our land will admit."[10] As for the slaves, the goal of the Church should be the amelioration of their treatment, not their emancipation.

Thus, the evangelical challenge to slavery in the late eighteenth century failed. The intransigence of slavery once again set the limits of the Christian egalitarian impulse, just as it had in colonial days for the Anglican mission. Rapid growth of the Baptist and Methodist churches forced an ineluctable accommodation to slaveholding principles rather than the overthrow of slavery. At the beginning of the nineteenth century, Robert Semple, another Baptist historian, described the change that came over the "outlandish" Baptists after 1790: "Their preachers became

much more correct in their manner of preaching. A great many odd
tones, disgusting whoops and awkward gestures were disused. . . . Their
zeal was less mixed with enthusiasm, and their piety became more rational. They were much more numerous, and, of course, in the eyes of the
world, more respectable. Besides, they were joined by persons of much
greater weight in civil society; their congregations became more numerous. . . . This could not but influence their manners and spirit more or
less."[11] Though both Methodists and Baptists rapidly retreated from antislavery pronouncements, their struggle with the established order and
their uneasiness about slavery gave slaves, at least initially, the impression that they were "friendly toward freedom." For a short time, revivalist evangelicalism breached the wall that colonial missionaries had built
between spiritual and temporal equality. Converting slaves to Christianity could have implications beyond the spiritual, a possibility slaves were
eager to explore.

Methodists and Baptists backed away from these implications in the
1790s, but they had already taken a momentous step, and it proved irreversible. The spread of Baptist and Methodist evangelicalism between
1770 and 1820 changed the religious complexion of the South by bringing unprecedented numbers of slaves into membership in the church
and by introducing even larger numbers to at least the rudiments of
Christianity. During the antebellum decades, Christianity diffused
throughout the slave quarters, though most slaves did not hold membership in regular churches. Those slaves who did attend church generally
attended with whites, but some—in greater numbers than historians
have realized—attended separate black churches, even in the antebellum South.

Thanks to the willingness of the evangelical churches to license black
men to exhort and preach, during the 1770s and 1780s a significant
group of black preachers had begun to pastor their own people. Mainly
Baptist, since the congregational independence of the Baptists gave
them more leeway to preach than any other denomination, the black
preachers exercised a ministry that was mostly informal and extraecclesial. It would be difficult to overestimate the importance of these early
black preachers for the development of an African-American Christianity. In effect, they mediated between Christianity and the experience of
the slaves (and free blacks), interpreting the stories, symbols, and events
of the Bible to fit the day-to-day lives of those held in bondage. And
whites—try as they might—could not control this interpretation or determine its "accuracy." Slave preachers, exhorters, and church-
appointed watchmen instructed their fellow slaves, nurtured their religious development, and brought them to conversion—in some cases
without any active involvement of white missionaries or masters whatso-

ever. By nurturing Christian communities among slaves and free blacks, the pioneer black preachers began to build an independent black church.

We tend to identify the development of the independent black church with free blacks in the North, but the spirit of religious independence also created separate black churches in the South. Several "African" churches, as they were called, sprang up before 1800. Some of these black congregations were independent to the extent that they called their own pastors and officers, joined local associations with white churches, and sent their own delegates to associational meetings. However, this early independence of black preachers and churches was curtailed during the antebellum period when, in reaction to slave conspiracies, all gatherings of blacks for whatever purpose were viewed with alarm. For slaves to participate in the organization, leadership, and governance of church structures was perceived as dangerous. Nevertheless, unlikely as it may seem, black churches continued to grow in size and number in the slave South. Though nominally controlled by whites, these separate congregations were frequently led by black ministers, some free and some slaves. Often the black congregations outnumbered the largest white churches in the local church associations. Although never numerous in the South, the separate black churches were extremely important, if limited, institutional expressions of black religious independence from white control.

In the North, the abolition of slavery after the Revolution gave black congregations and clergy much more leeway to assert control over their religious lives. Federal and state disestablishment of religion created an environment of voluntarism in which church organization flourished. Between 1790 and 1820, black Episcopalians, Methodists, Baptists, and Presbyterians founded churches, exercised congregational control where possible, and struggled with white elders, bishops, and associations to gain autonomy. Among the first to succeed in doing so was Bethel African Methodist Episcopal Church in Philadelphia. Founded in 1794 by Richard Allen, a former slave who had become a licensed Methodist preacher, Bethel was organized after discriminatory treatment drove black Methodists to abandon St. George's, the white church they had supported for years. When the white elders of St. George's tried to take control of the Bethel church property, the black congregation went to court to retain their rights to the church they had built themselves. They won.

Conflicts elsewhere between black Methodists and white elders prompted Allen to call for a convention of African Methodists to meet in Philadelphia in 1816. There, delegates organized an independent black denomination, the African Methodist Episcopal (A.M.E.) Church, and elected Richard Allen as its first bishop. Two other African Methodist denominations had organized by 1821. Though the black Methodists were the first to take independent control of their church property, finances, and governance on the denominational level, northern blacks in other churches also demonstrated their spirit of independence. In all denominations, the black churches formed the institutional core for the development of free black communities. Moreover, they gave black Christians the opportunity to articulate publicly their own vision of Christianity, which stood in eloquent testimony to the existence of two Christian Americas.

Of course, independent religious institutions were out of the question for the vast majority of black Americans, who were suffering the system of slavery in the southern states. If they attended church at all, they did so with whites or under white supervision. Nevertheless, slaves developed their own, extraecclesial "invisible institution" of religious life. In the slave quarters and brush arbors, they held their own religious meetings, where they interpreted Christianity according to their experience. Conversely, they also interpreted their experience by means of the myths, stories, and symbols of Christianity. They were even willing to risk severe punishment to attend forbidden prayer meetings in order to worship God free of white control. A former slave, Lucretia Alexander, explained why:

> The preacher came and . . . he'd just say, "Serve your masters. Don't steal your master's turkey. Don't steal your master's chickens. Don't steal your master's hawgs. Don't steal your master's meat. Do whatsomever your master tell you to do." Same old thing all the time. My father would have church in dwelling houses and they had to whisper. . . . Sometimes they would have church at his house. That would be when they want a real meetin' with some real preachin'. . . . They used to sing their songs in a whisper. That was a prayer meeting from house to house . . . once or twice a week.[12]

Inevitably the slaves' Christianity contradicted that of their masters. For the slaves knew that no matter how sincerely religious the slaveowners might be, their Christianity was compatible with slavery, and the slaves' was not. The division went deep; it extended to the fundamental interpretation of the Bible. The dichotomy between the faiths of black and white Christians was described by a white Methodist minister who pastored a black congregation in Charleston, South Carolina, in 1862:

> There were near fourteen hundred colored communicants. . . . [Their] service was always thronged—galleries, lower floor, chancel, pulpit, steps and all. . . . The preacher could not complain of any deadly space between himself and his congregation. He was positively breast up to his people,

with no possible loss of . . . rapport. Though ignorant of it at the time, he remembers now the cause of the enthusiasm under his deliverances [about] the "law of liberty" and "freedom from Egyptian bondage." What was figurative they interpreted literally. He thought of but one ending of the war; they quite another. He remembers the sixty-eighth Psalm as affording numerous texts for their delectation, e.g., "Let God arise, let his enemies be scattered"; His "march through the wilderness"; "The Chariots of God are twenty thousand"; "The hill of God is as the hill of Basham"; and especially, "Though ye have lain among the pots, yet shall ye be as the wings of a dove covered with silver, and her feathers with yellow gold." . . . It is mortifying now to think that his comprehension was not equal to the African intellect. All he thought about was relief from the servitude of sin, and freedom from the bondage of the devil. . . . But they interpreted it literally in the good time coming, which of course could not but make their ebony complexion attractive, very.[13]

What the preacher is describing is the end of a long process, spanning almost two hundred and fifty years, by which slaves came to accept the gospel of Christianity. But the slaves did not simply become Christians; they fashioned Christianity to fit their own peculiar experience of enslavement in America. The preacher, like many white Christians before and since, thought there was no distance between him and "his people," no possible loss of rapport. He learned belatedly that the chasm was wide and deep. As one freedman succinctly stated, "We couldn't tell NO PREACHER NEBER how we suffer all dese long years. He know'd nothin' 'bout we."[14]

EXODUS

No single symbol captures more clearly the distinctiveness of Afro-American Christianity than the symbol of Exodus. From the earliest days of colonization, white Christians had represented their journey across the Atlantic to America as the exodus of a New Israel from the bondage of Egypt into the Promised Land of milk and honey. For black Christians, the imagery was reversed: the Middle Passage had brought them to Egypt land, where they suffered bondage under a new Pharaoh. White Christians saw themselves as the New Israel; slaves identified themselves as the Old. This is, as Vincent Harding remarked, one of the abiding and tragic ironies of our history: the nation's claim to be the New Israel was contradicted by the Old Israel still enslaved in her midst.[15]

American preachers, politicians, and other orators found in the story of Exodus a rich source of metaphors to explicate the unfolding history of the nation. Each section of the narrative—the bondage in Egypt, the rescue at the Red Sea, the wandering in the wilderness, and the entrance into the Promised Land—provided a typological map to reconnoiter the moral terrain of American society. John Winthrop, the leader of the great Puritan expedition to Massachusetts Bay, set the pattern in his famous "A Modell of Christian Charity" sermon composed on his ship in 1630. Having elaborated the covenantal obligations that the settlers had contracted with God, echoing the Sinai covenant of Israel with Yahweh, Winthrop concluded his discourse with a close paraphrase of Moses' farewell instruction to Israel (Deuteronomy 30):

> Beloved there is now sett before us life, and good, deathe and evill in that wee are Commaunded this day to love the Lord our God, and to love one another, to walke in his wayes and to keepe his Commaundements and his Ordinance, and his lawes, and the Articles of our Covenant with him that wee may live and be multiplied, and that the Lord our God may blesse us in the land whither we goe to posess it: But if our heartes shall turne away soe that wee will not obey, but shall be seduced and worship . . . other Gods, our pleasures, and proffitts, and serve them; it is propounded unto this day, wee shall surely perishe out of the good Land whither wee passe over this vast Sea to possesse it. . . .[16]

Notice the particular application that Winthrop draws from the Exodus story: possession of the land is contingent upon observing the moral obligations of the covenant with God. It is a mark of the greatness of Winthrop's address that the obligations he emphasizes are justice, mercy, affection, meekness, gentleness, patience, generosity, and unity—not the qualities usually associated with taking or keeping possession of a land. Later and lesser sermons would extol much more active and aggressive virtues for the nation to observe.

Already in Winthrop's address there is an explicit notion of reciprocity between God's Will and America's Destiny: God has made a contract with us; if we live up to our part of the bargain, so will He. This pattern of reciprocity between Divine Providence and American Destiny had tremendous hortative power, which Puritan preachers exploited to the full over the next century and more in the jeremiad. In sermon after sermon, a succession of New England divines deciphered droughts, epidemics, Indian attacks, and other misfortunes as tokens of God's displeasure over the sins of the nation. Unless listeners took the opportunity to humble themselves, repent, and reform, they might expect much more of the same.

Implicit in this relationship of reciprocity there lay a danger: the danger of converting God's Will into America's Destiny. Winthrop was too good a Puritan to succumb to this temptation. Protected by his belief in the total sovereignty of God, he knew that the relationship between

God's Will and human action was one-sided and that the proper human attitude was trust in God, not confidence in man. God's Will was the measure of America's deeds, not vice versa. Of course, no American preacher or politician would have disagreed, but as time went on the salient features of the American Exodus story changed. As the actual experience of migration with all its fear and tenuousness receded, Americans tended to lose sight of their radical dependence upon God and to celebrate their own achievements as a nation.

We can catch sight of the change by comparing the tone of Winthrop's "A Modell of Christian Charity" with the mood of an election sermon entitled "The United States Elevated to Glory and Honor," preached by Ezra Stiles in 1783. Flushed with excitement over the success of the Revolution, Stiles dwelled at length on the unfolding destiny of the new nation. Quoting, like Winthrop, from the book of Deuteronomy, Stiles struck a celebratory rather a hortatory note:

> "And to make thee high above all nations which he hath made, in praise, and in name, and in honour; and that thou mayest be an holy people unto the Lord thy God. . . ." I have assumed [this] text as introductory to a discourse upon the political welfare of God's American Israel, and as allusively prophetic of the future prosperity and splendour of the United States. Already does the new constellation of the United States begin to realize this glory. It has already risen to an acknowledged sovereignty among the republicks and kingdoms of the world. And we have reason to hope, and I believe to expect, that God has still greater blessings in store for this vine which his own right hand hath planted, to make us "high among the nations in praise, and in name, and in honour." [17]

Stiles went on at great length to identify the reasons for his optimism about America's present and future preeminence, including the fact that "in our civil constitutions, those impediments are removed which obstruct the progress of society towards perfection." [18] It's a long way from Winthrop's caution to Stiles' confidence, from an "Errand in the Wilderness" to "progress towards perfection." In Stiles' election sermon we can perceive God's New Israel becoming the Redeemer Nation. The destiny of the New Israel was to reach the pinnacle of perfection and to carry liberty and the gospel around the globe.

In tandem with this exaggerated vision of America's Destiny went an exaggerated vision of human capacity. In an increasingly confident and prosperous nation, it was difficult to avoid shifting the emphasis from divine sovereignty to human ability. Historian Conrad Cherry has succinctly summarized the change in perception of America's destiny: "Believing that she had escaped the wickedness of the Old World and the guilt of the past, God's New Israel would find it all too easy to ignore her vices and all too difficult to admit a loss of innocence." [19]

Among the realities this optimistic vision ignored was the presence of another, darker Israel:

America, America, foul and indelible is thy stain! Dark and dismal is the cloud that hangs over thee, for thy cruel wrongs and injuries to the fallen sons of Africa. The blood of her murdered ones cries to heaven for vengeance against Thee. . . . You may kill, tyrannize, and oppress as much as you choose, until our cry shall come up before the throne of God; for I am firmly persuaded, that he will not suffer you to quell the proud, fearless and undaunted spirits of the Africans forever; for in his own time, he is able to plead our cause against you, and to pour out upon you the ten plagues of Egypt.[20]

So wrote Maria Stewart, a free black reform activist in Boston, in 1831. Her words were addressed to an America that projected itself as the probable site of the coming Millennium, Christ's thousand-year reign of peace and justice. From the perspective of slaves, and of free blacks like Maria Stewart, America was Egypt, and as long as she continued to enslave and oppress Black Israel, her destiny was in jeopardy. America stood under the judgment of God, and unless she repented, the death and destruction visited upon Biblical Egypt would be repeated here. The retribution envisaged was quite literal, as Mary Livermore, a white governess, discovered when she overheard a prayer uttered by Aggy, the slave housekeeper, whose daughter had just been brutally whipped by her master:

Thar's a day a comin'! Thar's a day a comin'. . . . I hear de rumblin' ob de chariots! I see de flashin' ob de guns! White folks' blood is a-runnin' on de ground like a riber, an' de dead's heaped up dat high! . . . Oh, Lor'! hasten de day when de blows, an' de bruises, an' de aches, an' de pains, shall come to de white folks, an' de buzzards shall eat 'em as dey's dead in de streets. Oh, Lor'! roll on de chariots, an' gib de black people rest an' peace.[21]

Nor did slaves share the exaggerated optimism of white Americans about human ability. Trapped in a system from which there seemed little, if any, possibility of deliverance by human actions, they emphasized trusting in the Lord instead of trusting in man. Sermon after sermon and prayer after prayer echoed the words that Moses spoke on the banks of the Red Sea: "Stand still and see the salvation of the Lord." Although the leaders of the three principal slave revolts—Gabriel Prosser in 1800, Denmark Vesey in 1822, and Nat Turner in 1831—all depended upon the Bible to justify and motivate rebellion, the Exodus story was used mainly to nurture internal resistance, not external revolution among the slaves.

The story of Exodus contradicted the claim made by white Christians that God intended Africans to be slaves. It seemed to prove that slavery was against God's will and that slavery would inevitably end, although the when and the how remained hidden in Divine Providence. Christian slaves thus applied the Exodus story, whose end they knew, to their own experience of slavery, which had not yet ended, and so gave meaning and purpose to lives threatened by senseless and demeaning brutality. Exodus functioned as an archetypal myth for the slaves. The sacred history of God's liberation of his people would be or was being reenacted in the American South. A white Union Army chaplain working among freedmen in Decatur, Alabama, commented disapprovingly on the slaves' fascination with Exodus: "There is no part of the Bible with which they are so familiar as the story of the deliverance of Israel. Moses is their *ideal* of all that is high, and noble, and perfect, in man. I think they have been accustomed to regard Christ not so much in the light of a *spiritual* Deliverer, as that of a second Moses who would eventually lead *them* out of their prison-house of bondage." [22]

Thus, in the story of Israel's exodus from Egypt, the slaves envisioned a future radically different from their present. In times of despair, they remembered Exodus and found hope enough to endure the enormity of their suffering. As a slave named Polly eloquently explained to her mistress, "We poor creatures have need to believe in God, for if God Almighty will not be good to us some day, why were we born? When I heard of his delivering his people from bondage, I know it means the poor Africans." [23]

By appropriating the story of Exodus as their own story, black Christians articulated their own sense of peoplehood. Exodus symbolized their common history and common destiny. It would be hard to exaggerate the intensity of their identification with the children of Israel. A.M.E. pastor William Paul Quinn demonstrated how literal the metaphor of Exodus could become when he exhorted black Christians, "Let us comfort and encourage one another, and keep singing and shouting, great is the Holy One of Israel in the midst of us. Come thou Great Deliverer, once more awake thine almighty arm, and set thy African captives free." [24] As Quinn's exhortation reveals, it was prayer and worship that made the identification seem so real. Sermons, prayers, and songs recreated in the imagination of successive generations the travail and triumph of Israel. Exodus became dramatically real, especially in the songs and prayer meetings of the slaves, who reenacted the story as they shuffled in the ring dance they called "the shout." In the ecstasy of worship, time and distance collapsed, and the slaves literally became the children of Israel. With the Hebrews, they traveled dry-shod through the Red Sea; they, too, saw Pharaoh's army "get drownded"; they stood beside Moses on Mount Pisgah and gazed out over the Promised Land; they crossed Jordan under Joshua and marched with him around the

walls of Jericho. Their prayers for deliverance resonated with the expe-
riential power of these liturgical dramas.

Identification with Israel, then, gave the slaves a communal identity
as a special, divinely favored people. This identity stood in stark contrast
with racist propaganda, which depicted them as inferior to whites, as
destined by nature and providence to the status of slaves. Exodus, the
Promised Land, and Canaan were inextricably linked in the slaves'
minds with the idea of freedom. Canaan referred not only to the condition of freedom but also to the territory of freedom—the North or Can-
ada. As Frederick Douglass recalled, "A keen observer might have de-
tected in our repeated singing of 'O Canaan, sweet Canaan, / I am
bound for the land of Canaan,' something more than a hope of reaching
heaven. We meant to reach the *North,* and the North was our Canaan."[25]
Slave owners, too, were well aware that the Exodus story could be a
source of unflattering and even subversive analogies. It took no genius
to identify Pharaoh's army in the slave song "My army cross ober, My
army cross ober / O Pharaoh's army drownded."

The slaves' faith that God would free them just as he had freed Israel
of old was validated by Emancipation. "Shout the glad tidings o'er
Egypt's dark sea / Jehovah has triumphed, his people are free!" the ex-
slaves sang in celebration of freedom. But it did not take long for the
freedmen to realize that Canaan Land still lay somewhere in the distance. "There must be no looking back to Egypt," a band of refugee
slaves behind Union lines were instructed by a slave preacher in 1862.
"Israel passed forty years in the wilderness, because of their unbelief.
What if we cannot see right off the green fields of Canaan, Moses could
not. He could not even see how to cross the Red Sea. If we would have
greater freedom of body, we must free ourselves from the shackles of
sin. . . . We must snap the chain of Satan, and educate ourselves and our
children."[26]

But as time went on and slavery was succeeded by other forms of
racial oppression, black Americans seemed trapped in the wilderness no
matter how hard they tried to escape. Former slave Charles Davenport
voiced the despair of many when he recalled, "De preachers would exhort us dat us was de chillen o' Israel in de wilderness an' de Lord done
sent us to take dis land o' milk and honey. But how us gwine-a take land
what's already been took?"[27] When race relations reached a new low in
the 1880s and 1890s, several black leaders turned to Africa as the black
Promised Land. Proponents of emigration, such as Henry McNeal
Turner, urged Afro-Americans to abandon the American wilderness for
an African Zion. Few black Americans, however, heeded the call to emi-
grate to Africa; most continued to search for their Promised Land here.
And as decade succeeded decade they repeated the story of Exodus,

which for so many years had kept their hopes alive. It was, then, a very old and evocative tradition that Martin Luther King, Jr., echoed in his last sermon:

> We've got some difficult days ahead. But it really doesn't matter with me now. Because I've been to the mountaintop. Like anybody I would like to live a long life. Longevity has its place. But I'm not concerned about that now. I just want to do God's will. And He's allowed me to go up to the mountain. And I've seen the Promised Land. And I may not get there with you. But I want you to know tonight that we as a people will get to the Promised land.[28]

A period of over three hundred years stretches between John Winthrop's vision of an American Promised Land and that of Martin Luther King. The people whom Winthrop addressed long ago took possession of their Promised Land; the people whom King addressed still wait to enter theirs. For three centuries, white and black Americans have dwelt in the same land. For at least two of those centuries, they have shared the same religion. And yet, during all those years, their national and religious identities have been radically opposed. It need not have been so. After all, Winthrop's version of Exodus and King's were not so far apart. Both men understood that charity is the charter that gives title to the Promised Land. Both taught that mercy, gentleness, and justice are the terms for occupancy. Both believed that the conditions of the contract had been set by God, not by man. At times in our history, the two visions have nearly coincided, as they did in the antislavery stance of the early evangelicals, or in the abolitionist movement, or in Lincoln's profound realization that Americans were an "almost chosen people," or in the civil rights movement of our own era. Yet, despite these moments of coherence, the meaning of the Exodus story for America has remained fundamentally ambiguous. Is America Israel, or is she Egypt?

NOTES

1. Peter Kalm, *Travels into North America*, 2d ed. (London: 1772), reprinted in vol. 13 of *A General Collection of the Best and Most Interesting Voyages and Travels*, ed. John Pinkerton (London: 1812), 503.

2. Thomas Secker, Bishop of London, *A Sermon Preached before the Incorporated Society for the Propagation of the Gospel in Foreign Parts . . . February 20, 1740–1* (London: 1741), reprinted in Frank J. Klingberg, *Anglican Humanitarianism in Colonial New York* (Philadelphia: Church Historical Society, 1940), 223.

3. Winthrop D. Jordan, *White over Black: American Attitudes toward the Negro, 1550–1812* (Baltimore, Md.: Penguin, 1969), 191.

4. Secker, "A Sermon Preached," 217.

5. Edgard Legare Pennington, *Thomas Bray's Associates and Their Work among the Negroes* (Worcester, Mass.: American Antiquarian Society, 1939), 25.

6. David Benedict, *Fifty Years among the Baptists* (New York: Sheldon & Company, 1860), 93–94.

7. Charles F. James, ed., *Documentary History of the Struggle for Religious Liberty in Virginia* (Lynchburg, Va.: J. P. Bell, 1900), 84–85.

8. Donald G. Mathews, *Slavery and Methodism: A Chapter in American Morality, 1780–1845* (Princeton, N.J.: 1965), 293–99.

9. David Barrow, *Circular Letter* (Norfolk, Va.: [1798]), 4–5; Robert B. Semple, *A History of the Rise and Progress of the Baptists in Virginia*, ed. George W. Beale (Philadelphia: American Baptist Publication Society, 1894), 105.

10. Francis Asbury, *The Journal and Letters of Francis Asbury,* ed. Elmer T. Clark, J. Manning Potts, and Jacob S. Payton, 3 vols. (Nashville, Tenn.: Abingdon, 1958), 2: 284; Wesley M. Gewehr, *The Great Awakening in Virginia, 1740–1790* (Durham, N.C.: Duke University Press, 1930), 240–41, 244–48.

11. Semple, *History of Baptists in Virginia,* 59.

12. George P. Rawick, ed., *The American Slave: A Composite Autobiography,* 19 vols. (Westport, Conn.: Greenwood, 1972), vol. 8, *Arkansas Narratives,* pt. 1, p. 35.

13. Abel McGee Chreitzberg, *Early Methodism in the Carolinas* (Nashville, Tenn.: Publishing House of the M[ethodist] E[piscopal] C[hurch], South, 1897), 158–59.

14. Austa Melinda French, *Slavery in South Carolina and the Ex-Slaves; or, The Port Royal Mission* (New York: W. M. French, 1862), 127.

15. Vincent Harding, "The Uses of the Afro-American Past," in *The Religious Situation, 1969,* ed. Donald R. Cutter (Boston: Beacon, 1969), 829–40.

16. John Winthrop, "A Modell of Christian Charity," in *Winthrop Papers* (Boston: Massachusetts Historical Society, 1931), 2: 282–84, 292–95. Reprinted in Conrad Cherry, *God's New Israel: Religious Interpretations of American Destiny* (Englewood Cliffs, N.J.: Prentice-Hall, 1971), 43.

17. Ezra Stiles, "The United States Elevated to Glory and Honor," in *A Sermon Preached before Gov. Jonathan Trumbull and the General Assembly . . . May 8th, 1783,* 2d. ed. (Worcester, Mass.: Isaiah Thomas, 1785), 5–9, 58–75, 88–92, 95–98. Reprinted in Cherry, *God's New Israel,* 82–84.

18. Ibid., in Cherry, *God's New Israel,* 84.

19. Cherry, *God's New Israel,* 66.

20. Marilyn Richardson, ed., *Maria W. Stewart, America's First Black Woman Political Writer: Essays and Speeches* (Bloomington: Indiana University Press, 1987), 39–40.

21. Mary A. Livermore, *My Story of the War: A Woman's Narrative of Four Years Personal Experience . . .* (Hartford, Conn.: A. D. Worthington, 1889), 260–61.

22. William G. Kephart to L. Tappan, May 9, 1864, American Missionary Association Archives, Decatur, Ala., Reel 2; also in *American Missionary* 8, no. 7 (July 1864), 179.

23. As cited in diary entry of 12 December 1857 by her mistress: Barbara Leigh Smith Bodichon, *An American Diary, 1857–1858,* ed. Joseph W. Reed, Jr. (London: Routledge & Kegan Paul, 1972), 65.

24. W. Paul Quinn, *The Sword of Truth Going "Forth Conquering and to Conquer"; The Origin, Horrors, and Results of Slavery Faithfully and Minutely Described . . .* (1834); reprinted in *Early Negro Writing, 1760–1837,* ed. Dorothy Porter (Boston: Beacon, 1971), 635.

25. Frederick Douglass, *Life and Times of Frederick Douglass: Written by Himself* (1892; reprint, New York: Crowell-Collier, 1969) 159–60.

26. American Missionary 6, no. 2 (February 1862): 33.

27. Norman R. Yetman, ed., *Voices from Slavery* (New York: Holt, Rinehart and Winston, 1970), 75.

28. Martin Luther King, Jr., sermon of April 3, 1968, delivered at Mason Temple, Memphis, Tenn., reprinted in *A Testament of Hope: The Essential Writings of Martin Luther King, Jr.,* ed. James Melvin Washington (San Francisco: Harper & Row, 1986), 286.

CHAPTER TWO

"Believer I Know"
The Emergence of African-American Christianity

Charles Joyner

Suffering produces endurance,
endurance produces character, and
character produces hope.
—ROMANS 5: 3–4

Glory Hallelujah
Believer I know
I done cross Jurden
Believer I know
—GEORGIA SLAVE SONG
SUNG BY KATIE BROWN

The little ship with its human cargo sailed up the Altamaha river. Major Pierce Butler had purchased a large number of Africans for his Georgia plantation in 1803. When the vessel arrived at Butler's Island, the Major's plantation manager informed him, "You have no people that can talk with them but they are so smart your young Wenches are Speculating very high for husbands."[1] In the new physical and social environment of the lowcountry, African men and women of various ethnic groups mixed in ways that did not occur in Africa. Similarly, the varied African cultures were increasingly fused in combinations that did not exist in Africa. A new culture, predominantly African in origin, but different from any *particular* African culture, began to take shape.

During the formative years of African-American culture, most of the mature slaves on many South Carolina and Georgia lowcountry plantations came either directly from Africa or from the Caribbean. According to a Georgia slave, "Doze Africans alluz call one anudduh 'countryman'. . . . Dey know ef dey come frum duh same tribe by duh mahk dey hab.

18

Some hab a long mahk an some hab a roun un. Udduhs weah eahring in duh eah. Some weahs it in duh lef eah an doze from anudduh tribe weahs it in duh right eah."[2]

There was a great mixture of African ethnic groups in the lowcountry, but African ethnic distinctions continued to be made among the slaves as long as slavery lasted. Coromantees from the Gold Coast were said to be ferocious and unforgiving, but hardy and therefore favored as field hands. Congos and Angolas were alleged to be handsome and docile, but weak and predisposed to run away. And Ibos from the Niger Delta were considered sickly, melancholy, and suicidal. On any given morning in a lowcountry rice field, an enslaved African would meet more Africans from more ethnic groups than he or she would have encountered in a lifetime in Africa.[3]

To underestimate the Africanity of African-American Christianity is to rob the slaves of their heritage. But to overestimate the Africanity of African-American Christianity is to rob the slaves of their creativity. Africans were creative in Africa; they did not cease to be creative as involuntary settlers in America. The African-American Christianity that developed was neither a dark version of the Christianity preached by slaveholders nor a continuation of African religion disguised as Christianity. The story of the emergence of African-American Christianity is a story of an emergent African-American culture as well as of residual African cultures, a story of innovation as well as of tradition, a story of change as well as of continuity.

MUSLIM SLAVES

The old man always wore a fez and a long coat, just as he would have done in Africa. He was the driver on Thomas Spalding's Sapelo Island plantation, near Darien, Georgia. A Georgia rice planter's daughter who visited the Spalding plantation in the 1850s wrote of the old man and his family many years later: "They were all tall and well-formed, with good features. They conversed with us in English, but in talking among themselves they used a foreign tongue that no one else understood. . . . These Negroes held themselves aloof from the others as if they were conscious of their own superiority." The old man's name was Bilali Mohomet, and he was the great-grandfather of Katie Brown and Shadrach Hall. According to Shad, Bilali and his wife "pray at sun-up and face duh sun on duh knees an bow tuh it tree times, kneelin on a lill mat." Katie added, "Dey wuz bery puhticluh bout duh time dey pray an dey ber regluh bout duh hour. Wen duh sun come up, wen it straight obuh head an wen it set, das duh time dey pray. Dey bow tuh duh sun an hab lill mat tuh kneel on. Duh beads is on a long string. Bilali he pull bead an he say, 'Belambi, Hakabara, Mahamadu.' Phoebe she say, 'Ameen, Ameen.' " When Bilali died, he was buried with his prayer rug and his Quiran. Many former Gullah slaves remembered their ancestors praying in the Muslim fashion.[4]

Bilali and other Muslim slaves on the Georgia coast carefully observed Muslim fasts and feast days. Katie Brown recalled the Muslim rice cakes made by her grandmother: "She make funny flat cake she call 'saraka'. She make um same day ebry yeah, an it big day. Wen dey finish, she call us in, all duh chillun, an put in hans lill flat cake an we eats it. Yes'm, I membuh how she make it. She wash rice, an po off all duh watuh. She let wet rice sit all night, an in mawnin rice is all swell. She tak dat rice an put it in wooden mawtuh, an beat it tuh paste wid wooden pestle. She add honey, sometime shuguh, an make it in flat cake wid uh hans. 'Saraka' she call um." Shad Hall remembered that his grandmother made the pieces of saraka into dumplings. Katie Brown said her grandmother rolled the rice paste into balls "the size of small fowls' eggs" and set them aside to harden. When the saraka was ready, the children were lined up so that the grandmother could make certain their hands were clean. Any child whose hands were not clean had to go wash them. The other children had to wait until everyone was ready. As she handed each child some of the saraka, the grandmother would say either "Saraka dee" or "Ah-me, Ah-me."[5]

It is important to note that Christianity enjoyed no religious monopoly among Gullah slaves. Christianity had to compete in a religiously diverse environment. African-born slaves, for instance, often maintained their traditional religious outlooks. "At the time I first went to Carolina, there were a great many African slaves in the country," recalled fugitive slave Charles Ball. "Many of them believed there were several gods; some of whom were good, and others evil." Other African-born slaves embraced Islam. There was a considerable Muslim presence in the Georgia and South Carolina lowcountry. "I knew several who must have been, from what I have since learned, Mohammedans," Ball noted. "There was one man on this plantation who prayed five times every day, always turning his face to the east." It has been estimated that as many as twenty percent of the enslaved Africans in America embraced Islam. There is evidence that Muslim slaves in coastal Georgia deliberately sought marriage partners of the same faith as late as the second generation. On some lowcountry plantations, Muslim slaves were given a ration of beef instead of pork.[6]

THE SLAVEHOLDERS' MISSION TO THE SLAVES

The Reverend Charles Colcock Jones stood in his Savannah pulpit and, in his ringing voice, delivered an eloquent sermon urging slaveholders to instruct their slaves in the principles of the Christian religion. Not only would religious instruction save the slaves' souls, he said, but it would also create "a greater subordination" among the slaves and teach them "respect and obedience [to] all those whom God in his providence has placed in authority over them." The Reverend Jones was not only pastor of Savannah's First Presbyterian Church but also the master of three rice plantations and more than one hundred slaves in Liberty County, Georgia. While he seemed genuinely concerned for the salvation of his slaves' souls, there is no question that he consciously and deliberately used religion as an instrument of discipline and control. A faithful servant, Jones believed, was more profitable than an unfaithful servant. So he attempted to tailor Christianity to keep bondsmen reconciled to their bondage. Jones and similarly inclined slaveholders wanted their slaves delivered from "savage heathenism" to the true light of the Christian gospel, preferably of the Episcopal or Presbyterian persuasion.[7]

Early low-country planters were reluctant to tolerate missionary efforts among their slaves. "There has always been a strong repugnance amongst the planters, against their slaves becoming members of any religious society," Charles Ball wrote in 1837. "They fear the slaves, by attending the meetings and listening to the preachers, may imbibe the morality they teach, the notions of equality and liberty, maintained in the gospel." Planters doubted that preachers could be depended upon to defend the Peculiar Institution. "The abolition measures have excited such a spirit of jealousy and suspicion that some planters will not listen to the introduction of religion on their places," wrote a Charleston clergyman in 1836. Gradually, however, at least some ministers won the trust of the slaveholders and began missionary work among the slaves. Henry Brown, a former slave near Charleston, recalled that his master's slaves "went to meeting two nights a week and on Sunday they went to Church, where they had a white preacher Dr. Rose hired to preach to them."

Masters came more and more to believe that religion sustained rather than threatened slavery, and slave churchgoing came to seem less and less threatening. By the 1830s, lowcountry masters were giving increased attention to controlling the *content* of slave religion. A Georgia planter's daughter remembered her father's efforts to evangelize his slaves. "There was Sabbath School each Sunday afternoon, under the big live oaks," she recalled. "My Father would read from the Bible and we would tell simple stories to the children and many grownups, who came with them."[8] In 1837 the Reverend Jones published a *Catechism* especially for slaves. One section was devoted to "Duties of Masters and Servants." In it Jones, too fastidious to call a slave a slave, addressed a series of questions to the "servants":

Q. What are the Servants to count their Masters worthy of?
A. All honour.
Q. How are they to try to please their Masters?
A. Please them well in all things, not answering again.
Q Is it right for a Servant when commanded to do anything to be sullen and slow, and answering his master again?
A. No.
Q. But suppose the Master is hard to please, and threatens and punishes more than he ought, what is the Servant to do?
A. Do his best to please him.
Q. Are Servants at liberty to tell lies and deceive their Masters?
A. No.
Q. If servants will faithfully do their duty and Serve God in their stations as Servants, will they be respected of men, and blessed and honoured of God, as well as others?
A. Yes.[9]

Slaveholders supported religious instruction partly out of sincere Christian concern for the salvation of the slaves. On his deathbed one Charleston master instructed his children, "I wish you also to give all the indulgence you possibly can to the negroes in going to Church, and making them repeat their questions, for this reason that if neglected we will have to answer for the loss of their souls." The Christianity disseminated by slaveholders, however, was very selective, emphasizing obedience in the here and now as much as salvation in the hereafter. The slaves were going to get religion whether their masters liked it or not, many masters reasoned, so making religion safe for slavery became a matter of high priority. South Carolina planter Robert F. W. Allston described his slaves as "attentive to religious instruction, and greatly improved in intelligence and morals, in domestic relations, etc. . . . Indeed, the degree of intelligence which as a class they are acquiring is worthy of deep consideration." If the planters evidenced a genuine concern for their slaves' spiritual welfare, they also recognized that religion was a more subtle, more humane, and more effective means of control than the whip.[10]

There are incessant references in the Jones family correspondence to the spiritual as well as physical welfare of the slaves. Sandy Maybank, then working as the head carpenter at Montevideo plantation in coastal Georgia, received a letter from the man who claimed to own him. "I trust," Charles Colcock Jones wrote to Maybank, "that you are holding on to your high profession of the Gospel of our Lord and Saviour Jesus Christ at all times, and constantly watch and pray." "You know our life and health are in His hands," Jones constantly counseled his driver Catoe, "and it is a great comfort to me to have a good hope that you love Him, and do put all your trust in our Lord and Saviour Jesus Christ, who is a precious Saviour to us in life and in death." And Jones was quite pleased when Catoe sent back such replies as "Your people all seem to be doing very well. They attend praise and go to church regularly whenever there is preaching in reach." Another Jones driver, Andrew, wrote, "About a month ago Revd Mr Law administered the sacraments in Sunbury and among several black people that joined the church was my daughter Dinah, and I trust that she may practice what she professes, for as Mas John says it is no light thing to be a christian, for we may play with the lightning and the rattle snake, but dont trifle with Almighty God 'lest he tear you to pieces in his anger and then be never to deliver you.'"[11]

To suggest that lowcountry slaveholders cynically reduced Christianity to patience, humility, and the fear of sin, or that they were more concerned with the discipline of slaves than with the salvation of souls, would be untrue to history. "In our philosophy, right is the highest expediency," James Henley Thornwell insisted, "and obedience to God the firmest security of communities as well as individuals. We have not sought the protection of our property in the debasement of our species; we have not maintained our own interests in this world, by the deliberate sacrifice of the eternal interests of the thousands who look to us for the way to salvation." Nevertheless, it would also be untrue to history not to point out that much of the slaveholders' missionary motivation was their understanding that preaching had a significant effect on slave discipline. Ministers went out of their way to appease the slaveholders by approaching slave religion with the utmost discretion. Masters knew that so long as the slaves were listening to a trusted white preacher, they could not (at least for the moment) be listening to a subversive black one.[12]

Some slaveholders opposed the religious education of slaves as useless. Certainly not all slaveholders believed that slave religion would promote slave control. One reason for doubt was their belief in black Christians' excessive propensity for backsliding. In fact, black Christians were no more and no less immune to backsliding than were white Christians, even with the constant religious instruction that was the stock-in-trade of such slaveholders as the Reverend Charles Colcock Jones. Others maintained that the slaves were not fully human creatures and were therefore incapable of reasoning and of learning the truths of the Christian religion. Still others feared the intense emotionalism preferred by the slaves as the appropriate form of worship. The Reverend Jones encountered considerable opposition from his fellow slaveholders until he was able to prove to their satisfaction that he favored only quiet and sedate worship services. Others, such as the Georgia slaveholders Pierce Butler and James Hamilton Couper, were simply indifferent to the reli-

gious education of their slaves. At Couper's showplace Georgia plantation, Swedish visitor Fredericka Bremer tried to teach a gathering of the
slave children to recite the Lord's Prayer. "The children grinned,
laughed, showed their white teeth," she said, "and evinced very plainly
that none of them knew what that wonderful prayer meant nor that they
had a Father in heaven."[13]

White preachers had to face the dilemma that their Christianity was—
at least potentially—subversive of slavery. During the 1834 South Carolina legislative debate over the prohibition on teaching slaves to read and
write, Whitemarsh Seabrook noted that anyone who wanted slaves to
read the *entire* Bible belonged in "a room in the Lunatic Asylum." To be
fair, the ministers were more than mere sycophants of cynical slaveholders. They did not select only the texts that promoted order and discipline among the slaves. But they could not fail to realize that while
Christianity promoted order among the slaves, it also contained the
seeds of disorder. They certainly would not preach to their congregations that Pharoah had enslaved the children of Israel and had held
them in bondage in Egypt, that the Lord had then visited plagues on the
slaveholders, or that Moses had led the slaves in a mass escape out of
bondage in Egypt to the Promised Land.[14]

If the white ministers shied away from scriptural passages with clear
analogies to the condition of the slaves, they did preach the equality of
all in the sight of God and the equality of human sinfulness. The Reverend James Henley Thornwell put it thus:

> It is a publick testimony to our faith, that the Negro is of one blood with
> ourselves—that he has sinned as we have, and that he has an equal interest
> with us in the great redemption. Science, falsely so-called, may attempt
> to exclude him from the brotherhood of humanity. Men may be seeking
> eminence and distinction by arguments which link them with the brute;
> but the instinctive impulses of our nature, combined with the plainest dec-
> larations of the word of God, lead us to recognize in his form and linea-
> ments—in his moral, religious, and intellectual nature—the same human-
> ity in which we glory as the image of God. We are not ashamed to call him
> our brother.

Christianity, such ministers preached, imposed obligations not just on
the slaves but on their earthly masters as well. Both master and slave on
this earth would be held to the same account before the heavenly Master. As the Bible taught servants to obey their masters, these ministers
preached, so it required masters to rule their servants wisely, and it required the rich to use their riches to do good.[15]

Thus was the slaveholders' theological dilemma posed: as Christians,
they were committed to the religious instruction of their slaves, but the

religion preached to the slaves also called the masters to account. Masters were as subject as slaves were to the requirements of Christianity. The idea of equality before God created a problem of role boundaries and emphasized tensions and anomalies within the institution of slavery that could not easily be ignored. Governor Robert F. W. Allston believed that the "best inducement to keep the slaves both Christian and quiescent" was "example on our part; next a just, consistent, systematic administration of domestic government."[16]

SLAVE WORSHIP

The preacher began softly and conversationally, his voice cool and level. But slowly and gradually he built toward a more pronounced, more powerful rhythm. The slaves in the congregation did not receive his words passively. As the rhythm rose and fell, they became participants as well. The congregational response was essential to worship, a religious requirement. Just as in Africa, such antiphony exemplified the solidarity of the community even as the sermon called forth the profoundest expression of the individual: neither I-Thou nor I-you, but the sacred link between the individual and the social body. The slaves *had* to talk back to the sermon. The preacher had not come to give his own opinions; he had come to preach the word of God to a people who refused to be passive and uncritical receptors. "Amen!" "Yes, Lord!" "Yes, Jesus!" "Yes! Yes!" Feet began to pat. Under the influence of congregational response, the preacher built steadily.

> An dem buckra dat beat dem nigger onjestly an onmusefully, jes kase de po nigger cant help e self, dems de meanest buckra ob all, an berry much like de sheep-killin dog dat cowud to take sumpn dat cant help e self.

"Preach the sermon!" someone shouted. "Yes, Lord!" "Yes, Jesus!" "Yes!" The preacher began to pace back and forth, raising his hands. Someone began to hum a mournful air, and the humming spread through the congregation. The slaves' bodies rocked, their heads nodded, their hands clapped, and their feet stamped a steady rhythm, pushing the preacher onward.

> Dat berry ting dat de nigger cant fend e self an helpless, mek de gentleman buckra berry pashunt an slow to punish dem nigger.

The preacher told them to put all their faith in the Lord. The Lord would deliver them from the House of Bondage as He had delivered the children of Israel from bondage in Egypt. The preacher also likened his flock of slave Christians to a flock of sheep.

> An de berry fack dat de Lawd sheep is po helpless ting, mek de Lawd pity
> an lub we mo, an mek we pen pun Him an cry fur Him in de time ob
> trouble an danejur. An dat wha de Lawd want, fur we feel we own weak-
> ness an trust in Him strenk. De mudder lub de morest de chile dats de
> weakest an dat need um de morest, and so wud de Sabeyur an e lettle wuns
> dat pend only pun Him.

As he moved his congregation toward a crescendo of exaltation, the
preacher broke into a chant. The response was no longer confined to
antiphonal amens but also included shouts and cries, the clapping of
hands and the stamping of feet, and the indescribable sounds of religious transcendence. The congregation worshiped with soul and body
in unison. Relying heavily on tone, gesture, and rhythm, the preacher
preached a sermon defiant enough to release pent-up frustrations
among the slave community, although neither so incendiary as to stir
hopeless revolts nor so blatant as to bring down the wrath of the masters
upon their heads. But expressing even such mild sentiments could be
dangerous. Who could tell when slaves might begin to ask the Lord not
merely to deliver them in the next world, but to aid them in casting off
the shackles of those who claimed to own them in this one? [17]

Slave preachers achieved renown in the slave community as "men of
words." They delivered sermons and prayers with memorable Biblical
imagery, imagery that seemed especially relevant to the slaves' own situ-
ations. "We're down here, Lord," they preached, "chewin' on dry bones
an' swallerin' bitter pills!" The slaves could identify with Moses leading
the children of Israel out of enslavement in Egypt after the Lord had
visited seven years of plagues upon the slaveholders. They could identify with the crucified Jesus, suffering through his time on the cross, as
the slave preacher chanted:

> They led him from hall to hall!
> They whipped him all night long!
> They nailed him to the cross!
> Don't y'u hear how the hammer ring?

It is not difficult to understand why the slaves preferred their own
preachers to the emotionless and self-serving platitudes of the white missionaries. [18]

To Christian slaves, the slave preachers were men of status. "My pa
was a preacher why I become a Christian so early," testified one. "He
used to tell us of hell an' how hot it is. I was so afraid of hell 'till I was
always tryin' to do the right thing so I couldn't go to that terrible place."
The slave preachers' continuing importance as men of words exemplified another adaptation of African traditions to African-American
Christianity. The linguistic inventiveness of the slave preachers was re-

lated to the ancient concept of *nommo:* the properly spoken word that results in appropriate action. Utilizing ritualized language and behavior as symbolic action, they transformed religious ritual through transcendental ecstasy into structured meaning, renewing and recycling the energies of the slave community. Such "gifted" men, straddling the sacred and secular worlds, were believed to exercise sacred powers within the secular domain. They often mediated between the slaves' Christian beliefs and the workaday world of the low country. The role they played as arbiters in settling disputes among the slaves was itself a product of their African heritage of the involvement of religion in everyday life. Through such mediation the preachers not only promoted social order but also played a major role in solidifying a sense of community among the slaves. In addition, as strong cultural personalities whose identities did not depend upon their positions as slaves, they served younger slaves as important role models.[19]

Slave preachers also sowed the seeds of discontent. The slaves' spiritual life was largely hidden from white observation. Often the slave preachers held services apart from the whites and without their knowledge. The major slave insurrections of the Old South—those of Gabriel Prosser, Nat Turner, and Denmark Vesey—were planned under the cover of such religious associations. According to Charleston's official account of the Vesey plot, "among the conspirators a majority of them belonged to the African church," a recently formed Methodist church described as "composed wholly of persons of color and almost entirely of blacks." The importance of the slaves' religion thus rested upon its capacity to serve them as a source not only of cultural values but also of an understanding of themselves, of their world, and of the relations between themselves and their world. It served them, in other words, both as a model *for* behavior and as a model *of* behavior. The power of African-American Christianity in supporting the social values of Gullah slaves rested upon its ability to make plain a world in which those values, as well as the forces opposing them, were primal elements.[20]

THE SPIRITUALS

The theological orientation of African-American Christianity is strikingly revealed in African-American spirituals collected in South Carolina in the 1860s. Because the spirituals were transmitted orally, it may be assumed that whatever did not correspond to the slaves' shared religious and poetic sensibilities was eliminated. Deriving their raw materials from Biblical passages, nature, work patterns, and other songs, slave poets often used material objects as poetic devices in the spirituals to amplify their artistry with the resonance of hidden meanings. In the spirituals, for instance, gates symbolically lead to a new and better life. "Children Do Linger," for instance, promises a reunion in the next world when "we'll meet at Zion Gateway." Gates imply passage into the new life for some, but exclusion for others. Not everyone will be allowed through the gates of heaven. In the spiritual "Heaven Bell A-Ringing," the slaves sang, "I run to de gate, but the gate shut fast." In this verse the anonymous slave poet voices the despair of the downtrodden sinner with little hope, a downtrodden sinner barred from entry into heaven. The same theme echoes through yet another spiritual, "Bell Da Ring." Sinners are excluded from the new life, for "the gates are all shut, when de bell done ring."[21]

Streets and roads undergo poetic transformation into symbols of deliverance in the spirituals. Streets are used to suggest that if one walks and lives in the right path, one will find redemption and success: "If you walk de golden street and you join de golden band / Sing glory be to my Emanuel," the slaves sang in "King Emanuel." One who lives on or walks down the golden street is on the path to deliverance. But the verses, by beginning with "if" clauses, also imply that not everyone will walk down the golden street or join the golden band. Roads fulfill a similar poetic function in the spirituals. Singers announce that they are traveling down the right road, the golden road—set apart from common, ordinary roads—because "I know de road, Heaven bell a'ring, I know de road." But roads in the spirituals are not always as "golden" as streets. Sometimes roads are ordeals, expressing the slaves' belief that one must travel the dark and stormy road of life—full of trials, tribulations, and temptations—if one hopes to reach the golden road to heaven. The road is long ("O walk Jordan long road") and hard ("Road so stormy, Bell da ring"). But the spirituals offer hope to the sinner, reminding believers that the golden road is farther along, beyond the misery of life in bondage ("If you look up de road you see Fader Mosey, join the Angel Band"). If the road is long and dark, "Sister Dolly light the lamp, and the lamp light the road." The road is long and hard, but it leads to Paradise ("I'se been on de road into heaven, My Lord!").[22]

A road itself implies movement, and the slaves always seem to be on the move in the spirituals. In "I Wish I Been Dere," the singer's family has died, and the singer expresses the desire to go with them to Heaven. "I wish I been dere to climb Jacob's ladder." The ascending motion of the spiritual was transcendent to slaves held down too long. The ladder, usually depicted as the Biblical Jacob's ladder, is another poetic transformation in the spirituals. It symbolizes social, economic, or religious climbing. To ascend the ladder is to reach a higher and better level of existence. The line "I wish I been dere to climb Jacob's ladder" reflects the slaves' aspirations to climb to a better place.[23]

Slave poets use ships, boats, and arks in the lowcountry spirituals to symbolize the transfer of people or souls from one place to another over impassable terrain. The Sea Island rowing song "Michael Row the Boat Ashore" utilizes this poetic transformation several times: "Michael row the boat ashore, Hallelujah. ... Michael boat a music boat. ... Sister help for trim dat boat. ... Michael haul the boat ashore, then you'll hear the horn they blow." The boat that carries the souls of men and women into heaven is recalled in such lines as "When de ship is out a-sailin, Hallelujah" and "O brudder will you meet us when de ship is out a-sailin?"[24]

Whereas many spirituals express a desire for change symbolized by traveling roads or climbing ladders, "Fare Ye Well" expresses a feeling that a new life must begin by sweeping the old life clean ("Jesus gib me a little broom, for to sweep 'em clean"). Brooms symbolize the power to become new and better by the act of cleansing, therefore leading the slave upward and forward toward God and a good life.[25]

Through the spirituals slaves were striving to climb higher, to get to a better place, to find a happier life. One way they might fulfill their desire for accomplishment was to build something with their own hands, something they could call their own. The act of building appealed to the slaves. When they sang "Build a house in Paradise / Build it widout a hammer or a nail," they added another dimension to their desire to build houses of their own. A house built without hammer or nail is more than just a house; it is transformed into something miraculous. The hammer and the nail recall Jesus on the cross. And the spiritual assured the slaves that there are many mansions in heaven built not with hammers and nails but with faith.[26]

All of these poetic transformations symbolize deliverance, the passage of souls from this world into the next. Believers either cross through the gates of heaven, enter heaven by sweeping their souls clean with a broom, ride in a boat to heaven, or enter heaven by passing over the streets and roads of righteousness. For some slaves, at least, these devices must also have symbolized the end of slavery and their passage into freedom.[27]

SPIRIT POSSESSION

African-American Christianity emerged from the fragmentation of a unified African religious outlook into separate streams in America. Fragmentation and re-formation were especially marked among the Gullah-speaking slaves of the South Carolina and Georgia lowcountry. One stream of inherited African cosmology included polytheism, the concept of rebirth, and spirit possession in religious ritual. In the South

Carolina and Georgia lowcountry, far from the African context of their
sacred cosmos, the slaves worshiped their new Christian God with the
kind of expressive behavior their African heritage taught them was appropriate for an important deity: a high degree of spiritualism in worship, including the use of chants and bodily movement to rhythmic
accompaniment, leading to trances and spirit possession. The phenomenon of spirit possession, one of the most significant features in African
religion (especially pronounced among the Bantu, the Yoruba, and the
Fante-Ashanti), was reinterpreted in Christian terms to become a central
feature of expressive behavior in African-American Christianity and a
necessary part of the conversion experience. Conversion was the climax
of a spiritual journey called "seeking." A prolonged period of praying
"in the wilderness" induced an ecstatic trance without which conversion
was not considered authentic. On Sapelo Island, Georgia, Katie Brown
sang

> The way to get to Heaven
> Believer I know
> Go in the wil'erness
> Believer I know
> Cry Lord have mercy
> Believer I know
> Cry Lord have mercy
> Believer I know
> Glory Hallelujah
> Believer I know
> I done cross Jurden
> Believer I know

Not until one had actually experienced spirit possession was one accepted as a church member; those who had not experienced it were still
regarded as sinners.[28]

Slave Christians often held secret meetings at night to pray, to sing,
and to "shout." "Shouting" was not the same as yelling or making a loud
noise. "Shouting" denoted bodily movements accompanied by singing,
handclapping, and foot-stomping. As late as the 1930s, the folklorist
John A. Lomax reported that in Murrells Inlet, South Carolina, he had
seen "young girls dive through the air and fall headlong on the hard
floor in defiance of bruised flesh and broken bones. The men were more
careful of bodily injuries, seemingly content to 'hold' the riotous females
temporarily under the influence of the words of the minister." White
observers often mistook shouting for dancing. In shouting, however, the
feet were not supposed to cross each other or to leave the floor; such
acts would be dancing, and dancing was regarded as sinful. Frederika
Bremer reported having heard that "the Methodist missionaries, who

are the most influential and effective teachers and preachers among the negroes, are very angry with them for their love of dancing and music, and declare them to be sinful." Such hostility seemed to her "a very unwise proceeding on the part of the preachers. Are not all God's gifts good, and may they not be made use of in His honor? . . . I would, instead, let them have sacred dances, and let them sing to them joyful songs of praise in the beautiful air, beneath the blossoming trees. Did not King David dance and sing in pious rapture before the ark of God?" Exemplifying the creative adaptation of the West African ring "dance," which was performed to complex drum rhythms, the shout consisted of body motions performed to the accompaniment of spirituals. Slaves improvised a substitute for the drums, with polyrhythmic hand-clapping and foot-stomping. While slave Christians often deprecated dancing, they shouted with great enthusiasm.[29]

When slave Christians gathered for praise meetings at one another's quarters, the soaring rhetoric of the prayers, the antiphonal singing, and the ecstatic shouts provided a release for pent-up emotions. For the slaves, religious services constituted not a relationship between a performer and an audience but a mutual performance. Just as the spirituals were marked by the strong call-and-response antiphony of African music, so prayers and sermons were punctuated by congregational responses.[30]

HAGS, HAUNTS, AND PLAT EYES

Her hair was plaited and tightly wrapped with white twine. Her garments hung loosely about her gaunt frame. Her name was Addie, and she came out of slavery times. Her windowless cabin had but one room. Her table consisted of a board and four sticks, her china of clam shells. A blue milk-of-magnesia bottle served as a flower vase. But in this cabin Addie had reared fourteen grandchildren and great-grandchildren. In her yard redbirds visited, sunflowers turned their faces to the sun, and crape myrtles displayed their colorful finery. Wild plum trees hugged the sides of her house, and green corn waved a bright promise in the fields beyond. In March of 1936, Addie sat on the porch of her cabin at Murrells Inlet, South Carolina, with Genevieve Willcox Chandler, a fieldworker for the Federal Writers Project, spinning out her memories of life in bondage. Addie's nose crinkled with the effort to put her life into words, to leave behind her testimony so that future generations could know what the slaves had been forced to live through. She was asked about "plat eyes," the most hideous and most malevolent of the occult spirits of the Georgia and South Carolina coast, evil spirits that changed shapes at will in order to lure victims into danger and rob them of their sanity. "De ole folks is talk bout Plat Eye," Addie recalled.

Dey say dey takes shape ob all kind da critter—dawg, cat, hawg, mule, varmint and I is hear tell ob Plat Eye takin form ob gator. I ain see dem scusing wan lettle time. You know dat leetle swamply place hind de Parsonage? Well, wan time—I hab meh bloom on me [was in her prime] een dem days. . . . En I bawg tru dat deep white sand en I passes de grabe yard entrance en I leabes de open en enters dem dahk woods whey de moss wabe low en brush een yuh face. En I been tink bout Plat Eye. De min come tuh me it wuz good time tuh meet um.

Den I bresh dem weepin moss aside en I trabble de wet mud een meh bare feets en my shoe been tie tuh meh girdle string. En wen I been come tuh de foot lawg . . . a cootuh [small turtle] slide offen de lawg at meh feets. En, clare tuh Gawd, I been fuh look up at dat cootuh en den I turn meh eye up en der wuz a cat—black cat wid he eye lak balls ob fire en he back all arch up en he tail twissin en er switchin en he hair stan on end. E move backward front ob me cross dat cypress lawg. En he been big. E been large ez meh leetle yearlin ox.

En I talk tuh 'em en try fuh draw close. En I say tuh um, "I ain fuh feah nuttin! Ain no ghos'! Ain no hant! Ain no Plat Eye! Ain no nuttin'!" En I'se try fuh sing,

> E carry me tru many ob danger
> Because he fus lubb me.
> E guard gainst hant en Plat Eye
> Because he fus lubb me.

En dat Plat Eye ain gib me back meh word. E mobe forward en he tail swish en swish same lak big moccasin tail wen e lash de rushes.

En de mind come to me, "Chile ob Gawd, doan you show no fear!" En I is brace up. En meh short handle leetle clam rake been een meh han', en I sing,

> Gawd will take care ob me.
> Walkin' tru many of dangers,
> Gawd will take care ob me.

En den de min [mind] come tuh me, "De Lawd heps dem wut heps deyself!" En I raise up meh rake en I come right cross dat critter head.

Ef dat had uh been a real cat, I'd uh pin um tuh dat lawg. Meh rake been bury deep, en de lawg hold um. En I clare tuh Gawd, e up en prance right under meh feets, dem eyes burnin holes een me en e tail swish, swish lak ole Sooky tail wen de flies bad.

En I gits mad. I fuh struggle wid meh rake en de lawg loosen e grip en I fuh pray, "Gib Addie strenth, O Gawd!" En down I come straight tru dat critter middle. . . . But dat critter ain feel meh lick.

En I'se rassel lak Jacob wid de angel. I been strong en hab meh bloom on me. It ain 'vail nuttin. No man! Mr. Plat Eye jes ez pert en frisky as fore he been hit. En I 'buse um en I cuss um en I say, "You debbil! Clare mah path!" En if dat critter didn't paw de air en jus rise up dat big bamboo vine an me fuh hit um ebry jump!

So, I tink, "Sinner, lebel dat lawg." De min' come to me, "Chile ob Gawd, trabbel de woods path!" En I tuhn back en I hit dat path. En I ain been tarry en jes ez I wuz gibbin Gawd de praise fuh delivuh me, DERE DAT CAT! Dis time he big ez meh middle size ox en he eye been BLAZE!

En I lam [strike at] en I lam. En dat rake handle been wire en been nail on. En jus ez I mek meh las' lam, dat critter rise up fore my eyes en dis time e been big ez cousin Andrew full grown ox. En he vanish up dat ole box pine ez yuh quits de deep woods.

I ain b'lieve een Plat Eye 'twell den, but I min's meh step since dem days. En wen I trabbles de deep woods whey de moss wabe low . . . en de firefly flickuh, I'se ready fuh um.

Uncle Murphy, e witch doctuh en e been tell me how fuh fend um off. Gunpowder en sulphur. Dey is say Plat Eye can't stan' dem smell mix. Dat man full ob knowledge. E mus hab Gawd min' een um. So I totes meh powder en sulphur en I carries meh stick een meh han en I puts meh truss een Gawd.[31]

Addie's plat eye narrative illustrates a second stream of African cosmology, a stream that proved less compatible with African-American Christianity than rebirth and spirit possession. Many slaves in the South Carolina and Georgia lowcountry continued to embrace African supernatural beliefs that were not incorporated into African-American Christianity but instead persisted in a kind of parallel stream. Addie's defense against plat eyes, in its ingenious blend of creativity, tradition, and common sense, may be seen as a metaphor for the emergence of African-American Christianity.[32]

"Hags"—or "boo hags"—were one example of these supernatural beliefs. Hags were the disembodied spirits of witches or "conjure men" who were believed to leave their skins behind in order to fly through the air and give people nightmares, or "ride" them. Especially bothersome creatures, hags were believed able to fly through the air to midnight rendezvous, and to sail through keyholes by placing the bone of a black cat in their mouths. It was said that hags could bewitch people merely by looking at them. Even accusations of cannibalism attached to those suspected of witchcraft. Old Grace, an elderly slave on St. Simons Island, was rumored by her neighbors to be a hag. Local children were warned to stay away from her cabin because she allegedly boasted that she had eaten children in her native land. Slaves could take precautions, however, to keep hags from riding them: "conjure balls" (hair balls filled with roots, herbs, and other substances) were sometimes successful in keeping them at bay. But the only certain preventive was to eliminate the hag. That could best be done by the traditional African method of salting and peppering the skin while she had left it behind to go out "hagging."[33]

"Haunts"—the spirits of the dead—returned from time to time to trouble the living, in a modified version of the Congo *zumbi* or the Haitian *zombi*. The process of dying, according to West African belief, was not complete for up to five years. The spirits of the ancestors—the living dead—were the closest link between the world of the living and the world of the spirits, because they straddled both worlds.[34]

Haunts were most likely to appear at certain times, such as during a full moon or on Friday nights when the moon was young, although they were believed also to show themselves in broad daylight at certain places. Some believed that haunts rose up in every graveyard on the stroke of twelve; one haunt—the spirit of the oldest dead—would stay behind to guard the vacated graves while the others roamed the roads and entered houses. At slave funerals, efforts were made to contain the spirits of the ancestors; the living sought to prevent the dead from remaining behind as malign spirits.[35]

CONJURATION

Many features of African religion thus either converged or coexisted with Christianity. A third stream of African cosmology maintained a subterranean existence outside of and inimical to African-American Christianity. This element of slave religion continues to be largely unknown and at least partly unknowable. Documentation of voodoo, or hoodoo (as African conjuration was called in the New World), is inevitably scanty, as such magical shamanism was practiced clandestinely. Still, sufficient evidence remains to testify to the existence of an underground stream of magical shamanism, not only throughout the slavery period, but long beyond.[36]

Illness was regarded as supernatural in origin; thus it was necessary, through sorcery, to summon the spirits of the dead to offer advice or to perform cures. Voodoo, or hoodoo, could be used for either protective or malevolent purposes: it could cure an illness, kill an enemy, or secure someone's love. All misfortune, including (presumably) slavery, was regarded as the result of magical shamanism. The only way a slave could gain protection from sorcery was by stronger countersorcery. With some variation, voodoo was known throughout the slave societies of the New World.[37]

The survival of African sorcery seems to have been most pronounced in the South Carolina and Georgia lowcountry, where slaves were concentrated in significant numbers. Voodoo grew with the arrival of slaves from the West Indies or directly from Africa, who adapted African snake cults to a new environment. High in the African pantheon, the snake god of the Ewe, Fon, Bantu, Dahomey, Ouidah, and Yoruba symbolized the cosmic energy of nature, the dealer of fortune or misfortune. The African names for the voodoo gods were lost; their personalities converged with those of Judeo-Christian prophets and saints, demons and devils. They continued to comfort believers and to wreak havoc on the wicked. Only the snake god's sorcerers could invoke his protective power. Snakeskins were prominent in initiation rituals. Snake charming was featured in some rites. All sorts of supernatural might were attributed to serpents in the snake lore of lowcountry slaves.[38]

Voodoo in the lowcountry never approached the complexities of Haitian Vodun; nevertheless, it achieved a distinctive character above the level of simple, unorganized sorcery. Gullah slaves took their physical or personal problems more often to local conjurers—the priests of the old religion—than to their masters. Such conjurers often enjoyed considerable power within the slave community, even among some of the Christians. They were spoken of with great awe, and some were considered invulnerable. No feat of black magic was considered beyond their ability to perform. Conjurers gained and held their influence over the slaves by various methods and especially by fear. Their patrons relied upon them both for protection and relief from spells and for casting spells upon their enemies.[39]

The sorcerer's spells could be benign as well as malign. If conjurers were considered the source of most misfortunes, they were also held in high esteem as healers. The positive role played by the sorcerers in treating slave illnesses demonstrates the role religion played in every aspect of life among the slaves. Voodoo allowed the slaves the exalted feeling of direct contact with the supernatural in attempting to cope with their ailments.[40]

Not all Gullah slaves believed in magical shamanism; the sorcerers neither commanded universal adherence nor approached the political power of the priests of Obeah, Myalism, or Vodun in the West Indies. Most Christian slaves—if they did not summarily reject the appeal of sorcery—considered the shaman's powers to be evil, hostile to the spirit of Christianity. Nevertheless, conjurers exercised an extraordinary influence over the lives of other slaves that they could have neither gained nor maintained if they had not fulfilled a real function. Even if they are often considered frauds and extortionists, sorcerers served their fellow slaves in times of suffering. They were interpreters of those unobservable spirits whose activities directed everyday life; they were awesome beings whose supernatural powers could be enlisted in the redress of grievances. Gullah Jack, one of the organizers of the Denmark Vesey plot, enlisted his occult powers in the cause of the slave revolt. Sorcerers

in the lowcountry bridged for Gullah slaves the precarious life of servitude in this world and the mysteries of the spirit world. They turned
human behavior into a perceived cosmic order and projected images of
that order onto the plane of the slaves' everyday experience. They created a buffer against mental and emotional submission for the slaves
who believed in them. Many—perhaps most—of the slaves abandoned
shamanistic traditions, but those who held on tenaciously to their beliefs
helped to preserve and extend an autonomous African heritage, making
an important contribution to community and survival.[41]

THE CREATIVITY OF SLAVE CHRISTIANITY

Thus the once-unified religious cosmology fragmented. Adherence to
the various components was by no means uniform. Some Gullah slaves
abandoned belief in all forms of non-Christian supernaturalism; many
selectively adhered to some beliefs and abandoned others. Some undoubtedly continued African religious practices under cover of Christianity. What may have appeared to the slaveholders to be the Christian
cross may well have referred, in the mind of a given slave, to the Yoruba
belief in sacred crossroads or the Kongo symbol for the four points of
the sun. How easily Christianity might be interpreted in the same "primitive" terms that Western scholars apply to African religions is pointed
up by Zora Neale Hurston in a letter she wrote, with mock naïveté, to
her anthropological mentor, Franz Boas:

> Is it safe for me to say that baptism is an extension of water worship as a
> part of pantheism just as the sacrament is an extension of cannibalism?
> Isn['］t the use of candles in the Catholic chu[r]ch a relic of fire worship?
> Are not all the uses of fire upon the altars the same thing? Is not the
> christian ritual rather one of attenuated nature-worship, in the fire, water,
> and blood? Might not the frequently mentioned fire of the Holy Ghost not
> be an unconscious fire worship. May it not be a deification of fire?"[42]

Despite a large number of "survivals" of African cultural patterns,
what is most obvious from a truly Afrocentric perspective is the creativity of slave culture in the lowcountry. Most of the slaves' culture was
neither "retained" from Africa nor "adopted" from white slaveholders.
Rather, it was created by the slaves from a convergence of various African cultural patterns, white cultural influence, and the necessities de-
manded by new environment.[43]

The religion created by enslaved Africans shaped as much as it reflected their worldview. The Christianity of African-Americans reveals
both their mental picture of the unalterable shape of reality and their
deepest, most comprehensive concepts of cosmic order. For them, reli-

gion functioned to portray their ethical and aesthetic preferences as normative—given the imposed conditions of reality—while it also supported such preferences by invoking deeply felt ethical and aesthetic beliefs as evidence of their truth. The African contribution to African-American Christianity was enormous. The slaves did not simply adopt the God and the faith of the white missionaries. In establishing a spiritual life for themselves, they reinterpreted the elements of Christianity in terms of deep-rooted African religious concerns. Africa was not culturally homogeneous, nor did it bequeath to its exiles in the African diaspora a legacy of static survivals. In fact, religious expression in Africa was diverse, and borrowings among ethnic groups were common. Rising above the variety of beliefs and practices, however, was a shared bond—a concept of the sacred cosmos in which virtually all experience was religious, from the naming of children to planting, hunting, and fishing practices. Underlying the various African cultures were shared cognitive (or "grammatical") orientations—mental rules governing appropriate behavior—that profoundly affected the slaves' adoption, adaptation, and application of Christianity.[44] The originality of African-American Christianity, then, lies neither in its African elements nor in its Christian elements, but in its unique and creative synthesis of both. Examination of the selective Christianity evangelized to the slaves may provide some perspective on the process by which lowcountry slaves mixed both elements and adapted both to the realities of slave life.

Despite unusually strong continuities of Islam and of traditional African religions, most Gullah slaves embraced Christianity. In their praise meetings, in their ecstatic prayers and exuberant shouts, and especially in their transcendent spirituals, they found a source of strength and endurance that enabled them to triumph over the collective tragedy of enslavement.

NOTES

Part of this essay was written while the author was an associate of the W. E. B. Du Bois Institute for Afro-American Research at Harvard University. The support of the Du Bois Institute is gratefully acknowledged. Earlier versions of this paper were presented in the New Christianities series at the University of Utah and in the symposium on the History of African-American Christianity at the Harvard Divinity School, Cambridge, Mass., December 8–9, 1989. I am grateful to Randall Burkett, Ronald Coleman, Robert L. Hall, Paul Johnson, Albert Raboteau, Margaret Washington, and David Wills for their helpful comments.

1. Roswell King to Pierce Butler, May 13, 1803, quoted in Malcolm Bell, Jr., *Major Butler's Legacy: Five Generations of a Slaveholding Family* (Athens: University of Georgia Press, 1987), 132.

2. Interviews with Robert Pinckney, Wilmington Island, and Ryna Johnson, St. Simons Island, in Savannah Unit, Federal Writers Project [eds.], *Drums and Shadows: Survival Studies among the Georgia Coastal Negroes* (Athens: University of Georgia Press, 1940; reprint, 1987), 106, 176. Cf. Daniel C. Littlefield, *Rice and Slaves: Ethnicity and the Slave Trade in Colonial South Carolina* (Baton Rouge: Louisiana State University Press, 1981).

3. One of the most controversial topics in the controversial literature of American slavery is the nature and origin—the intellectual and spiritual sources—of the religion of the slaves. One school of thought, deriving from the work of the black sociologist E. Franklin Frazier, emphasizes the influence of white culture upon enslaved Africans. Some leading contemporary scholars of slavery emphasize that the values and practices of white Christians penetrated deeply into black Christianity, and the black church became perhaps the most important agency in "Americanizing" enslaved Africans and their descendants. See John Boles, *Black Southerners, 1619–1869* (Lexington: University of Kentucky Press, 1983), 153–68; John Boles, ed., *Masters and Slaves in the House of the Lord* (Lexington: University of Kentucky Press, 1988); and John Blassingame, *The Slave Community: Plantation Life in the Antebellum South,* 2d ed. (New York: Oxford University Press, 1979), 98. An opposite school of thought, emphasizing the "Africanity" of slave religion, derives from the work of the white anthropologist Melville J. Herskovits. Sterling Stuckey, for example, argues that the Christianity of the slaves was "shot through with African values." A leading contemporary spokesman for Africanity, Stuckey interprets the culture of the African diaspora using African rather than European ideals. "By operating under cover of Christianity," Stuckey writes, "vital aspects of Africanity, which were considered eccentric in movement, sound, or symbolism, could more easily be practiced openly." As Stuckey sees it, slave Christianity was simply "a protective exterior beneath which more complex, less familiar (to outsiders) religious principles and practices were operative." Writing from an Afrocentric critical perspective, Stuckey insists that the distinctive attributes of slave Christianity were outward and visible manifestations of inward and invisible African cognitive orientations, reflecting "a religious outlook toward which the master class might otherwise be hostile." What John Blassingame describes as "the 'Americanization' of the bondsman" Stuckey calls the "Africanization of Christianity." See Sterling Stuckey, *Slave Culture: Nationalist Theory and the Foundations of Black America* (New York: Oxford University Press, 1987), 54, 35–36, 57. Cf. Blassingame, *Slave Community,* 98. A third school of thought, exemplified by Mechal Sobel, sees the emergence of slave religion as a convergence of European and African religious values. In her study of the colonial Chesapeake, Sobel contends that stressing the relative autonomy of slave culture overlooks the cultural interaction of Africans and Europeans. Enslaved Africans, she argues, adopted Christian eschatology, while their white neighbors adopted African practices of spirit possession and the African sense of life as a spiritual pilgrimage. Thus, not only was black culture shaped by exposure to white culture, but emergent forms of white culture were also shaped by close association with bearers of African tradition. See Mechal Sobel, *The World They Made Together: Black and White Values in Eighteenth-Century Virginia* (Princeton, N.J.: Princeton University Press, 1987), esp. 11, 137, 221, 233. To acknowledge the convergence of African and European elements

in African-American Christianity, however, is not to imply that Europe and Africa always converged in relatively equal proportions. In such places as the South Carolina and Georgia lowcountry, enslaved Africans and their descendants constituted 80 to 90 percent of the population for most of the eighteenth and nineteenth centuries. In such places, African cultural influences necessarily outweighed European ones.

4. Georgia Bryan Conrad, "Reminiscences of a Southern Woman," *Southern Workman* 30 (1901): 13; see also her *Reminiscences of a Southern Woman* (Hampton, Va.: [1901]). Interview with Shad Hall, Sapelo Island, Georgia, in Savannah Writers Project, *Drums and Shadows,* 166; interview with Katie Brown, Sapelo Island, Georgia, ibid, 161. The name is transcribed Bi-la-li, Bu Allah, or Ben Ali in various sources. See also Clyde Ahmad Winters, "Afro-American Muslims from Slavery to Freedom," *Islamic Studies* 17 (1978), 187–90; Alan D. Austin, *African Muslims in Antebellum America* (New York: Garland, 1984).

5. Katie Brown, in Savannah Writers Project, *Drums and Shadows,* 162; Katie Brown, quoted in Lydia Parrish, *Slave Songs of the Georgia Sea Islands* (New York: Creative Age Press, 1942; reprint, Athens: University of Georgia Press, 1991), 27; Shad Hall, in Savannah Writers Project, *Drums and Shadows,* 166.

6. Charles Ball, *Slavery in the United States: A Narrative of the Life and Adventures of Charles Ball, A Black Man, Who Lived Forty Years in Maryland, South Carolina and Georgia, as a Slave* (New York: John Taylor, 1835), 164–65; Ball Family Papers, South Caroliniana Library, University of South Carolina, Columbia. According to Sterling Stuckey, "the great bulk of the slaves were scarcely touched by Christianity": *Slave Culture,* 37–38.

7. Charles Colcock Jones, *Suggestions on the Religious Instruction of the Negroes in the Southern States* (Philadelphia: Presbyterian Board of Publication, 1847), quoted in Robert S. Starobin, ed., *Blacks in Bondage: Letters of American Slaves* (New York: New Viewpoints, 1974), 42.

8. Ball, *Slavery in the United States,* 164–65, 201–3; Rev. Edward Thomas to Rt. Rev. R. W. Whittingham, March 10, 1836, quoted in Eugene D. Genovese, *Roll, Jordan, Roll: The World the Slaves Made* (New York: Pantheon, 1974), 187; Paul Trapier, *The Religious Instruction of the Black Population: The Gospel To Be Given to Our Servants* (Charleston, S.C.: 1847), 14; Henry Brown, Charleston, interviewed by Jessie A. Butler, in *The American Slave: A Composite Autobiography,* ed. George P. Rawick (Westport, Conn.: Greenwood, 1972), vol. 2, sec. 1, 120; Sarah Hodgson Torian, ed., "Antebellum and War Memories of Mrs. Telfair Hodgson," *Georgia Historical Quarterly* 27 (1943): 351. Cf. William W. Freehling, *Prelude to Civil War* (New York: Harper and Row, 1966), 336–37; Luther P. Jackson, "Religious Instruction of Negroes, 1830–1860, With Special Reference to South Carolina," *Journal of Negro History* 15 (1930): 72–114.

9. Charles Colcock Jones, *A Catechism of Scripture, Doctrine and Practice for Families and Sabbath Schools. Designed Also for the Oral Instruction of Colored Persons* (Savannah and New York: Observer Office Press, 1844), 127–30, quoted in Bell, *Major Butler's Legacy,* 152–63.

10. John Rogers, "My Dear Children," April 5, 1842, quoted in Genovese, *Roll, Jordan, Roll,* 190; Robert F. W. Allston, quoted by Ulrich B. Phillips, "Racial Problems, Adjustments, and Disturbances," in *The South in the Building of the Nation,* ed. Julian A. C. Chandler, Franklin L. Riley, James C. Ballagh, John

Bell Henneman, Edwin Mims, Thomas E. Watson, Samuel Chiles Mitchell, and Walter Lynwood Fleming, (Richmond, Va.: Southern Historical Publishing Society, 1909–12), 4: 210.

11. Charles Colcock Jones to Sandy Maybank, quoted in Starobin, *Blacks in Bondage*, 42; Charles Colcock Jones to Catoe, January 28, 1831, ibid., 44; Catoe to Charles Colcock Jones, September 3, 1852, ibid., 48; Andrew to Charles Colcock Jones, September 10, 1852, ibid., 51–52.

12. James Henley Thornwell, *The Rights and Duties of the Masters: A Sermon Preached at the Dedication of a Church Erected in Charleston, S.C. for the Benefit and Instruction of the Colored Population* (Charleston, S.C.: Walker and James, 1850), 11; *Public Proceedings Relating to Calvary Church and the Religious Instruction of Slaves* (Charleston, S.C.: Walker and James, 1850), 19.

13. Frederika Bremer, *Homes in the New World: Impressions of America* (New York: Harper, 1853), 1: 491.

14. Whitemarsh Seabrook, quoted in Freehling, *Prelude to Civil War*, 335; Whitemarsh Seabrook, *Essay on the Management of Slaves* (Charleston, S.C.: Miller and Brown, 1834), 15, 28–30. On the revolutionary potential of African-American Christianity, see Orville Vernon Burton, *In My Father's House Are Many Mansions: Family and Community in Edgefield, South Carolina* (Chapel Hill: University of North Carolina Press, 1985), 152–58.

15. Thornwell, *Rights and Duties of Masters*, 11; Alexander Glennie, *Sermons Preached on Plantations to Congregations of Slaves* (Charleston, S.C.: 1844), 1–5, 21–27. Cf. John Blassingame, *The Slave Community: Plantation Life in the Ante-Bellum South* (New York: Oxford University Press, 1972), 170.

16. Robert F. W. Allston, *Essay on Sea Coast Crops* (Charleston, S.C.: A. E. Miller, 1854), 41. On the problem of role boundaries in culture, see Mary Douglas, *Purity and Danger: An Analysis of Concepts of Pollution* (London: Praeger, 1966), 143.

17. This is a composite of descriptions of slave religious services in Bremer, *Homes in the New World*, 1: 289–90; William Wyndham Malet, *An Errand to the South in the Summer of 1862* (London: Richard Bentley, 1863), 49–50, 74; Laurence Oliphant, *Patriots and Filibusters; or Incidents of Political and Exploratory Travel* (Edinburgh: Blackwood, 1860), 140–41; Sir Charles Lyell, *A Second Visit to the United States of America* (London: John Murray, 1849), 1: 269–70, 2: 213–14; A. M. H. Christensen, "Spirituals and Shouts of the Southern Negroes," *Journal of American Folk-Lore* 7 (1894): 154–55; H. G. Spaulding, "Under the Palmetto," *Continental Monthly* 4 (1863): 196–200; Daniel E. Huger Smith, "A Plantation Boyhood," in *A Carolina Rice Plantation of the Fifties*, ed. Alice R. Huger Smith and Herbert Ravenel Sass (New York: William Morrow, 1936), 75; C. Vann Woodward, ed., *Mary Chestnut's Civil War* (New Haven, Conn.: Yale University Press, 1981), 213–14; and John G. Williams, *De Ole Plantation: Elder Coteney's Sermons* (Charleston, S.C.: Walker, Evans, and Coggswell, 1895), 2–11. The text is quoted from Williams, *De Ole Plantation*, 40. I recorded a similar African-American religious service at New Bethel Baptist Church on Sandy Island, S.C., January 16, 1972. William Faulkner includes a literary description of such a service in the "Dilsey" section of *The Sound and the Fury* (New York: Jonathan Cape and Harrison Smith, 1929). See also analyses of African-American preach-

ing styles in W. E. B. Du Bois, "Religion of the Southern Negro," *New World* 9 (1900); Grace Sims Holt, "Stylin' Outta the Black Pulpit," in *Rappin' and Stylin' Out*, ed. Thomas Kochman (Urbana: University of Illinois Press, 1972), 189–95; Le Roi Jones, *Blues People: Negro Music in White America* (New York: William Morrow, 1963), 45–46; Henry H. Mitchell, *Black Preaching* (Philadelphia: J. B. Lippincott, 1970); Bruce A. Rosenberg, *The Art of the American Folk Preacher* (New York: Oxford University Press, 1970), 7, 10, 14, 17, 40, 47, 51, 115–16; Gerald L. Davis, *I Got the Word in Me and I Can Preach It, You Know* (Philadelphia: University of Pennsylvania Press, 1987); W. D. Weatherford, *American Churches and the Negro: An Historical Study from Early Slave Days to the Present* (Boston: Christopher Publishing House, 1957), 114–15; Carter G. Woodson, *History of the Negro Church* (Washington, D.C.: Association for the Study of Negro Life and History, 1921), 41; Clarence E. Walker, *A Rock in a Weary Land: The African Methodist Episcopal Church during the Civil War and Reconstruction* (Baton Rouge: Louisiana State University Press, 1982), 61. On the status of the slave preachers in the slave community, see John W. Blassingame, "Status and Social Structure in the Slave Community," in *The Afro-American Slaves: Community or Chaos,* ed. Randall M. Miller (Malabar, Fla.: Robert Krieger, 1981), 114, 120–21. *Buckra* means white person.

18. Parrish, *Slave Songs,* 166.

19. Henry Brown interview in Rawick, *The American Slave,* vol. 2, sec. 1, 126. Cf. Albert J. Raboteau, Jr., *Slave Religion: The "Invisible Institution" in the Antebellum South* (New York: Oxford University Press, 1978), 136–37; Roger Bastide, *African Civilisations in the New World,* trans. Peter Green (New York: Harper and Row, 1971), 92. On the social position of the preacher in the slave community, see Blassingame, "Status and Social Structure," 114, 120–21. On the social position of the man of words elsewhere in the African diaspora, see Roger D. Abrahams, *The Man of Words in the West Indies* (Baltimore, Md.: Johns Hopkins University Press, 1983). On the social position of the man of words in African societies, see S. A. Babalola, *The Content and Form of Yoruba Ijala* (Oxford: Clarendon Press, 1966), 40–55; Dan Ben-Amos, *Sweet Words: Storytelling Events in Benin* (Philadelphia: Institute for the Study of Human Issues, 1975), and his "Two Benin Storytellers," in Richard M. Dorson, ed., *African Folklore* (Garden City, N.Y.: Doubleday, 1972), 103–14; Ruth Finnegan, *Limba Stories and Storytelling* (Oxford: Clarendon Press, 1966), 64–85; and Judith Irvine, "Caste and Communication in a Woloj Village" (Ph.D. dissertation, University of Pennsylvania, 1973). For a discussion of the "phenomenon of mid-transition"—of one who straddles sacred and secular worlds—see Victor W. Turner, *The Forest of Symbols: Aspects of Ndembu Ritual* (Ithaca, N.Y.: Cornell University Press, 1967), 110; and Victor W. Turner, ed., *Celebration: Studies in Festivity and Ritual* (Washington, D.C.: Smithsonian Institution, 1982). See also Kenneth Burke, *Language as Symbolic Action: Essays in Life, Literature, and Method* (Berkeley and Los Angeles: University of California Press, 1971), 391; and Peter Berger and Thomas Luckmann, *The Social Construction of Reality: A Treatise in the Sociology of Knowledge* (Garden City, N.Y.: Doubleday, 1966), 47–49.

20. Lionel H. Kennedy and Thomas Parker, *An Official Report of the Trials of Sundry Negroes Charged with an Attempt to Raise an Insurrection in the State of South Carolina* (Charleston, S.C.: James R. Schenk, 1822), 14–15, 50, 54, 61. Other

contemporary accounts include Edwin C. Holland, *A Refutation of the Calumnies against Southern and Western States: An Account of the Late Intended Insurrection among a Portion of the Blacks of this City,* 3d ed. (Charleston, S.C.: A. E. Miller, 1822) 22–23, 30; [James Hamilton, Jr.], *Narrative of the Conspiracy and Intended Insurrection among a Portion of the Blacks in the State of South Carolina in the Year 1822* (Boston: Joseph W. Ingram, 1822); and [Thomas Pinckney,] *Reflections, Occasioned by the Late Disturbances in Charleston* (Charleston, S.C.: A. E. Miller, 1822). There is a manuscript trial transcript in [Thomas Bennett], Governor's Message No. 2, November 2, 1822, Governor's Papers, South Carolina Department of Archives and History, Columbia. Book-length secondary accounts of the Vesey plot include John Lofton, *Denmark Vesey's Revolt: The Slave Plot that Lit a Fuse to Fort Sumter* (Kent, Ohio: Kent State University Press, 1983); and Robert S. Starobin, ed., *Insurrection in South Carolina: The Slave Conspiracy of 1822* (Englewood Cliffs, N.J.: Prentice-Hall, 1970). Cf. Clifford Geertz, *The Interpretation of Cultures* (New York: Basic Books, 1973), 123–31.

21. William Francis Allen, Charles P. Ware, and Lucy McKim Garrison, eds., *Slave Songs of the United States* (Boston: A. Simpson, 1867), 51, 55, 20, 34. Cf. John Lovell, Jr., *Black Song: The Forge and The Flame. The Story of How the Afro-American Spiritual Was Hammered Out* (New York: Macmillan, 1972), 244–50.

22. Allen, Ware, and Garrison, *Slave Songs of the U.S.,* 6, 13, 26, 28, 34, 39, 42, 50, 63, 66, 75, 81.

23. Ibid., 67, 29.

24. Ibid., 23, 50–51.

25. Ibid., 93.

26. Ibid., 68, 29.

27. Charles Joyner, *Folk Song in South Carolina* (Columbia, S.C.: University of South Carolina Press, 1971), 62–95.

28. Katie Brown, in Parrish, *Slave Songs,* 131–32; Chalmers S. Murray, "Edisto's Ghosts Fond of Whiskey," Chalmers S. Murray Papers, South Carolina Historical Society, Charleston (hereinafter abbreviated SCHS). Cf. Julia Peterkin, *Green Thursday* (New York: Alfred A. Knopf, 1924), 94–101; and Roland Steiner, "Seeking Jesus," *Journal of American Folklore* 14 (1901): 672. For comparative examples of the convergence of African spirit possession with Christianity in African-American cultures, see Erika Bourguignon's "Ritual Dissociation and Possession Belief in Caribbean Negro Religion," in Norman E. Whitten, Jr., and John F. Szwed, eds., *Afro-American Anthropology: Contemporary Perspectives* (New York: Free Press, 1970), 87–101; Elsa Goveia, *Slave Society in the British Leeward Islands at the End of the Eighteenth Century* (New Haven, Conn.: Yale University Press, 1965), 247–48; Edward Brathwaite, *The Development of Creole Society in Jamaica, 1770–1820* (Oxford: Clarendon Press, 1971), 219; George E. Simpson, "'Batismal,' 'Mourning,' and 'Building' Ceremonies of the Shouters of Trinidad," *Journal of American Folklore* 79 (1965): 537–50; and George E. Simpson, *The Shango Cult in Trinidad* (San Juan, P.R.: Institute of Caribbean Studies, 1965), 155.

29. John A. Lomax, Field Notes 1935–1937, John A. Lomax Papers, Archive of Folk Culture, Library of Congress; Bremer, *Homes in the New World,* 1: 290; Chalmers S. Murray, "Tom-Toms Sound for Edisto Rites," in Murray Papers, SCHS; Smith, "A Plantation Boyhood," 75–76; Charlotte Forten, "Life on the

Sea Islands," *Atlantic Monthly* 13 (1864): 593–94, and *The Journal of Charlotte L. Forten,* ed. Ray L. Billington (New York: Dryden Press, 1953), 153, 184, 190, 205; Allen, Ware, and Garrison, *Slave Songs of the U.S.,* xiv; Thomas Wentworth Higginson, "Negro Spirituals," *Atlantic Monthly* 19 (1867): 685–94, and his *Army Life in a Black Regiment* (Boston, 1870), 197–98; Elizabeth Ware Pearson, ed., *Letters from Port Royal* (Boston: W. B. Clarke, 1906), 22–28; Rupert S. Holland, ed., *Letters and Diary of Laura M. Towne: Written from the Sea Islands of South Carolina, 1862–1884* (Cambridge, Mass.: 1912), 20–23; Society for the Preservation of Spirituals, *The Carolina Low Country* (New York: William Morrow, 1931), 198–201; Zora Neale Hurston, "Shouting," in Nancy Cunard, ed., *Negro: An Anthology* (London: Wishart, 1934), 49–50; Willie Lee Rose, *Rehearsal for Reconstruction: The Port Royal Experiment* (Indianapolis, Ind.: Bobbs-Merrill, 1964), 91. The symbolic significance of drums to both blacks and whites is illustrated in Edward G. Mason, "A Visit to South Carolina in 1860," *Atlantic Monthly* 53 (1884): 244. The importance of shouting in African-American Christianity is underlined by an exchange between a Gullah preacher and a white folklorist in 1936. After a field trip to All Saints Parish in the South Carolina low country, John A. Lomax wrote in his field notes, "Once I asked the Reverend Aaron Pinnacle of Heavens Gate Church, South Carolina, why he deliberately attempted in his sermons to influence his congregation to 'shout'. . . . The Reverend Pinnacle, coal black [illegible] replied without hesitation: 'If I did not preach shoutin' sermons, my congregation would pay me nothing.' Even in religious matters, the economic factor is dominant. We can't get away from it." See Lomax, Field Notes, 1935–1937, Lomax Papers, Library of Congress.

30. Trapier, *Religious Instruction,* 4; Almira Coffin to Mrs. J. G. Osgood, May 10, 1851, in J. Harold Easterby, ed., "South Carolina through New England Eyes: Almira Coffin's Visit to the Low Country in 1851," *South Carolina Historical Magazine* 45 (1944): 131.

31. "Truss Gawd or Ad's Plat Eye," collected by Genevieve Willcox Chandler, Murrells Inlet, South Carolina, WPA Manuscript Collection, South Caroliniana Library (hereafter, SCL), University of South Carolina, Columbia. "Memories of an Island," 90–94; "Conjure Horses Have Passed," "Edisto Treasure Tales Unfruitful," and "Negroes Plagued by Edisto Ghosts," in Murray Papers, SCHS; John Bennett Papers, MS vol., 60, 63–64, SCHS; Ben Washington, Eulonia, Georgia, in Savannah Writers Project, *Drums and Shadows,* 136; Peterkin, *Green Thursday,* 77–78. Cf. Henry C. Davis, "Negro Folk-Lore in South Carolina," *Journal of American Folklore* 27 (1914), 248; Newbell Niles Puckett, *Folk Beliefs of the Southern Negro* (Chapel Hill: University of North Carolina, 1926), 130; and Ambrose E. Gonzales, *The Black Border: Gullah Stories of the Carolina Coast* (Columbia, S.C.: The State Company, 1922), 33.

32. MS vol. 10–17, 61–76, 103–104, 112, in Bennett Papers, SCHS; "Boo-Hags," "Conjer-Horses," and "Edisto Reveres Old Time Magic," in Murray Papers, SCHS. Cf. Davis, "Negro Folk-Lore," 247; Puckett, *Folk Beliefs,* 147; William R. Bascom, "Acculturation among the Gullah Negroes," *American Anthropologist* 43 (1941): 49. In Josephine Pinckney's novel *Great Mischief* (New York: Viking Press, 1948), a retelling of the Faust legend, a nineteenth-century Charleston apothecary becomes enmeshed in black magic and is lured to his doom by a charming hag. For a comparative perspective, see Bastide, *African Civilisations,*

108–10. For an African derivation, see E. E. Evans-Pritchard, *Theories of Primitive Religion* (Oxford: Clarendon Press, 1965), 17.

33. MS vol. 10–17, 61, 76, 103, 112, in Bennett Papers, SCHS; "Conjer Horses Have Passed," "Edisto's Ghosts Fond of Whiskey," and "Edisto Reveres Old Time Magic," in Murray Papers, SCHS. Cf. Bascom, "Acculturation among Gullah Negroes," 49; F. C. Bartlett, *Psychology and Primitive Culture* (New York: Macmillan, 1923), 63, 110, 117–18.

34. Jack Wilson, Old Fort, Georgia, in Savannah Writers Project, *Drums and Shadows*, 7; Shad Hall, Sapelo Island, Georgia, ibid., 167.

35. Solbert Butler, Hampton County, interviewed by Phoebe Faucette, in Rawick, *The American Slave*, vol. 2, sec. 1, 161–65; Isaiah Butler, Hampton County, interviewed by Phoebe Faucette, ibid., vol. 2, sec. 1, 160; MS vol. 45–50 in Bennett Papers, SCHS; "Gullahs Nearer to Spirit World," "Edisto Negroes Close to Spirits," and "Voodoo Gods Yet Alive on Islands," in Murray Papers, SCHS. Cf. Bastide, *African Civilisations*, 108–10.

36. "Voodoo Survivals Traced on Edisto," "Tom-Toms Sound for Edisto Rites," and "Edisto Reveres Old Time Magic," in Murray Papers, SCHS; James R. Sparkman, "The Negro," in Sparkman Family Papers, SCL. For a similar portrayal of the fragmentation of African religion in Jamaica, see Bastide, *African Civilisations*, 103. That all three streams should be considered aspects of slave religion is suggested by Anthony F. C. Wallace's definition of religion as "that kind of behavior which can be classified as belief and ritual concerned with supernatural beings, powers, and forces" in his *Religion: An Anthropological View* (New York: Random House, 1966), 5; and by Mary Douglas, in her *Edward Evans-Pritchard* (New York: Viking, 1980), 25–26.

37. MS vol., 18–24, 39A, 81–87, 158 in Bennett Papers, SCHS; "Voodoo Gods Yet Alive on Island," "Voodoo Survivals Traced on Edisto," and "Memories of an Island," 193–96, in Murray Papers, SCHS. Cf. George Eaton Simpson, "The Shango Cult in Nigeria and Trinidad," *American Anthropologist* 54 (1962): 1204–29, and his *Shango Cult in Trinidad;* Harold Courlander, *The Dream and the Hoe: The Life and Lore of the Haitian People* (Berkeley and Los Angeles: University of California Press, 1960); Alfred Metraux, *Voodoo in Haiti,* trans. Hugo Charteris (New York: Oxford University Press, 1959); Melville J. Herskovits, *Life in a Haitian Valley* (New York: Alfred A. Knopf, 1937); John Mbiti, *African Religions and Philosophy* (Garden City, N.Y.: Doubleday, 1969), 83; Bastide, *African Civilisations,* 59–60, 101–3; Martha Beckwith, "Some Religious Cults in Jamaica," *American Journal of Psychology* 34 (1923): 32–45; Donald Hogg, "The Convince Cult in Jamaica," in Sidney Mintz, ed., *Papers in Caribbean Anthropology* (New Haven, Conn.: Yale University, Department of Anthropology, 1960); George Eaton Simpson, "Jamaican Revivalist Cults," *Social and Economic Studies* 5 (1956): 321–42; Puckett, *Folk Beliefs,* 167–310; E. Horace Fitchett, "Superstitions in South Carolina," *Crisis* 43 (1936): 360–71; Monica Shuler, "Afro-American Slave Culture," in Michael Craton, ed., *Roots and Branches: Current Directions in Slave Studies* (Toronto, Ontario: Pergamon Press, 1979), 129–37.

38. "Voodoo Gods Yet Alive on Islands," "Edisto Overrun by Rattlesnakes," "Voodoo Survivals Traced on Edisto," and "Conjer-Men Keep Den of Reptiles," in Murray Papers, SCHS; *Account of the Late Intended Insurrection,* 23. Cf. Davis,

"Negro Folk-Lore in South Carolina," 245; Benjamin A. Botkin, " 'Folk-Say' and Folk-Lore," in William T. Couch, ed., *Culture in the South* (Chapel Hill: University of North Carolina Press, 1934), 590; Bastide, *African Civilisations*, 134–47; Paul D. Escott, *Slavery Remembered: A Record of Twentieth-Century Slave Narratives* (Chapel Hill: University of North Carolina Press, 1979), 105; Genovese, *Roll, Jordan, Roll*, 220; John Blassingame, *The Slave Community*, 41; Zora Neale Hurston, *Mules and Men* (Philadelphia: J. B. Lippincott, 1935), 247, and her "Hoodoo in America," *Journal of American Folklore* 44 (1931), 317–417; Leonora Herron and Alice Bacon, "Conjuring and Conjure-Doctors," *Southern Workman* 24 (1895): 118. Julia Peterkin's novels of African-American folk life in South Carolina are veritable catalogs of such folk beliefs: see, e.g., *Black April* (Indianapolis, Ind.: Bobbs-Merrill, 1927), 147–48, 245, and *Bright Skin* (Indianapolis, Ind.: Bobbs-Merrill, 1932), 59.

39. Kennedy and Parker, *Official Report*, 15–16, 78; "Memories of an Island," 108, 193–97, and "Edisto Reveres Old Time Magic," in Murray Papers, SCHS; MS vol., 18–24, and "Edisto Negroes Close to Spirits" in Bennett Papers, SCHS. Cf. Davis, "Negro Folk-Lore," 245–48; Fitchett, "Superstitions," 360–71; Puckett, *Folk Beliefs*, 200; Herron and Bacon, "Conjuring and Conjure-Doctors," 193–94; Blassingame, *Slave Community*, 109; Gilbert Osofsky, ed., *Puttin' On Ole Massa* (New York: Harper and Row, 1969), 37; Du Bois, "Religion of the Southern Negro," 618; W. E. B. Du Bois, *The Souls of Black Folk* (Chicago: A. C. McClurg, 1903), 144; "Lizard in the Head," collected by Genevieve Willcox Chandler, WPA Manuscript Collection, SCL; Peterkin, *Green Thursday*, 158–63, *Black April*, 123, and *Bright Skin*, 114.

40. "Edisto Reveres Old Time Magic," in Murray Papers, SCHS. Cf. Peterkin, *Black April*, 7; Julia F. Morton, *Folk Remedies of the Low Country* (Miami, Fla.: E. A. Seaman, 1974), Davis, "Negro Folk-Lore," 247; Wayland D. Hand, *Popular Beliefs and Superstitions from North Carolina* (Durham, N.C.: Duke University Press, 1961), 858–62; Roland Steiner, "Breziel Robinson Possessed of Two Spirits," *Journal of American Folklore* 13 (1900), 226–28; Charles W. Chesnutt, "Superstitions and Folklore of the South," *Modern Culture* 13 (1901), 231–35; Herron and Bacon, "Conjuring and Conjure-Doctors," 210–11. The distrust of white medicine is well portrayed in Peterkin, *Black April*, 71, 275, 281–83. For a comparative perspective, see Metraux, *Voodoo in Haiti*.

41. Isaiah Butler, Hampton County, interviewed by Phoebe Faucette, in Rawick, *American Slave*, vol. 2, sec. 1, 160; "Edisto Negroes Close to Spirits," in Murray Papers, SCHS; Kennedy and Parker, *Official Report*, 76.

42. Zora Neale Hurston, Eau Gallie, Florida, to Franz Boas, New York, April 21, 1929, in Zora Neale Hurston Papers, American Philosophical Society Library, Philadelphia, Pa. I am grateful to Amy Horowitz for bringing this letter to my attention. A quilter on Johns Island, South Carolina, explained to folklorist Mary Arnold Twining in the 1970s that the cross in her quilt pattern was not a Christian cross. Instead, "it represented danger, evil, and bad feelings." See Mary Arnold Twining, "An Examination of African Retentions in the Folk Culture of the South Carolina and Georgia Sea Islands" (Ph.D. dissertation, Indiana University, 1977), 188. Cf. Peterkin, *Bright Skin*, 51; Leland Ferguson, "The Cross Is a Magic Sign: Marks on Pottery from Colonial South Carolina" (Paper

presented at "Digging the Afro-American Past: A Research Conference on Historical Archaeology and the Black Experience," University of Mississippi, May 18, 1989).

43. I have elsewhere described this process of convergence as the *creolization* of slave culture. See Charles Joyner, *Down by the Riverside: A South Carolina Slave Community* (Urbana: University of Illinois Press, 1984); my "The Creolization of Slave Folklife: All Saints Parish, South Carolina, as a Test Case," *Historical Reflections / Reflexions Historiques* (Waterloo, Ontario) 6 (1979): 435–53; and my "Creolization," *Encyclopedia of Southern Culture*, ed. William R. Ferris and Charles Reagan Wilson (Chapel Hill: University of North Carolina Press, 1989, 147–49.

44. Cf. Geertz, *Interpretation of Cultures*, 89–90, 119; Darryl Forde, ed., *African Worlds: Studies in the Cosmological Ideas and Social Values of African Peoples* (London: Oxford University Press, 1954); Meyer Fortes, *Oedipus and Job in West African Religion* (Cambridge: Cambridge University Press, 1959); Geoffrey Parrinder, *African Traditional Religion* (Westport, Conn.: Greenwood Press, 1962); William R. Bascom, *Ifa Divination: Communication between Gods and Men in West Africa* (Bloomington: Indiana University Press, 1969); E. E. Evans-Pritchard, *Nuer Religion* (Oxford: Clarendon Press, 1956), and his *Witchcraft, Oracles, and Magic among the Azande* (Oxford: Clarendon Press, 1937); W. E. Abraham, *The Mind of Africa* (Chicago: University of Chicago Press, 1962), chap. 2; R. S. Rattray, *Religion and Art in Ashanti* (Oxford: Clarendon Press, 1926); Mbiti, *African Religions and Philosophy*, chap. 3; Melville J. Herskovits and Frances S. Herskovits, *An Outline of Dahomean Religious Belief* (Menasha, Wisc.: American Anthropological Association, 1933); Martha Warren Beckwith, *Black Roadways: A Study of Jamaican Folk Life* (Chapel Hill: University of North Carolina Press, 1929), chaps. 2, 6; Dominique Zahan, *The Religion, Spirituality, and Thought of Traditional Africa*, trans. Kate E. Martin and Lawrence M. Martin (Chicago: University of Chicago Press, 1979); Mechal Sobel, *Trabelin' On: The Slave Journey to an Afro-Baptist Faith* (Westport, Conn.: Greenwood Press, 1979). The importance of a continuing Yoruba and Ashanti influence and declining Bantu religious influence in African-American religion, despite Bantu demographic dominance in the New World, is discussed in Bastide, *African Civilisations*, 104–15.

CHAPTER THREE

Community Regulation
and Cultural Specialization
in Gullah Folk Religion

Margaret Washington

God done gib de white folk a heap of things, . . . but he ain't forgotten us,
. . . 'cause he gib us Religion and we have a right to show it out to all de
world. De Buckra [white people] deys got de knowing of the whys and
hows of religion, but dey ain't never got de feel of it yet. I tink God ain't
have much respect for no kind of religion without de feeling. De Book say,
"They that worship me must worship me in spirit and in truth." There
might be some truth in deys-all religion, but there ain't much spirit in a
religion that's all in de head.[1]

So Sam Polite told his praise house congregation. Sam Polite was senior
praise house elder on Benjamin Fripp's plantation on St. Helena Island
in South Carolina until well into the twentieth century. "His hair was
white and his face looked worn and lined," even in the dim praise house
light. Unsure of his exact age, Polite had "ben a man fore 'gun shoot' "
(i.e., the Battle of Port Royal, November, 1861). Those who had observed him for many years insisted that his "wisdom" and "vision" were
"God's free gift" for the service of faith and hope that "Prophet" Polite
had rendered his people[2]—the Gullah people residing in the coastal
lowlands and islands of South Carolina and Georgia. The most numerous, isolated, and culturally self-contained Gullahs were the island folk,
slave producers of the famous high-quality, long-staple cotton.

The time of "gun shoot" brought northern military occupation to the
area, along with a kind of prelude to Reconstruction: the Port Royal
experiment. From nearly every northern state, abolitionists, ministers,
journalists, teachers, college students, photographers, and others followed the army to the Port Royal region of the South Carolina Sea Islands. The rest of the state was still in Confederate hands, but at Beaufort and the surrounding islands, Gideon's Band, as the group was
called, had an opportunity to ameliorate the ravages of bondage while

the war continued. It was a social experiment aimed at instructing slaves in education, religion, and industriousness. But the endeavor was also a profit-making venture: along with Gideon's Band came U.S. Treasury agents to supervise picking, packing, and shipping the bounteous Sea Island cotton crop which the southern planters had left in their hasty early morning flight. Two issues were uppermost in the minds of the Yankees: would free labor succeed among slaves, for southerners had always maintained it would not; and would the slaves fight, for even Abraham Lincoln had said that "if we were to arm them, I fear that in a few weeks the arms would be in the hands of the rebels." The Gullahs proved themselves on both accounts. They labored willingly in the cotton fields for wages, with which they hoped to purchase confiscated and abandoned lands. And when Lincoln finally issued a call for black troops, Sea Island men comprised the first black regiment: the First South Carolina Volunteers.[3]

Northerners were struck by this "very peculiar people," who were "pure" black, with a "strange" way of speaking and a "foreign" culture. "Their language is extravagant," wrote one teacher, who found that, despite their limited vocabulary, "their conversation is full of strong expression and graphic images." Some observers noted that it was "easier to understand a foreign tongue" than to comprehend Gullah. "Talk we get dinner" meant "do you mean that I shall get dinner?" If asked how they got from one place to another, the answer was "I took my foot." If asked about work to be done, one response was "I will strike in on that tomorrow and fight on with him till I get him done, den drop back on the next thing them is." Although nearly all Gullahs professed to be Baptists, they embraced a host of non-Christian beliefs. They believed in the power of conjuration and of the "evil eye" as well as in the healing power of a "good eye." They believed in the power of ancestors to return and commune with the living. Gideon's Band was most impressed with Gullah music: work songs, boat songs, haunting chants about slave life, uplifting shout tunes, prayer songs, and rearranged Methodist hymns adopted to their call-response technique and use of minor chords and keys. "Oh, I wish you and all my friends could have heard these Africs sing!" wrote Arthur Sumner from St. Helena Island. "I never listened to more impressive music than this. The singing was intrinsically good; the songs strange and beautiful and their swaying to and fro with the melody, seemed to have a sort of oceanic grandeur to it."[4]

As the flurry of wartime interest subsided, a few northerners remained on the islands, setting up schools and participating daily in black life without attempting to alter significantly the people's culture (although some practices had to go underground). Later, early twentieth-century artists and social scientists, impressed with Gullah language, folklore, music, and decorative art, often depicted the Sea Island region as a quaint, mysterious, picturesque corner of America. Yet few noted that Gullah culture, born in slavery, was grounded in a social cohesiveness that was nurtured by the people's folk religion.

RELIGION AND THE ART OF DOMINATION

The Gullahs called themselves "a peculiar people," a phrase directly from the New Testament: "But ye are a chosen generation, a royal priesthood, an holy nation, a peculiar people that ye should shew forth the praise of him who hath called you out of darkness into his marvelous light."[5] Prophet Polite's oration recreates the spirit of that biblical passage. For, in bondage and in freedom, Gullahs proudly viewed their religion as a special gift with a unique essence. However, Sam Polite's address can also be read as binding the oppressed to the oppressor religion. Evidence affirms that Christianity was employed to control slave life and enforce plantation management. This essay explores the issue of domination through religious influence. More significantly, it examines Gullah life in terms of its socioreligious significance for bondspeople and its value as a community compact. Gullah religion not only served spiritual needs, but also built internal community regulation and contributed largely to cultural creativeness. My focus thus also challenges interpretations of Christian conversion which emphasize white cultural influence and negate the impact of African memory. I maintain that the Gullahs' acceptance of Protestantism was eclectic rather than complete. If whites used Christian instruction to secure the plantation system, slaves practiced selective disengagement by refashioning Christianity according to their reality and their collective historical vision.

Historically, religious instruction was not a popular cause in South Carolina. Planters considered such instruction inimical to their interests, and only some of the Methodist churches challenged such thinking. Opinions were further polarized following Denmark Vesey's conspiracy of 1822. Planning the aborted rebellion in the massive, illegally formed African Methodist Church, lowcountry slaves, mainly from Charleston, had "made a desperate struggle to recover their rights." Vesey was literate, and a leader in the Methodist church. He used weekly class meetings in the church to point out antislavery elements of the scriptures. "He read to us from the Bible, how the Children of Israel were delivered out of bondage," an informant reported. Vesey justified rebellion by pointing out discrepancies between the oral instruction of the white ministers and planters, who insisted that black slavery was divinely ordained, and biblical passages in Exodus and Zachariah which condemned slaveholding as punishable by death. Following discovery of the conspiracy, many slaveholders felt vindicated in distrusting the Methodists' teaching of slaves and insisted that such instruction cease altogether. Others counseled that if Christianity had played any role in the conspiracy, it was the result of either a misguided interpretation of holy writ inspired by northerners infiltrating the South, or of the superstitious, "primitive" notions taught by African-born slaves. Some even argued not only that it was the *duty* of southerners to convert slaves, but that a concerted program conducted by "southern men with southern principles" was the best preventative against insurrection. Both opinions gained adherents as 1831 brought the rebellion led by Nat Turner, which went well past the planning stage and established an even sharper contradiction between biblical scripture and black bondage.[6]

Once frenzy over the Vesey Conspiracy had waned somewhat, the South Carolina Methodist Conference, supported by a few influential planters, led the way in advocating openly the religious instruction of slaves and engaging actively in instituting plantation missions. The movement began in 1829 and concentrated mainly in the lowcountry, where Methodists insisted that thousands were living and dying without ever hearing the gospel and consequently were "as destitute as if they were not inhabitants of the Christian land."[7]

The conference recognized that many of the conspirators had been avowed Methodists; some had even been class leaders in the white church before deciding to form their own congregation. Thus, in the minds of many slaveholders, the Methodist Episcopal Church had been implicated in the planned insurrection. While denying any association with the black strike for freedom, the Methodist hierarchy insisted that offering slaves "true" religion would secure the public safety while fulfilling spiritual obligation. The 1822 plotters, Methodists argued, had been beguiled by black leaders preaching a false Christianity mixed with African superstitions. *"The Christian Negro looks to heaven,"* wrote Georgia Bishop James Andrew in 1831.

> He feels that this world is but a temporary home, and although his condition here may be a hard one, yet God can sanctify every hardship to an abundant increase of his spiritual comfort. He serves his master from *principle* not from *fear*. It is a service rendered to God; and he regards his master's interests as his own. They are therefore safe in his hands.[8]

Sensitive to planter hostility and allegations about antislavery underpinnings, the South Carolina Conference reiterated frequently the Church's belief in slavery as an institution of Divine Providence, outside of Church jurisdiction. William Capers, Superintendent of the Missions to the Slaves and himself a slaveholder, wrote:

Holy Scriptures . . . do unequivocally authorize the relation of master and slave. . . . Our missionaries inculcate the duties of servants to their masters, as we find these duties stated in the Scriptures. . . . We hold that a Christian slave must be submissive, faithful and obedient. . . . We would employ no one in the work who might hesitate to teach this; nor can such a one be found in the whole number of preachers in this Conference.[9]

Capers prepared a textbook for the plantation missionaries which reflected how whites expected blacks to internalize Christianity. Aside from prayers and hymns, the Commandments, the Creed, a description of the Fall of Adam and Eve, and portions of scripture related to service formed the bulk of Caper's catechism. The remainder was in a question-and-answer format designed for children. Missionaries often chose texts from St. Paul for sermons. One former slave who later became an abolitionist lecturer wrote of the narrow latitude of white preaching:

I often heard select portions of the Scriptures read. . . . On Sunday we always had one sermon prepared expressly for the colored people. . . . So great was the similarity of the texts that they are always fresh in memory: "Servants, be obedient to your masters—not with eye-service, as men-pleasers." "He that knoweth his master's will and doeth it not, shall be beaten with many stripes"; and some of this class. Similar passages with but few exceptions, formed the basis of most of these public instructions. . . . I will not do them the injustice to say that connected with these . . . was not mingled much that was excellent. . . . One very kind-hearted clergyman . . . was very popular with the coloured people. But after he had preached a sermon from the Bible that it was the will of Heaven from all eternity that we should be slaves, and our masters be our owners many of us left them, considering, like the doubting disciple of old, "This is a hard saying, who can hear it."[10]

Steady outpourings of preaching and teaching stressed obedience and duty among adult slaves. Catechizing children was also a major thrust, since they represented a future generation of black workers who, from childhood, would imbibe the Christianity taught by whites. For adults, "grown up in ignorance," a personal approach was employed. Class meetings were used to examine Gullahs about their beliefs and to relate dramatic portions of scripture. The sincerity and concern some missionaries expressed about the slaves' daily life inspired their confidence and gratitude. "It is not only the duty of the missionary to catechize the children and preach to the adults," wrote A. M. Chreitzberg from the Sea Islands, "but also to visit the sick and aged, and it is here that many a triumph has been achieved for his Lord." Such individual attention, wrote Chreitzberg, brought "many a dark and benighted soul into the light and liberty of the Gospel." Furthermore, added Chreitzberg, the missionary should prepare for pulpit exercises by learning the way to the slaves' hearts, and by becoming acquainted with their ideas of God and religion:

> The negro knows that his minister is not ashamed to enter his smoky cabin, to take him by his rough and toil-hardened hand, and talk to him about the way to heaven, or to kneel beside his bed, offer prayer in his behalf, and to pour into his heart the consolation of God's word. It is this that frequently takes his heart captive, and binds him to the cross.[11]

In spite of these intense efforts to shape their beliefs, Gullahs often discarded incongruous and discordant features of the instruction and absorbed what they considered relevant.

One of the most significant effects of Methodist teaching was its influence on the creation of the slaves' religious music. Some writers argue that Gullah religious songs are traceable to Methodist hymns and camp meeting tunes. Slaves began adopting these hymns in the colonial era. Some other so-called Negro songs were actually of white origin. The influence of the domestic slave trade, black-white cultural borrowing, and diffusion were all factors in the creation of black music.

At least two types of religious music evolved: those songs and hymns learned from whites, and those representing the slaves' own creativity and originality—their prayer songs. Methodist missionaries' preaching and counsel often provided Gullahs with raw material for their songs and interpretations of sacred rites. In addition, from past spiritual traditions, African-Americans inherited a mysticism, a sense of drama, and an oral communication already rich in symbolic imagery. This background merged with biblical apocalypse, narrations, and miraculous interpretation. Aspects of Gullah life and the sense of human frailty also brought forth the poetry from within—in response to floggings, illness, fatigue, the loss of family, and the ubiquity of death. One Methodist missionary described officiating in the 1830s at the burial of a young Gullah woman who had died "in full hope of immortal life." As was customary, the burial took place at night. The plantation was large, and most of the slave community was present as the corpse was conveyed to the burial ground. The procession moved slowly "with lighted torches interspersed through the ranks." The scene was solemn and silent except for the thrilling note of the whippoorwill, whose home was this lonely retreat amid graves of all sizes. "I have attended many of my fellow beings to the grave," wrote the missionary, "but never did I witness a more solemn time, and yet I felt it a blessed time." It was also a time of weeping: "some of the most stubborn were melted into tears." The deceased's husband and infant were near her grave. "He, before a careless man," observed the missionary, "now wept aloud—and since that period has shown his grief was not of a worldly kind. He has offered himself to the Church, and his child has been baptized. Many others on the plantation have become serious, and are now on trial." [12]

Such a burial scene gives insight to the spiritual and emotional poignancy which prompted creation of prayer songs such as the one described during the Civil War by Colonel Thomas Wentworth Higginson as "the most poetic of all their songs":

> I know moon-rise, I know star-rise;
>   Lay dis body down.
> I walk in de moonlight, I walk in de starlight
>   To lay dis body down.
> I'll walk in de graveyard, I'll walk through de graveyard,
>   To lay dis body down.
> I'll lie in de grave and stretch out my arms;
>   Lay dis body down.
> I go to de Judgment in de evenin' ob de day
>   When I lay dis body down.
> And my soul and your soul will meet in de day
>   When I lay dis body down. [13]

As professors of Christianity, Gullahs looked forward to a "heavenly home." But they were not resigned to their circumstances, as the missionaries encouraged them to be. The bondspeople's reactions to Christianity under Methodist tutelage were complex. They responded positively to Methodist expressions of warmth and personal concern. More significantly, the Gullahs identified with the spiritual message of regeneration (or rebirth) and with its symbol, Jesus Christ. As *African* Americans, Gullah people came from cultures where the achievement of spiritual regeneration was the turning point in life. For Africans, the regenerative process involved pain, as it had for Jesus who had died to bring collective redemption. Thus, for Gullahs, the travails of bondage had regenerative power. Also, like their forebears, the Gullahs fused the sacred and the secular into one ethos, and redemption was not only spiritual but physical. Hence, it was not their Jesus who had ordained bondage; it was the doing of humankind. Therefore, acts of defiance against the plantation system were not sins. The paradoxes and contradictions in the oral Christian instruction received from the Methodists was not lost on the Gullahs.

Few white Methodists resided in the Sea Island region; the denomination was present mainly in its plantation missions. In contrast, the Baptist sect was the most numerous in the area and counted many of the wealthiest slaveholders among its numbers. Consequently, antislavery sentiments were never expressed among Sea Island Baptists as they were during early debates elsewhere in the South. These Calvinist-oriented

(or Particular) Baptists rejected evangelism in favor of Augustinian pre-
destination, and they restricted church membership. Thus, both their
religious proclivities and their economic self-interest caused them to resist converting their slaves. On the contrary, lowcountry Baptists were
historically suspicious of all missionaries, even "southern men with
southern principles," who emphasized obedience, docility, and submission.[14]

Methodist "knights of the saddlebags" experienced difficulty on the
denominational front. Even after 1830, Baptist slaveholders were skeptical at best, and many refused to allow Methodists on their plantations.
Episcopalian planters were less hostile, but remained unconvinced of the
enterprise's worthiness. Opinions shifted in 1844–1845 following the regional rupture of the churches, when northern denominations de-
nounced the southern churches' proslavery stance. The organization of
the Southern Baptist Convention and of the Methodist Episcopal
Church South assuaged slaveholders' fears of exposing the bondspeople
to abolitionist-minded clergy and prompted recalcitrant planters to re-
think the question of Christian instruction. Many were convinced that a
"suitable," selective type of Christian indoctrination was more effective
against black insurrection than statutes were.

In efforts to convince recalcitrant slaveholders, southern churches
stepped up publication of sermons specifically for black audiences, emphasizing the life of "meek and lowly Jesus," his ability to suffer quietly,
and his abhorrence of violence and disorder. Presbyterians and Episcopalians led in publishing literature on the positive aspects of Christianiz-
ing slaves. A prominent Charleston Presbyterian, Reverend James
Thornwell, "the jewel of the Southern Church," consistently expostu-
lated about how well Jesus' teaching suited bondspeople. Jesus was "no
stirrer up of strife, no mover of sedition." Christianity alone could curb
passions and accord each group its due: "to the laborious, the reward of
their industry; to the rich, the enjoyment of their wealth, to the nobles,
the preservation of their honors, and to the princes, the stability of their
thrones."[15]

Baptists were the least active in the movement for religious instruction. They lacked a structured church hierarchy, their interest was superficial, and their methods were neither systematic nor thorough.
However, after 1845 they permitted baptism and church membership
on a large scale. In the Sea Island region, African-Americans were
thereafter more attracted to the Baptist denomination than to others.
For one thing, Baptists were anxious to keep bondspeople on the plantations; this seclusion facilitated black autonomy, since Gullahs could practice their religious beliefs without much white supervision. Gullah ritu-

als, concepts of spirituality, and sacred world view fostered community regulation and social cohesion in the slave quarters.

Instead of having bondspeople attend churches in the region, Baptists organized praise houses among existing black societies on individual plantations. Black societies were under the jurisdiction of a Baptist planter, who often relinquished spiritual responsibility to a black elder. This elder was responsible for oversight of black Christians, for determining who was ready for baptism, and for exhorting among the people. The black elder was also expected to report breaches of church discipline. Through this latter function, white Baptists attempted to use black religious leaders for their own purposes.

Church discipline is an old concept designed to govern personal behavior by applying Old Testament biblical tenets. Early Charleston Baptists and their low-country extensions emphasized discipline among members through the authority of a committee. Once their attention was focused on slave conversion, Baptist churches revived the discipline committees and broadened their functions. In the Baptist church at Beaufort, South Carolina, with its massive slave membership, eight men, all substantial planters, sat on the discipline committee. They met monthly, heard cases of slave depredations, and recommended action on breaches of plantation discipline. All manner of "lapses in moral conduct" and plantation "crimes" came before the committee. Entries of the discipline committee of Beaufort Baptist Church read as follows:

Lizzy, Excommunicated, running away and insolent to owner.

Charles, Excommunicated, stealing corn and breaking into corn house.

Nell, Excommunicated, theft.

Joe, Excommunicated, drunkenness and running away.

Bacchus, Suspended, selling whiskey in violation of the law, publicly punished for it in stocks.

Other so-called lapses in moral conduct consisted of "barn burning," "hog stealing," "Sabbath breaking," and "fornication." One slave woman named Betty was suspended for fleeing, and her Tom suffered the same fate for "harboring above Betty." [16]

The discipline committee confronted bondspeople with their "sins" as would their heavenly Master in a future tribunal. The interests of both "masters" were represented as being the same. One former slave recalled that her old master "wouldn't miss de catechism," and children "was taught they must be faithful to the Missus and Marsa's work like you would to your heavenly Father's work." Slaves on St. Helena Island recalled "Good Billy" Fripp, a Baptist master referred to as good not because of his temperament but because of his avowed piety and strict sense of biblical discipline. This "leading Baptist" carried his Bible out to the fields, showed slaves "Moses' law," and then flogged them "acordin.' "[17]

Baptist planters anticipated that black societies, as religious associations, would uphold plantation discipline. Theft from plantation stores was a serious "church" offense and, if discovered, was brought before the disciplinary tribunal. Masters expected black societies and praise house associations to encourage submission. Instead, these organizations encouraged community loyalty and they illustrate how slaves used religion for their own purposes.

THE WEAPONS OF A COUNTER-HEGEMONIC CULTURE

The Methodists were more aware than were resident Episcopalian planters of how deftly Gullah people deviated from their instruction, since these missionaries actually had a closer spiritual relationship with some of the slaves. In the 1830s, when they first arrived in the Sea Island region, Methodists found tightly knit slave communities clinging to patterns of social behavior and modes of worship that were largely a mystery to whites. The first obstacle to surmount was verbal communication. "Their language," wrote one missionary, "though understood by themselves, cannot be by one unaccustomed to them without great study and application."[18] Other hindrances stemmed from the Gullahs' sense of independence, their internal moral code, and their loyalty to black leadership.

For example, in 1833, Methodist missionary Thomas Turpin was assigned to the southernmost region of the South Carolina Sea Islands. Frustrated by his lack of success, Turpin wrote the home office regarding the state of religion in the region, and his "Missionary Sketch" was published in the *Christian Advocate and Journal*. He had access to about a thousand adult slaves, one third of whom were reportedly in the Baptist church and in the "negro societies, and all of them under Baptist influence." In Turpin's opinion, this affiliation was not a good sign. The slaves rarely saw the pastor or the church, he wrote, since it was in Savannah and was pastored by Andrew Bryan, a black man. Instead, island people had "societies organized among themselves." Furthermore, Turpin insisted, "these societies are very corrupt." Turpin noted that at one black society gathering on Bull's Island, he had observed slaves engaged in a peculiar type of penance as punishment for sin, which by all appearances was contrary to Christian practice:

They had three degrees of punishment, and . . . the punishment was inflicted agreeably to the magnitude of the crime, according to their view of the crime. If the crime was of the first magnitude, the perpetrator had to pick up a quart of benne seed . . . poured on the ground by the priest; and if of the second, a quart of rice; and if of the third a quart of corn. . . . And they also had high seats and low seats, but incorrect views relative to those who ought to be punished. . . . It was also a rule among them never to divulge the secret of stealing: and if it should be divulged . . . that one had to go on the low seat or pick up the benne seed.[19]

Turpin's report caused a stir among Baptist planters in the Sea Island region and within the Missionary Society of the Methodist Episcopal Church. Baptists believed Turpin had suggested they knowingly allowed slaves to practice un-Christian rituals. Methodists were more than ever convinced that ignorance and superstition reigned in the Sea Islands south of Charleston, and it became their avowed mission to spread Christianity in the low country. "It appears," wrote Turpin, that the report "injured the feelings of many . . . Baptist friends. . . . It has been said that I have 'shot a ball particularly at the Baptists, and in its glance it has hit the Episcopalians.' "[20]

The benne seed ritual is another example of how Gullahs melded the sacred and the temporal, and how they reached back to African traditions and memory. Theft was dealt with as a breach of sacred trust. However, a "sin" was committed not by the slave who stole from the master, but by the one who divulged the act. This aspect of communal morality was not subverted by Christian dogma. While stealing from "Maussa" was not a sin, regardless of church discipline, it was wrong and against collective interests for Gullahs to steal from each other. Two Gullah soldiers testifying before the American Freedmen's Inquiry Commission in 1863 explained that slaves stole from masters but not from each other. Slaves' moral values went further. During the Civil War, a white officer of the First South Carolina Volunteers told Charlotte Forten, a black northern teacher, that he had never seen a regiment where men were so honest. "In many camps the colonel and the rest of us would find it necessary to place a guard before our tents. We never do it here," he said. "Yet nothing has ever been touched." During the same period, Laura M. Towne, a teacher and osteopath working among the Gullahs, wrote, "The men and women come crowding here at all times begging to be allowed to buy clothing, and though they stand about for hours in the sun, we have never missed the slightest thing."[21]

Gullahs' moral philosophy forbade stealing from whites simply because they were white, but the people were not naive. They maintained a shrewd sense of justice toward both black and white. One avaricious man, the Reverend Phillips, who was on full salary from a missionary organization, also drew a salary from the government as a plantation superintendent, including house-rent and rations. Still, he charged the Gullahs for ministerial duties, demanding a half dollar per church member for half a year. With over a thousand Gullahs claiming membership in the little Brick Baptist Church on St. Helena Island, Phillips intended to collect a hefty sum. But the people refused to pay. On another occasion, Gullahs discovered that a white minister sent by the American Missionary Association was cheating them out of a just price for their labor. They refused to attend the minister's services or work in the cotton fields he supervised. The people's patience had its limits. When government cotton agents on St. Helena charged over twice as much for store items as was being charged in Beaufort, their stores were broken into "and robbed of a good deal of clothing." As one northerner noted, it was "impossible to deal unjustly by them and succeed."[22]

The plantation black society was the institutional nucleus of Gullah religion. Its origin is unknown, but Methodist missionaries found these societies already existent and attempted to crush their influence. Baptist planters, on the other hand, attempted to use them to promote a Christianity suitable to plantation interests.[23] Gullahs used black societies to control their own practical, communal, and spiritual concerns and as training centers for black leadership. The latter function was a special foil to Methodist influence and Baptist hegemony.

Slaves' familiarity with the concepts of secret society membership and social regulations suggest a relationship to African institutions, reinforced by Christian ideas of a community of believers. Like the formation of Gullah language, the syncretic evolution of Gullah folk Christianity was a gradual process, occurring as diverse African groups framed a spiritual commonality and belief system which incorporated, reformulated, and appropriated Christianity. Gullah religious training often came from black rather than white teachers, hence contributing to the persistence of African norms, thought, and ceremony. But, as the benne seed ritual suggests, the presence of black "Christians" in the slave quarters undoubtedly produced debates, challenges, acknowledgments, and selective adaptation even before the Christian conversion movement was fully implemented.

Throughout the antebellum era, Methodists wrangled with black leaders and were often foiled by Baptist planters as well. One St. Helena absentee planter who supported Methodist instruction and disparaged black societies considered the Baptist church "a place of resort" and "almost entirely under the control of Negro leaders." Nearly all of his bondspeople wanted "tickets to get baptized" in the Baptist church. Methodist missionaries agreed with the planter's assessment. From

Beaufort Mission, T. E. Ledbetter wrote, "We combat a great many false notions, and . . . fatal doctrines which have been early imbibed by the colored population through the instrumentality of ignorant and superstitious teachers among themselves. . . . Many of them are opposed to us."[24]

Though officially affiliated with the Baptist church, Gullahs continued to prefer black leaders and their own mode of worship. Despite Methodist efforts, the Sea Island region remained "a very unpromising" field of labor, "all owing to the prejudices of the negroes." The ceremonious manner in which Baptists initiated converts and the nonhierarchical, informal worship impressed the Gullahs. They especially identified with total immersion: "We cannot . . . find fault with the negroes . . . for preferring another communion to our own," wrote a Methodist missionary. "But our voice will ever be lifted against them, for refusing the bread of life, because, forsooth it comes not to them . . . from the hands of one who has 'gone down into or come up out of the water.' "[25]

Planters chose black elders they considered "tried and true," while Methodists granted black leaders little authority. William Capers insisted that black leadership was merely "a feeble staff" not to be "leaned upon." Slaves, cautioned Capers, could "no more do the missionary's work than a staff can walk." Missionaries in the field concurred, insisting that most black leaders professing Christian knowledge represented "the very essence of ignorance and superstition." Although occasionally Methodists reported successful preaching where "precious seasons," and "effusions of tears would ensue," they remarked that Gullahs would immediately desert them for "one of their own":

> Let it be known that one of these is to preach on such a day and there is such a rush . . . that they may have the pleasure of hearing one of their own color. What else than mischief can be expected from the teaching of an ignorant enthusiast who knows nothing of God's word, and puts his own delusions in the place of divine truth? . . . And they say that, whenever they come to hear me, it is from duty . . . because I am employed by their owners.[26]

Despite Methodist skepticism, by the time of the Civil War most Gullahs considered themselves Christians and had accepted the Baptist faith. When northern occupation of the Sea Islands began in November 1861, representatives of freedmen and missionary associations were on the scene as soon as it was considered reasonably safe. They were impressed with Gullah spirituality, noting that Gullahs were a "religious people," easily inspired to sing and pray profusely. "Jesus," stated one observer, is "a common theme in their conversation." Even the children sang of Jesus, although their songs often reflected secular meanings.

At the newly established schools, the children's rich, spontaneous voices harmonized such "spirituals" as

> Patrol around me Tank God he no ketch me
> Oh Lord, yes my Lord

or

> In de mornin' when I rise,
> Tell my Jesus Huddy ho

Northern teachers marveled at how quickly the children memorized school lessons. Yet their religious knowledge was strangely confused with current events transforming their lives. One teacher, after "plainly" explaining to a Sunday school class of large boys the origin of the Ten Commandments and how they had been given to Moses, asked the children who had written the Ten Commandments. She was given such answers as "Uncle Sam," "General Saxby" (Rufus Saxton, military commander of the region), and "Columbus." On another occasion, officers in Sherman's army quizzed a group of island youth, asking "children who is Jesus Christ?" At first there was a "paralyzed silence." Finally, a small boy ventured loudly, "General Saxby sar!" An older boy then gave his classmate "a vigorous thrust in the back," and proclaimed, "Not so boy! Him's Massa Linkum!"[27] So much for the effectiveness of either Methodist catechism or Baptist Sunday school!

Adult knowledge of Christianity was also quite limited, despite the Gullahs' attraction to "things of the spirit." Gullahs knew little of Christian doctrine, as exemplified by their attitude toward Christmas. Although these African-Americans revered Jesus, few understood the significance of Christmas as the day of Christ's birth. But they knew that Christmas was a joyous, festive season, marked by a rare allocation of fresh meat, a two- or three-day cessation of labor, and possibly a new suit of clothing. Mary Ames taught among the Gullahs of Edisto and Wadmalaw Islands, where Methodism was reportedly especially effective. Yet she was surprised at how little the people knew of Christ's life, "not knowing even of his birth." "But," she added, "they are all familiar with his sayings." Elizabeth Botume, a Hilton Head teacher, remembered one jubilant Christmastime among the Sea Island "contrabands" when they asked her to preach:

> I replied that there was but one sermon fitting for the occasion, and I read the whole of Christ's Sermon on the Mount, first explaining to them the meaning of the evergreens, typical of Christ's life and teachings. They gave breathless attention to all this ejaculating from time to time, "My Lord! is dat so?"

I know now they understood very little of all I said, but no speaker ever had more interested and attentive listeners. When I sat down, one of the leaders chanted rather than spoke a touching prayer, in which he styled me his "dear imperial preacher."

Then the white friends sang, "Joy to the world, the Lord has come." By this time the entire audience was aroused and ready to pray and sing all night. In each prayer the speaker tried to introduce, in his uncouth phraseology, some of the passages of Scripture he had heard read.[28]

Though lacking a firm background in basic biblical knowledge, and unclear about the historical importance of Christ, Gullahs strongly identified with his suffering, crucifixion, and resurrection. This for them was Christianity, and given their confidence that their earthly lives so closely paralleled that of Jesus, becoming Christians was an apocalyptic fulfillment.

Some biblical messages were not lost on Gullahs. For instance, they were easily inspired by Exodus, an identification "talked up" by the 1822 Charleston rebels. The commander of Gullah troops, Thomas Wentworth Higginson, stated that his men's memories were a "vast, bewildered chaos of Jewish history and biography," and most great events of the past up to the American Revolution were instinctively attributed to Moses. One Civil War missionary noted:

Last week I read to the *church full* the account of the escape of the Children of Israel from Egyptian bondage. I was amazed at the impression it seemed to make. The remarks the old men made were graphic and eloquent. It made them recount with praise to God their escape. The little church seemed like dreamland to me almost when they got stirred to talk.[29]

Thus, while grasping the concepts behind the Ten Commandments might have been difficult, the story of the Jews leaving Egypt was collectively symbolic and inspiring. More significantly, while Gullahs did not have a complete intellectual grasp of the identity of Jesus Christ, and they did not totally comprehend the words of the Sermon on the Mount, they nevertheless saw their worldly existence as closely harmonizing with that of Christ. As a people, they were wholly within the philosophical drift of that sermon. And while their exposure to Christianity was sometimes superficial, their acceptance and reinterpretation was generally practical and original.

The center of the Gullah slave community was either the cabin of a religious leader or later, in the antebellum era, the praise house. By the 1840s, many planters had erected such plantation meeting houses to afford slaves a place of worship and to deprive those from various plantations of an opportunity to mingle. The slave quarters were called "the street," and the first building on "the street" was the praise house, described as a paintless, cheerless-appearing edifice that "looked as if a heavy gale might lay it low."[30] Several nights during the week and on Sundays, the praise house bell's welcoming, soothing sound brought the people on "the street" together for assembly. Even after the Civil War, when trouble befell their community, Gullahs gathered at the praise house—the center of group life and the key to personhood.

More than a meeting place for prayer and exhortation, the praise house operated as a town hall where members of the plantation gathered, using prayer, song, and exhortation to comfort each other. J. Miller McKim, a northern musicologist, wrote in 1862:

> I asked one of these blacks (Prince Rivers, Sergeant, 1st. Reg. S.C.V.)—where they got these songs. "De make 'em, sah." "How do they make them?" After a pause, evidently casting about for an explanation, he said: "I'll tell you, its dis way. My master call me up, and order me a short peck of corn and a hundred lash. My friends see it, and is sorry for me. When dey come to de praise-meeting dat night dey sing about it.

Sergeant Rivers' comment illustrates how religion served both sacred and secular ends. Gullahs did not completely separate the two realms. The multiple functions of the praise house provide one example of this continuity; the formation of spirituals offers another. During the Civil War, Gullah soldiers singing about black drivers called their song a "spiritual," whereas observers considered it quite secular in character.

> Fust ting my mammy tell me,
> O' gwine away!
> Tell me bout de nigger-driver,
> O' gwine away!
> Nigger-driver second debil
> O' gwine away![31]

The black drivers were foremen who supervised their fellow slaves; they derived their authority directly from the master. Their position of privilege came at the expense of their own people. Drivers often had the power to punish on their own as well as the responsibility of carrying out any punishment decreed by the master or overseer. Although exceptions existed, the interests of the black driver and those of the black community were generally inimical. The creation and singing of the above spiritual at the praise house was consistent with the slaves' conviction that no black driver could ever get to heaven because "he could not see God's face in peace." This belief caused one distraught black driver to pray for forgiveness in accepting Christianity. Expressing not only a Christian ethos but an association with African traditional religion, the driver stated, "To that *tree* every night I went to pray; at last God, for Christ sake, pardoned my sins." The man became convinced that, despite his opprobrium, "Christ is able to save a driver as well as anybody else," and he hoped that "people will see at least one driver in heaven."[32]

THE DUAL MEANING OF PRAISE HOUSE MEMBERSHIP

The most important people in the slave quarters rendered important service to their community. There were two types of religious leaders within this hierarchy. The first were the male elders (also called *deacons* or *watchmen*), who were approved by white authority. Sam Polite became such an elder. These experienced church members expressed Christian beliefs more literally than did the other group of leaders, referred to as spiritual leaders. Black elders were the liaisons between the black membership and the white Baptist churches (which most slaves never attended). Often they were permitted to assemble slaves for "praise meeting" without the legally required white presence. Elders were exemplary people, walking the thin line between keeping slaveholders' trust and commanding their people's respect. They ostensibly embodied non-threatening features of Christianity—obedience, docility, and a "turn the other cheek" attitude. As guardians of the community and articulators of group values, elders counseled patience, sometimes encouraging conservatism in the quarters. Stern about their extensive duties of oversight, direction, watchcare, and advisement, elders nevertheless used their positions with measure. Their message of love and steadfastness, which inspired moral confidence, was based on verbal ability, grave deportment, a consistent record of integrity, and a strong character.[33]

An example of the elder's role in the Gullah community is provided by Laura M. Towne, who lived out her life on the islands, becoming the Gullahs' constant champion and supporter. In May 1862, Gullah men were conscripted into the Union Army at bayonet point by General David Hunter, a zealous abolitionist. Because the Gullahs feared the worst—that, as masters had warned, they were being sold to Cuba—expressions of grief abounded on the islands. The men were herded off amidst crying children, grieving women, and indignant northern sympathizers. Towne wrote that it was an exceedingly low point for the Gullahs, who had already withstood so much:

> We, anxious and depressed, talked in low tones over this extra ordinary proceeding. . . . That evening we ladies went to the praise house and heard good, old Marcus exhort, Dagus pray and all sing. Marcus said he had often told all the brethren they must be just like birds when the gunner is

about, expecting a crack every minute. "De ain't neber know what gwine
befal dey, pore black folks must wait and hab faith. . . . Massa laff one day.
Ask me if I tink Christ want black nigger in heben. One ting I sure. We'uns
gwine to be where de crucify Lord am. And if dat place be Hell, He gwine
make it heben for we." [34]

The second group of religious leaders were spiritual parents; this
group contained a large female component. Although outside the purview of planters or missionaries, spiritual parents, like elders, were respected and highly regarded. Their influence belonged to another tradition, which had adapted to Christianity. From St. Helena Island, Laura
Towne wrote:

"I went to-day to see Maum Katie, an old African woman who remembers
worshipping her own gods in Africa, but who has been nearly a century in
this country. She is bright and talkative, a great "spiritual mother," a fortune teller, or rather prophetess, and a woman of tremendous influence
over her spiritual children. [35]

Spiritual parents' responsibilities began with the initial decision to "seek
Jesus" and extended through each individual Christian conversion. The
resulting bond between the convert and the altar parent was lifelong.
Spiritual parents interpreted dreams, signs, and visions. They taught the
"seeker" how to pray and emphasized loyalty to the praise house and the
importance of dealing justly with others in the slave community. Manners were especially important. "A Christian is mannerable," the Gullahs
insisted. All of these composites were essential to Gullah concepts of
spiritual rebirth. Both types of leaders—elders and altar parents—were
significant in the slave community. But the existence of altar parents in
particular expressed the bondspeople's judiciousness in creating a socioreligious sphere which reflected their own status system and their concepts of community obligation.

Observance of the Gullah method of admission to the praise house
and to black society membership reveals how black elders and spiritual
parents manifested divergent traditions and elements of syncretism
within Gullah folk religion. To be accepted into the praise house and
black society, a candidate had to relate a satisfactory experience based
on soul grappling: a series of traumatic confrontations between the individual and some higher power. The successful experience involved a
personal rebirth sensation and spiritual and moral transformation, cul-
minating in full membership in the socioreligious community. The tran-
sitional period between expressing a desire to become a Christian and
acceptance into the praise house was called "seekin'" (and sometimes
"strivin'"). This term was introduced to the Gullahs by Methodist missionaries who, at the close of preaching sessions, inquired whether any-

one wished to come forward and "seek Jesus." Those professing such a desire went "on trial" until deemed ready for baptism. For Methodists, readiness meant acceptance of their teaching and knowledge of the Creed, the sacraments, and the Lord's Prayer. Once they were deemed ready, slaves were eligible for "sprinkling" baptism.

Few slaves attempted to meet these requirements; nevertheless, slaves embraced the term "seekin' " and even devised an original interpretation of "seeking Jesus" that Methodists believed bore no resemblance to Christianity:

> When one of these people becomes serious, or "begins to pray" as he would say,—this is seldom the result of preaching, but most commonly a "warning in a dream,"—it is customary for him to select, by the direction of "the spirit" of course, some church member of influence, as his spiritual guide. Females are often chosen. Soon after the "vision" in which his teacher is pointed out, he makes known . . . his revelation and puts himself under . . . instruction.[36]

The instruction was twofold, coinciding with the twofold character of the spiritual teacher. The teacher as "prophet" taught the seeker proper conduct, particularly how to pray. The teacher was also an interpreter of visions "to whom the seeker relates all . . . *travels*." Missionaries were especially perplexed by the seeker's professed travels, considering this process the most peculiar and incomprehensible. "This word *travel*," wrote one missionary, "is one of the most significant in their language, and comprehends all those exercises, spiritual, visionary and imaginative, which make up an 'experience'. . . . These travels may differ in some things; and in others they all agree. Each seeker meets with warnings—awful sights or sounds, and always has a vision of a white man who talks with him, warns him, and then sometimes makes him carry a burden, and in the end leads him to the river."[37]

After the teacher was satisfied with the seeker's travels, the pronouncement "He git thru" indicated readiness for church membership. "This decision is never questioned," wrote the missionary. "Thus the case is settled. The man's religion is endorsed by an authoritative imprimatur and heaven is sure." After observing this entire process of religious conversion, the missionary expressed disbelief that he had witnessed any change of heart in the convert. There was, he stated,

> no solitary conviction to the true nature of sin, no genuine repentance to embitter sin to the soul, no distant apprehension of the sacrifices of the Savior and the merit of his death as the atonement for sin, and the great procuring cause of pardon: in a word, no distant element of the Christian experience involved in the whole affair.[38]

Several other paramount aspects of the "seekin' " experience shed light on Gullah concepts of spiritual transformation. First, the seeker was expected to shun all worldly pleasures. Second, the seeker went into "de wilderness," where the visions and "de trabbel" occurred. The latter requirement involved approved and unapproved night vigils. Grave-yards (normally taboo except during burials), the cotton or corn fields, and the marshes were all favorite praying grounds for seekers. No mat-ter where "de trabbel" occurred—in "de fields," "de ponds," or "de bush," all was defined as "de wilderness." Gullahs believed that "notin' won't hurt you while you been seekin'."[39]

Furthermore, seekers refrained from most social interaction and communicated only with the spiritual parent. They did not speak even to family members unless absolutely necessary. During this time of utter prostration, untidy and exceptionally unkempt appearance was ex-pected. Female seekers often covered their faces with ash. All seekers wore a white cloth or white string around their heads during the entire process "just to mark deyselbes diffren." During the Civil War, northern teachers working in the Sea Islands remarked that children "on trial" or "strivin' " were taken out of school. Since "de trabbel" lasted for months, sometimes the entire school was disrupted. One teacher wrote:

> In the winter most of the children were "seeking and praying." The older people said "They do hang they heads and pray"; and they are not allowed to do much of anything else for fear that they would "be turned back". . . .
>   These religious revivals are a source of much disturbance in school rou-tine. . . . We cannot call these "religious excitements"; the young seekers were in a stupid and lethargic condition. Some children were not allowed to come to school for fear they would be turned back.[40]

This spiritual compact and attachment to community membership derived from both Christian and African traditions of sacred ethos. Just as African memory profoundly impacted Gullah culture in the decora-tive arts, language formation, and oral tradition, so the socioreligious heritage was deeply rooted in Africanity.[41] The Gullahs' mystical con-version experience and strong emphasis on community integration was, as the Methodists suspected, linked to traditions outside Protestantism. The Gullah creed, which taught that leadership, sacred transformation, personhood, and social cohesion evolved from spiritual unity, invoked memories of the secret cultural associations of West Africa. Significant features of African spirituality and collectivity were practiced within and to some extent reinforced by Christianity.

The Gambia, Sierra Leone, and Liberia regions, referred to as Upper Guinea, supplied more slaves to coastal Carolina than any other region except Kongo-Angola. The large majority of the non-Moslem peoples of Upper Guinea had historically shared common cultural features, maintained by two associations which regulated the sacred, social, political, and—to some degree—economic life of the communities. These institutions were generally named *Poro* for men and *Sande* for women (although the names varied between groups). Upper Guinea contained a multiplicity of ethnic peoples bound together by these male and female organizations.[42] Their affinity was so strong that early travelers, explorers, and traders often referred to them as one society, under the generic name of *Sapi*, observing that political centralization and social homogeneity was maintained through the common secret societies.

Poro and Sande were not organizations of exclusivity, but means of introducing all members into adulthood. Each individual underwent a lengthy seclusion, secret training, the bestowing of a new name, graduation, and celebration as a full member of society. In these "bush schools" youth were instructed in social knowledge and conduct, group history and lore, and the activities peculiar to one's station and gender. Marriage, sexual relations, and holding property were prohibited to a noninitiate. Regardless of biological age, a noninitiate was considered a child with no significant position in the community. Poro and Sande were secret only to the uninitiated and other outsiders. The privacy of these bush activities was paramount on pain of death. Even in the twentieth century, these associations, though greatly altered, have proved resilient, and efforts to obtain eyewitness accounts of their activities are generally futile.[43]

Withdrawal from village society was a ritualistic death. Initiates were taken into a sacred grove by Poro priests and Sande priestesses, called "altar parents." Here they symbolically took leave of earth and journeyed down into the spirit world—the land of the dead. Among some ethnic groups, these spirits were ancestors. For others, they were nameless, capricious, quasi-human beings, sometimes occupying rocks, rivers, mountains, and trees. In any case, encounters with them were manifested in dreams and prayers—the most common forms of revelation and spiritual communication—and represented a form of earthly demise. Experiences during the "travel" into "the belly of the devil" were recounted to the altar parent for interpretation. During this journey through the spirit world, the initiate's soul was in an anxious, confused state, seeking to recover itself.[44]

Much as Gullah seekers did, female African initiates covered themselves with white clay, and all initiates tied white cloths around their heads. White symbolized habitation in the world of the dead; it indicated spiritual transparency. White was commonly viewed as a sacred color in West Africa because of its link with ancestors and its association with death. White was also associated with water, and the spirit world of the

dead was under water. In river beds, in the sea, and in other bodies of
water resided transpicuous spirits with varying degrees of power and
supernatural import.[45] The white spirit that led the Gullah seeker to a
river, as recorded by the Methodist missionary, may have represented a
non-Christian personification.

Initiation was a limbo status. One of its aims was to control the person's spirit, mainly through symbolic travel, rebirth, transformation, ceremony, ritual, mediation, medicine, and exclusive contact. This was
done by acquainting the initiate with both negative and positive spirit-
forms during the travel. Seclusion also signified a means of challenging
and triumphing over the natural environment. Equally important was
one's restraint over one's self, achieved by suspending elements of fear,
selfishness, and uncontrolled individualism, all considered detrimental
to society. A noninitiate was a shadow, a mere image, an imitation. During the stay in the sacred grove, the initiate became a "little spirit of the
bush." After graduation, the neophyte was a citizen, a full member of
the society.[46] Thus, secret society association directed forces of collective
human existence through a common theme of spiritual regeneration
and community integration. The initiate was in the power of the spiritual leader, far removed from kin who might condone or overlook frail-
ties. One entered the bush as a helpless, irresponsible being with no social sense. Guided by the altar parent, the initiate underwent a thorough
physical, mental, and moral test which eliminated unsuitable behavior.
The bush experience ended by either profound transformation or
death. Some initiates did not return from the sacred grove. In ancient
days, "weaklings" and homosexuals were allowed to die.[47]

African initiates returned from the sacred grove "reborn," having
"crossed the water." Former animosities, debts, and crimes were obliterated; former behavior was forgiven. Assumption of new responsibilities
and stature meant serving the village and accepting guidance from the
Poro Council. Reintegration was marked by a washing ritual in a creek
or river, dressing in finery, and "a public ceremony" in which "they are
handed over to their parents with great acclamation."[48]

Nearly all West African peoples had various kinds of sacred and secret associations, and, although membership was generally not manda-
tory except in Upper Guinea, many involved rites of passage into community membership, professional training, and adulthood.[49] In the
sacred, ceremonial character of these African institutions and their role
in community formation, they are analogous to African-American
group association. Group association took various forms in antebellum
black life, particularly in benevolent, mutual aid, and masonic societies.
As in African culture, these African-American societies were imbued
with both sacred and secular significance. Thus, while many aspects of

the Gullah experience were not unique, their geographical isolation and rootedness in the culture of the past encouraged a more visceral, tendentious Africanity than that of blacks elsewhere in the U.S. The spiritual travel, visions, mentoring, and final examination hark back to Africanity.

Other elements of the rite of passage, which followed the actual transforming experience, suggest a creative fusion of African and Judeo-Christian traditions into a community as well as spiritually binding enterprise. Once an individual "experience" had proved satisfactory, the seeker was examined publicly by the black elder. If the candidate passed this interrogation of spiritual and communal readiness, the water burial occurred on a "communion Sunday," the first Sabbath of the month. In the antebellum era, a record was set in 1857 when 220 slaves joining Beaufort Baptist Church "were all on Sunday morning . . . Baptized by our Pastor." During the Civil War, teacher David Thorpe wrote of one occasion when "upwards of one hundred and forty people," of all ages, were baptized on occupied St. Helena Island. It was "a strange and picturesque scene," as people gathered from "far and near," in all manner of vehicles and "every kind of attire." Candidates "dressed for the water" wore "miserable looking clothing," but nearby were mule carts loaded with new garments for the neophytes when they emerged from the river. The white minister read off each candidate's name, "Old Pa Tom" nodded his approval of the person's examination, and all headed for the water:

> The ceremony was performed by the roadside near a bridge. . . . "Siah," "leader" at "Good William Fripp's" took the arm of Mr. Phillips and together they entered the water. Around on every side were hundreds of people arrayed in their Sunday best. Their shiny black faces surmounted by bright turbans and white turbans. . . . They presented a beautiful sight. . . . Truly the sun shone out on a beautiful scene. . . . —Near the water stood a large band of singers and they sent up hymn after hymn. . . . Candidates . . . seemed to be attended by several friends or relatives. . . . Mr. Phillips took . . . each by one shoulder while Siah laid hold of the other and together they immersed them. . . . their friends received them . . . and hurried them off. It took a long time . . . but after . . . it was over . . . we all went back to church. All the candidates came out in shiny robes. . . . Then we had a long service, . . . the right hand of fellowship was given . . . and the sacrament was administered.[50]

Just as total immersion was the only means of true water burial and rebirth, so the ring shout was ceremonial recognition of "true believer" membership, of safe passage into "de ark ob safety." The ring shout did not involve random shrieking, wailing, or actual shouting. Instead, the shout was an atavistic, synchronous set of simultaneous motions involving foot stomping, hand clapping, and torso motions in unison, accompanied by singing. Usually one person in the middle of the ring "lined out" the songs while the congregation, in typical call-response fashion, repeated the lyrics and shuffled counterclockwise around the enclosed leader, who was in a state of "possession" or trance. Traveling through the South Carolina and Georgia Sea Island in 1848, Charles Lyell noted that on plantations frequented by Methodist missionaries, slaves replaced forbidden violins, dancing, and worldly singing with a religious exercise: "They are permitted to move round rapidly in a ring, joining hands in token of brotherly love, presenting the right hand and then the left." This "spiritual boulanger," according to Lyell, served as a substitute for the dance.[51]

Some accounts indicate that three or four people, rather than one, stood outside of the ring singing, clapping, and gesticulating, while shouters moved on their heels in a circle, bending the knees slightly. They began with a slow gait, with a few going around and others joining in vocally and kinetically. Then the rhythm went faster and faster, "till at last only the most marked part of the refrain is sung and the shuffling, stamping and clapping get furious." A watchful elder scrutinized the shout to ensure no crossing of legs, as this would signify worldly dancing.[52]

Some Methodists who observed the shout discouraged this rite and other forms of outward emotionalism. Slaves, they insisted, should be instructed in "distinguishing between animal feeling and a real work of grace." They should learn prepared catechism and recite memorized texts. Methodists wanted worship to be formal and emotional spontaneity to be eradicated, just as violins and banjos had been silenced. Gullahs embraced some Methodist teaching, but remained unconvinced that physical expressions of worship were "worldly." They insisted that "the angels shout in heaven," and that shouting was approved fellowship with the spirit world. This altered state of consciousness was also recognition of human communion and group solidarity. William Capers, Superintendent of Missions, instructed that slaves be allowed to "be themselves," and some white religious teachers permitted the ring shout, although not as part of the regular service.[53]

The ring shout was uniquely an African-American creation, although it was grounded in African spirit possession. Charlotte Forten, a black Northern teacher, described a shout scene she witnessed:

> At the close of the Praise-Meeting, they all shake hands in the most solemn manner. Afterward, as a kind of appendix, they have a grand "shout" during which they sing their own hymns. . . . The first shout that we witnessed impressed us very much. The large gloomy room, with its blackened walls—the wild whirling dance of the shouters,—the crowd of dark,

eager faces gathered around,—the figure of the old blind man, whose excitement could hardly be controlled, and whose attitude and gestures while singing were very fine—and over all, the red glare of the burning pine-knot, which shed a circle of light of the room—these all formed a wild, strange, and deeply impressive picture, not soon to be forgotten.[54]

Collectively, possession behavior, travel, visions, and the ring shout may have been a society's attempt to join the natural and supernatural worlds. Since the shout was a public ceremony, it was a sharing and solidifying experience, communicated through socioreligious interaction. But it also reinforced individual self-worth, and each shouter's skill was noted. Many years after bondage, descriptions of shouts observed on the Sea Islands reveal that the ceremony was an important means of "welcoming and initiating" individuals into the praise house. Yet ring shouts were also behavior inspired and controlled by an outside agent. While the outside agent was ostensibly the Holy Spirit, the American ring shout may, like the African circle dance, represent personalities displaced by ancestors and communion with spirits. Sterling Stuckey argues for the universality of the ring among African-Americans.[55] Perhaps, like the associations and secret societies, the ring shout affirms the longevity of shared African memories nestled within accepted aspects of American religious culture.

Just as Poro-Sande initiation went beyond the assumption of adult responsibilities or a simple rite of passage, so praise house membership involved more than conversion in a Christian sense. No aspect of West African life was truly secular, and Poro-Sande sociopolitical power symbolized relationships between the sacred and the temporal order. The foundation of Poro-Sande prerogative was mystical, and its spiritual significance was pervasive. The institution was "made by god, not by man." Poro-Sande spirits (priests, priestesses, and the "bush-devil"), although human, assumed godhead and, as earthly manifestations of supernatural power, remained hidden behind masks. Their leadership authority was highly respected and unchallenged, and crossed group boundaries. The Poro Council, consisting of senior members of both societies, stopped village quarrels, tried and condemned social criminals, and even gave permission to declare war. Each group's nominal ruler was a chief, who ruled via temporal power. But Poro Council law was supreme, and the council could depose a chief.[56]

The authority of the praise house religious court, like that of the Poro Council, came from God, the ultimate source of virtue, order, and goodness. The religious court was composed of spiritual parents with authority over sacred and community matters. Both the religious court and the council were God-given regulators, functioning as primary psychological and spiritual coercive agents for the common good. Gullahs referred to religious conversion and praise house membership as having "caught sense." "Catching sense" meant full plantation membership; it meant accepting the politico-jural authority of the praise house, as embodied in its religious court. All members answered to the religious court system when discord arose, and all were expected to abide by its rulings. Gullahs defined it as "just law," while white law was "unjust law." Long after slavery, this system effectively held members responsible for good behavior; it explains why crimes were rarely committed in Gullah communities. Thus, apart from the spiritual function of the praise house, the communal aspect of praise house membership and of religious court regulation was also essential.[57]

The relationship between Gullah folk religion, secret society regulation, and cultural specialization is perhaps best recapitulated by Kenneth Little:

> The secret societies are an embodiment of . . . supernatural power. Collectively, they provide an institutional structure which bears similarity to the medieval church in Europe. . . . They lay down various rules of conduct, prescribe certain forms of behavior and are the sole agency capable of remitting certain sins.[58]

In both African and Gullah society, allegiance was based on an institution's supernatural force, which was used to establish law, authority, accountability, security, and social cohesion. Individual experience and self-esteem were also promoted through personal training, symbolic travel, and rebirth. Nearly all Africans brought to America came from groups in which some type of initiation process had been practiced and secret societies had existed. Yet no others contained the distinctive, structurally inclusive elements of Poro and Sande. Because so many ethnic groups from Poro-Sande traditions were transported to the low country (and perhaps elsewhere), conceivably some of the more adaptive and useful elements of Poro-Sande institutions remained, despite the trauma of capture, the long march, and the Middle Passage. To be sure, this tradition represents merely one possible relationship between Gullahs and their various forebears, just as the strong BaKongo influence affecting Gullah concepts of sacred medicine, healing, and funeral practices represents another. Nevertheless, one way of understanding the significance of Gullah folk religion is through its force as a cultural and community-building phenomenon and a means of instilling individual dignity among bondspeople.

Anthropologist Gerald Sider's discussion of Newfoundland fishermen—a study in hegemony and counter-hegemony—provides a theoretical vision for understanding religious instruction, the Gullah socioreligious community, and Gullah expressions of symbolic protest. Sider defines culture as "the form and manner in which people perceive, define, articulate and express their mutual relations." Hegemony, says Sider, "is that aspect of culture which, usually in the face of struggle, most directly seeks to unify production and appropriation, and to extend appropriation beyond the productive act itself into neighborhood, family, forms of consumption—in sum into daily life." This type of "assertive" hegemony (Christian religious instruction for Gullahs) explains counter-hegemonic cultural tendencies and manifestations of popular resistance (Gullah folk religion) *which may borrow from symbols of elite cultural domination.*[59]

Admittedly, this borrowing places limitations on resistance. But the "very experience of opposition," by exposing the contradictions within the existing hegemonic model, heightens consciousness. Like other forms of culture, counter-hegemonic strategies emerge not merely from individual thoughts, actions, and experiences, but also from a mutual understanding of social relations.[60] The complexity may not have been lost to praise house leaders such as Sam Polite. While he extolled the religion of his "peculiar people," perhaps he recognized the contradictions of that religion, as expressed in a prayer he prayed when over one hundred years old, "The Long Look":

> Do not pass we by, My Jesus, as you go on de road from Jericho to de new Jerusalem, but tarry at de door and speak de word of hope to we heart and blow de breeze of blessing upon us. Almighty and eternal Father, we de prisoners of Hope, turn to de stronghold and begs oona [you] fur give we de long look . . . dat we could have 'couragement fur go forward. . . . Do God, if it so please you, Massa Jesus, Gib me de long look like Moses, so I could see into de Promised Land from de mount, if my weary feet ain't never guine to walk in de New Jerusalem with my people.[61]

Prophet Polite was neither the first nor the last black leader to ask for a look at the promised land. Certainly solemn Denmark Vesey and stoic Nat Turner went to the gallows with a vision of a "long look." And, one hundred years after the Emancipation Proclamation, another black religious leader would ask for the "long look."[62]

African Americans have been aware of self-interested interpretations of biblical scripture ever since their Christian instruction began. They also recognized the power, knowledge, and wisdom of spiritual discourse. Gullahs embraced edifying features of Protestantism, grafted onto it elements of Africanity, and created a religion which challenged slavery's assertive cultural hegemony. Christian experience was expressed through communal fulfillment, and, for the slaves, plantation life had aspects of an African village in microcosm. They attempted to exert control over their environment as had their forebears. Gullahs lived under an oppressive socioeconomic system that challenged their self-esteem. In response, they molded a strong community and used their spirituality to create a personal and collective culture which served them under enslavement and mitigated the yoke of bondage.

NOTES

1. "The Long Look," n.d., miscellaneous correspondence, vol. 17, Penn School Papers, Southern Historical Collection, University of North Carolina, Chapel Hill. Sam Polite's sermon was recorded by Rosa Cooley in 1934. Cooley was superintendent of Penn School on St. Helena Island at the time.

2. Ibid.

3. Willie Lee Rose, *Rehearsal for Reconstruction: The Port Royal Experiment* (Indianapolis, Ind.: Bobbs-Merrill, 1964); Lincoln's quote is from Leon F. Litwack, *Been in the Storm So Long: The Aftermath of Slavery* (New York: Vintage, 1980), 66.

4. David Thorpe to William Weld, November 9, 1864, and David Thorpe to John Mooney, January 25, 1863, both in Dabbs Papers, Thorpe Series; Arthur Sumner to Lt. Joseph Clark, January 23, 1863, and Arthur Sumner to Nina Hartshorn, July 7, 1862, both in Penn School Papers, vol. 4; all may be found in the Southern Historical Collection, University of North Carolina, Chapel Hill.

5. 1 Peter 2:9.

6. Harriott Pinckney Rutledge to Edward Rutledge, August 5, 1822, Pinckney Papers, South Carolina Historical Society, Charleston; Lionel Kennedy and Thomas Parker, *An Official Report of the Trials of Sundry Negroes, Charged with an Attempt to Raise an Insurrection . . . and in an Appendix, a Report of the Trials of Four White Persons on Indictments for Attempting to Excite the Slaves to Insurrection* (Charleston: James R. Schenck, 1822), 13–14, 67–69; Luther Porter Jackson, "Religious Instruction of Negroes, 1830–1860," *Journal of Negro History* 15 (1930): 70–79; Stephen B. Oates, *The Fires of Jubilee: Nat Turner's Fierce Rebellion* (New York: Harper and Row, 1975).

7. Charles C. Pinckney, *An Address Delivered in Charleston before the Agricultural Society of South Carolina, At Its Annual Meeting, 18th August, 1829* (Charleston, S.C.: A. E. Miller, 1829), passim; James O. Andrew, "The Southern Slave Population," *Methodist Magazine and Quarterly Review* 31 (1831): 315–17; *Southern Christian Advocate,* January 26, 1838.

8. Andrew, "Southern Slave Population," 316–19, 322.

9. "Report of the Missionary Society," in Minutes of South Carolina Conference of the Methodist Episcopal Church, February 10, 1836, p. 20, Historical Society of the South Carolina Conference, Methodist Church Archives, Wofford College, Spartanburg, S.C.; William W. Wightman, *Life of William Capers, Including an Autobiography* (Nashville, Tenn.: J. B. McFerrin, 1858), 295–96; *Southern Christian Advocate,* January 26, 1838.

10. William Capers, *A Catechism for the Use of the Methodist Missions* (Charleston, S.C.: J. S. Burges, 1833), passim; *Southern Christian Advocate,* January 31, 1851; slave's passage quoted in John Spencer Bassett, *The Southern Plantation Overseer, As Revealed in His Letters* (Northhampton, Mass: Smith College, 1925), 14–15.

11. Charles C. Pinckney to William Capers, January 24, 1835, Historical Soci-

ety of the South Carolina Conference; Wightman, *Life of William Capers*, 298–99; *Christian Advocate and Journal*, April 10, 1833, September 9, 1833, January 24, 1835, and June 26, 1835; *Southern Christian Advocate*, July 7, 1843, December 22, 1843, and February 23, 1847; Mason Crum, *Gullah: Negro Life in the Carolina Sea Islands* (Durham, N.C.: Duke University Press, 1940), 218.

12. *Christian Advocate and Journal*, August 18, 1837.

13. Thomas Wentworth Higginson, *Army Life in a Black Regiment* (1870; reprint, New York: Collier Books, 1962), 71–72.

14. Joe Madison King, *A History of South Carolina Baptists* (Columbia, S.C.: General Board, South Carolina Baptist Convention, 1964), 26–35; A. H. Newman, *A History of the Baptist Church in the United States* (New York: Christian Literature, 1894), 1–79, 221–26, 242–52; Sidney E. Ahlstrom, *A Religious History of the American People* (New Haven, Conn.: Yale University Press, 1972), 171–72; *Christian Advocate and Journal*, November 20, 1835, January 22, 1836; Wightman, *Life of William Capers*, 295–96; Charles C. Jones, *Religious Instruction of the Negroes in the United States* (1842; reprint, New York: Negro Universities Press, 1969), 86.

15. John H. Tucker to T. D. Grimke, n.d. [ca. early 1845], South Carolina Historical Society; *Proceedings of the Meeting in Charleston, South Carolina, May 13–15, 1845 on the Religious Instruction of the Negroes* (Charleston, S.C.: B. Jenkins, 1845), 71–72; Pastoral Address, Minutes of the South Carolina Conference of the Methodist Episcopal Church, December 25, 1844, pp. 14–15, Historical Society of the South Carolina Conference; John B. Adger, *A Sermon Preached by the Rev. J. B. Adger of the Second Presbyterian Church, Charleston, S.C., May 9, 1847* (Charleston, S.C.: T. W. Haynes, 1847), 12–13; Rev. Alexander Glennie, *Sermons Preached on Plantations to Congregations of Negroes* (Charleston, S.C.: A. E. Miller, 1844), passim; Rev. A. F. Dickson, *Plantation Sermons* (Philadelphia, Penn.: Presbyterian Board of Publication, 1855), passim; Donald Blake Touchstone, "Planters and Slave Religion in the Deep South," (Ph.D. dissertation, Tulane University, 1973), 71–85; Rev. J. H. Thornwell, *The Rights and Duties of Masters: A Sermon Preached at the Dedication of a Church Erected in Charleston, S.C., for the Benefit and Instruction of the Colored Population* (Charleston, S.C.: Steam-Power Press, 1850), 48–51.

16. James Leo Garrett, Jr., *Baptist Church Discipline: An Historical Introduction to the Practices of Baptist Churches, With Particular Attention to the Summary of Church Discipline Adopted in 1773 by the Charleston Association* (Nashville, Tenn.: Broadman Press, 1962), 3–4, 10–18, 28; King, *South Carolina Baptists*, 62–63; Ahlstrom, *A Religious History;* 440–43; Minutes of the Euhaw Baptist Church, South Caroliniana Library, University of South Carolina, Columbia; Janet Duitsman Cornelius, "God's Schoolmasters: Southern Evangelists to the Slaves, 1830–1860," (Ph.D. dissertation, University of Illinois at Urbana-Champaign), 228–40; Minutes of the Beaufort Baptist Church, October 8, 1840, p. 11, April 9, 1841, p. 15, May 14, 1842, p. 34, July 8, 1842, p. 34, August 12, 1843, pp. 61–62, September 8, 1843, p. 63, October 1, 1853, p. 180, April 5, 1855, pp. 203–4, Baptist Collection, Furman University, Greenville, S.C.

17. George P. Rawick, ed., *The American Slave: A Composite Autobiography*, 19 vols. (Westport, Conn: Greenwood Publishing, 1972), vol. 2, *South Carolina Narratives*, part 2, 184; Diary of William F. Allen, pp. 23, 57, William F. Allen Family Papers, 1775–1937, State Historical Society of Wisconsin, Madison.

18. *Southern Christian Advocate*, May 1, 1840.

19. *Christian Advocate and Journal*, January 31, 1834, and June 20, 1834.

20. Ibid., June 20, 1834.

21. John W. Blassingame, ed., *Slave Testimony: Two Centuries of Letters, Speeches, Interviews and Autobiographies* (Baton Rouge: Louisiana State University Press, 1977), 374, 381; Charlotte Forten, "Life on the Sea Islands: Part 1," *Atlantic Monthly* 13 (May 1864): 668; Diary of Laura M. Towne, vol. 2, p. 15, Penn School Papers, Southern Historical Collection, University of North Carolina, Chapel Hill.

22. Allen Diary, 37, 71, 87–88; Rev. W. T. Richardson to Reverend Whipple, July 3, 1863, Papers of the American Missionary Association, Amistad Research Center, Tulane University, New Orleans, La.; Henry Noble Sherwood, ed., Introduction, "Journal of Miss Susan Walker, March 3d to June 6, 1862," *Historical and Philosophical Society of Ohio* 7 (January–March 1912): 32–33, 40–41; Thorpe to Weld, Nov. 9, 1864.

23. *Christian Advocate and Journal*, January 31, 1834; John Field to George Washington Moore, March 21, 1833, Historical Society of the South Carolina Conference; Minutes, Beaufort Baptist Church, October 7, 1859 (see "Origin of the Colored Societies," business meeting in which the organization of the societies is discussed), pp. 271–74, January 7, 1842, passim, and November 11, 1840, p. 12, Baptist Collection, Furman University, Greenville, S.C.

24. Field to Moore, March 21, 1833; *Christian Advocate and Journal*, July 22, 1836.

25. *Southern Christian Advocate*, July 7, 1843, August 21, 1840, February 3, 1841, and September 29, 1843.

26. *Christian Advocate and Journal*, January 31, 1834, November 20, 1835, and July 22, 1836; *Southern Christian Advocate*, May 1, 1840, April 8, 1842, June 26, 1843, and July 28, 1843.

27. W. T. Richardson to Rev. S. S. Jocelyn, June 19, 1863, and Lydia Fuller to Rev. S. S. Jocelyn, July 5, 1864, both in Papers of the American Missionary Association; Allen Diary, 96, 127–28, 144, 151–52; Edward L. Pierce, "The Freedmen at Port Royal," *Atlantic Monthly* 12 (September 1863): 304; Laura M. Towne to James McKim, February 1, 1862, Antislavery Papers, Rare Book Room, Cornell University; Elizabeth Hyde Botume, *First Days Amongst the Contrabands* (1893; reprint, New York: Arno Press and New York Times, 1968), 91–92; 112–14.

28. Mary Ames, *From a New England Woman's Diary in Dixie* (1906; reprint, New York: Negro Universities Press, 1968), 68; Botume, *Amongst the Contrabands*, 74–75.

29. Kennedy and Parker, *Trial of Sundry Negroes*, 46, 58–59; Robert Starobin, ed., *Denmark Vesey: The Slave Conspiracy of 1822* (Englewood Cliff, N.J.: Prentice-Hall, 1970), 25, 50, 61, 64; Higginson, *Army Life*, 49; Edwin Williams to Rev. S. S. Jocelyn, January 28, 1863, Papers of the American Missionary Association.

30. Mrs. William R. Wister, "Recollections of a Southern Plantation and School," Penn School Papers, vol. 5, p. 15, Southern Historical Collection, University of North Carolina, Chapel Hill.

31. William F. Allen, Charles Pickard Ware, and Lucy McKim Garrison, *Slave*

Songs of the United States (1867; reprint, New York: Oak Publications, 1951), xviii; Higginson, *Army Life*, 210–11.

32. *Southern Christian Advocate*, August 11, 1843.

33. David Thorpe to John Mooney, January 25, 1863, Dabbs Papers, Thorpe Series, Southern Historical Collection; Rev. Augustine Roots to Rev. S. S. Jocelyn, February 8, 1863, Papers of the American Missionary Association; Thomas J. Woofter, *Black Yeomanry* (New York: Henry Holt, 1930), 243–54; Jenkins Mikell, *Rumblings of the Chariot Wheels* (Columbia, S.C.: The State Co., 1923), 128; Samuel Lawton, "The Religious Life of Coastal and Sea Island Negroes" (Ph.D. dissertation, George Peabody College for Teachers, 1939), 36–37, 62–63, 69–72; Patricia Guthrie, "Catching Sense: The Meaning of Plantation Membership on St. Helena, South Carolina" (Ph.D. dissertation, University of Rochester, 1977), chapters 4 and 5.

34. Towne Diary, vol. 6, p. 26, Penn Papers.

35. Rupert Holland, ed., *Letters and Diary of Laura M. Towne* (1912; reprint, New York: Negro Universities Press, 1969), 145, 162; Margaret Washington, "Cultural Transmission and Female Diviners in Gullah Slave Society" (Paper presented at the Southern Historical Association, Lexington, Ky., November 9, 1989), passim.

36. *Southern Christian Advocate*, October 30, 1846 and October 30, 1847; Lorenzo D. Turner, *Africanisms in the Gullah Dialect* (1949; reprint, New York: Arno Press and New York Times, 1969), 271–75. "Seekin' " was practiced among other African-American slaves in various parts of the South; see Charles A. Raymond, "The Religious Life of the Negro Slave," *Harper's New Monthly Magazine* 27 (October 1863): part 2, 680–82.

37. *Southern Christian Advocate*, October 30, 1847.

38. Ibid.

39. Mikell, *Chariot Wheels*, 137–39; Raymond, "Religious Life of Slaves," part 2, 680–81; Higginson, *Army Life*, 191–95; Rosa B. Cooley, *School Acres* (New Haven, Conn.: Yale University Press, 1930), 151–53; Lawton, "Religious Life of Island Negroes," 143–45; Allen Diary, 155; Elsie Clews Parsons, *Folk-lore of the Sea Islands of South Carolina* (Cambridge, Mass.: American Folklore Society, 1923), 204–5.

40. Allen Diary, 155; Botume, *Amongst the Contrabands*, 254–55.

41. See Parsons, *Folk-lore of Sea Islands;* Turner, *Africanisms in Gullah;* Robert Farris Thompson, *Flash of the Spirit: African and Afro-American Art and Philosophy* (New York: Vintage, 1983); Joseph Cornet, *The Four Moments of the Sun: Kongo Art in Two Worlds* (Washington, D.C.: National Gallery of Art, 1981); John M. Vlach, *The Afro-American Tradition in Decorative Arts* (Cleveland, Ohio: Cleveland Museum of Art, 1978); Charles Joyner, *Down By the Riverside: A South Carolina Slave Community* (Urbana and Chicago: University of Illinois Press, 1984); Sterling Stuckey, *Slave Culture and the Foundations of Nationalist Theory* (New York: Oxford University Press, 1987); Margaret Washington Creel, *"A Peculiar People": Slave Religion and Community Culture among the Gullahs* (New York: New York University Press, 1988).

42. John Matthews, *A Voyage to the River Sierra Leone* (1788; reprint, London: Frank Cass, 1966), 82–83; Nicholas Owen, *Journal of a Slave Dealer: A View of*

Some Remarkable Axedents in the Life of Nicholas Owen on the Coast of Africa and America from the Year 1746 to the Year 1757 (London: George Routledge, 1930), 30–31; Warren L. d'Azevedo, "The Setting of Gola Society and Culture: Some Theoretical Implications in Time and Space," *Kroeber Anthropological Society Papers* (Berkeley: University of California, 1959), 67–68; Kenneth Little, *The Mende of Sierra Leone* (London: Routledge & Kegan Paul, 1951) 7–8, 240–42, his "The Poro as Arbiter of Culture," *African Studies* 7 (March 1948): 1, and his "The Political Function of the Poro: Part 1," *Africa* 35 (October 1965): 349–50; Walter Rodney, *A History of the Upper Guinea Coast, 1545–1800* (Oxford: Clarendon Press, 1970), 32–33, 65–67.

43. Mark Hanna Watkins, "The West African 'Bush' School," *American Journal of Sociology* 48 (1943): 667–70, 674–75; Little, "Poro as Arbiter of Culture," 5–6, his "Political Function of Poro," 349–56, and his *Mende*, 240–53; Warren L. d'Azevedo, "Gola Poro and Sande: Primal Tasks in Social Custodianship," *Ethnologische Zeitschrift Zurich* 1 (1980): 15–16; Carolina H. Bledsoe, "Stratification and Sande Politics," ibid., 143–45; Svend Holsoe, "Notes on the Vai Sande Society of Liberia," ibid., 97–107.

44. Watkins, " 'Bush' School," 66–67; James L. Gibbs, Jr., "The Kpelle of Liberia," in James L. Gibbs, Jr., *Peoples of Africa* (New York: Holt, Rinehart and Winston, 1965), 219–22; Warren L. d'Azevedo, "Common Principles of Variant Kinship Structures among the Golas of Western Liberia," *American Anthropologist* 64, no. 3 (1962): 505, his *Gola of Liberia* (New Haven, Conn.: Human Relations Area Files, 1972) 2: 312–13, and his "Gola Poro and Sande," 98–104; M. C. Jedrej, "Structural Aspects of a West African Society," *Ethnologische Zeitschrift Zurich* 1 (1980): 136; Bledsoe, "Stratification and Sande," 143–45; Holsoe, "Notes of Vai Sande," 97–107; Michael Jackson, *The Kuranko: Dimensions of Social Reality in a West African Society* (London: C. Hurst, 1977), 34, 182–84, 202–04; George Harley and George Schwab, "The Mano of Liberia," in *A Reader in General Anthropology*, ed. Carleton S. Coon (New York: Henry Holt, 1960), 348–49, 359–60, 364–65, 369.

45. *Tribes of the Western Province and the Denwoin People*, Folkways Research Series (Monrovia, Liberia: Dept. of Interior, 1955), 11–22; *Traditional History and Folklore of the Glebo Tribe* (Monrovia, Liberia: Dept. of Interior, 1961), 2: 83, Sylvia Boone, *Radiance from the Water: Ideals of Feminine Beauty in Mende Art* (New Haven and London: 1986); Creel, *Peculiar People*, chapters 2 and 10.

46. Watkins, " 'Bush' School," 66–68; Gibbs, "The Kpelle," 219–22; Jackson, *Kuranko*, 34, 182–84, 202–7; Harlen and Schwab, "The Mano," 348–49, 359–69; Little, *The Mende*, 225–27; d'Azevedo, *Gola of Liberia* 2: 83, and his "Gola Poro and Sande," 98–104.

47. Gibbs, "The Kpelle," 221–22; Watkins, " 'Bush' School," 666–68, 670–72.

48. Watkins, " 'Bush' School," 673–74; Jackson, *Kuranko*, 214, n. 1; *History of Gola* 2: 15–21; Sibley and Westermann, *Liberia*, 228–29; Holsoe, "Notes on Vai Sande," 103.

49. Betty M. Kuyk, "The African Derivation of Black Fraternal Orders in the United States," *Comparative Studies in Societies and History* 25, no. 4 (October 1983): 559–94.

50. Minutes of the Savannah River Baptist Association, November 26, 1853, pp. 10–11, November 25, 1854, p. 16, and November 14, 1857, pp. 10–11, Baptist Collection, Furman University, Greenville, S.C.; Minutes, Beaufort Baptist Church, July 12, 1857, pp. 2–3, 35, November 7, 1847, pp. 241–43; Thorpe to Mooney, January 25, 1863, Dabbs Papers.

51. Sir Charles Lyell, *A Second Visit to the United States* (New York: Harper & Brothers, 1849), 1: 269–70.

52. H. G. Spaulding, "Under the Palmetto," *Continental Monthly* 4 (August 1963): 202–03, 195–99; Holland, *Letters and Diary*, 22–23; Higginson, *Army Life*, 41; Cooley, *School Acres*, 150–51.

53. Lyett, *Second Visit*, 1: 269–70; *Southern Christian Advocate*, May 1, 1840, April 8, 1842, June 26, 1843, September 15, 1843, and September 6, 1850.

54. Charlotte Forten, "Life on the Sea Islands," part 2, *Atlantic Monthly* 13 (June, 1864), 672.

55. Robert Simpson, "The Shout and Shouting in Slave Religion in the United States," *Southern Quarterly* 23, no. 3 (Spring 1958): 34–40; Lawton, "Religious Life," 77–79; Stuckey, *Slave Culture*, passim, especially chapter 1.

56. Watkins, "'Bush' School," 671; Little, "Political Function of Poro," 557–58, and his "Poro as Arbiter of Culture," 4–10; Harley, "Notes on Poro," 6–7, 15, 19–20, 31; S. N. Eisenstadt, "Primitive Political Systems: A Preliminary Comparative Analysis," *American Anthropologist* 61 (1959): 202–03, 208; Fulton, "Functions of Poro in Kpelle," 121, 226–27; d'Azevedo, "Common Principles of Kinship among Golas," 513–14, and his "Setting of Gola Society and Culture," 70–76.

57. Patricia Guthrie, "Catching Sense: The Meaning of Plantation Membership in St. Helena Island, South Carolina" (Ph.D. dissertation, University of Rochester, 1977), chapters 4 and 5; Parsons, *Folk-lore of Sea Islands*, 205–6; Lawton, "Religious Life," 61–70; Mikell, *Chariot Wheels*, 138.

58. Kenneth Little, "The Role of the Secret Society in Cultural Specialization," *American Anthropologist* 51 (1949): 199.

59. Gerald Sider, "The Ties That Bind: Culture and Agriculture, Property and Propriety in the Newfoundland Village Fishery," *Social History* 5 (January 1980): 24–26.

60. Ibid.

61. "The Long Look," Penn School Papers.

62. Martin Luther King's last address, April 3, 1968, Memphis, Tennessee (see chapter 1 of this book).

CHAPTER FOUR

The Politics of "Silence"

Dual-Sex Political Systems and Women's Traditions of Conflict in African-American Religion

Cheryl Townsend Gilkes

Let your women keep silence in the churches: for it is not permitted unto them to speak.

—PAUL, I CORINTHIANS 14: 34 (KJV)

The "proper" place of women in the church is an age-old debate and from all appearances it seems that it perhaps will be an eternal one—for most mortals at least.

—BISHOP O. T. JONES, CHURCH OF GOD IN CHRIST, CA. 1950

As the Bible is an iconoclastic weapon—it is bound to break down images of error that have been raised. As no one studies it so closely as the Baptists, their women shall take the lead.

—MARY COOK, AMERICAN NATIONAL BAPTIST CONVENTION, 1887

Religion and politics, we are told, do not mix. Yet any superficial observation of religion in contemporary society will demonstrate that religious organizations contain within them structures and mechanisms which allocate power and authority. Religious systems are political systems, and very religious people can be quite political. Indeed, Alexis de Tocqueville in his travels through the United States commented on the political enterprise of the nation's preachers and the religious fervor of its politicians. The most dramatic contemporary religious politics revolve around issues of gender—specifically the power, authority, and prominence of women in churches and in public religious life. Because many Christian churches have recited Paul's admonition to the women in Corinth to "be silent," the proper activities of women in leadership roles have been problems to be resolved in dramatic, public contests of power. In addition to these gender conflicts, the African-European confrontation persists in our national life. It is not only a politico-economic conflict; it is also a cultural confrontation, and at the core of culture is religion.

The responses of Africans and their descendants to Christianity, we are now discovering, highlight the contrasts and contradictions between European and African worldviews. In one area alone—that of church polity and women's roles—we can recognize many of the tensions that existed between Western logic, which selected Paul's admonitions as privileged parts of the canon, and African logic, which tolerated a high degree of religious diversity, emphasized community and experience over doctrine and dogma, recognized women's religious authority, and gave a prominent place to the feminine in its cosmology. One result of these tensions is that a part of the religious experience of African-Americans involves coming to workable terms with European organizational forms that presume the subordination and marginalization—that is, the silence—of women.

This analysis attempts to confront and interpret the experience of African-American women in their churches. Women have emerged in every African-American religious tradition as persons with significant power, in spite of the overwhelming resistance of the largest church bodies to women's ordination. On the issue of ordination there is pluralism. Even in episcopal polities, where the practice is ostensibly "illegal," some bishops will ordain women. Women's roles in the African-American tradition have been constructed largely through the assertiveness and enterprise of women within a system of contested gender relations. That system was shaped in a societal context of competing cultural forces. I call this confrontation between the women and the larger system "the politics of silence."

Within this tradition one must examine the women, their religious roles, practices, and ideas, and then the entrenched conflicts that exist in the churches. First, I describe briefly some of the distinctive aspects of African-American women's experience. Then I look at the distinctive religious emphases fostered in slavery and nurtured thereafter in a wide variety of settings. I focus on those aspects specially related to the shaping of women's roles and to gender relations. Finally, I examine some of the conflicts that persist in the complex institutional arrangements of religious life.

AFRICAN-AMERICAN WOMEN'S EXPERIENCE

Although students of race relations and social change have acknowledged the primary importance of religion in the social and political life of the black community, there exists a critical lack of understanding of the historical process of the institutionalization of black religious traditions and their cultural importance. At the same time, the role of women has become an important question in the formal study of religion and in contemporary expressions of Jewish, Christian, and Islamic traditions. While material concerned with the historical importance of African-American religion and with the role of women in society is expanding at an unprecedented rate, far less has been written about the role of women in African-American religious traditions.

The legal, economic, and social status of African women, Paula Giddings (1984) argues, was perhaps the foundation upon which the unique experience of Africans and their descendants in the United States was constructed. Sexuality, cultural roles, and gender relations early became central problems in the organizational and cultural responses of African-Americans to their enslavement and to their subsequent experiences. Those responses, of which religion and church were integral parts, fashioned a complex community whose diversity has existed in a historical tension with its need for unity (Blackwell, 1982). Women, through their networks of ideologically and practically diverse organizations and constituencies, have been keys to that unity in the face of diversity. Deborah King (1988) employs the terms "multiple jeopardy" and "multiple consciousness" to develop an integrated theoretical approach to the experiences of African-American women. Instead of an image of abject victimization and paralysis, she points to race / ethnicity, class, and gender as terms that both locate and constrain experience at the same time as they interact to provide a unique perspective on culture and society. This multiple consciousness enables African-American women to shape a multifaceted critique of oppression and its diverse expressions as well as to develop strategies aimed at social change. Thus, in the face of crushing victimization and brutalization one finds a complex basis for resistance and self-actualization.

This resistance has manifested itself in the observations and writings of African-American women throughout their history in the United States. Frances Ellen Watkins Harper and Nannie Helen Burroughs, to select just two, insisted that the role of African-American women involved an assertive and persistent solidarity with their communities. They also pointed to a strength and pride that emerged from African-American women's resistance to the slave experience. Harper in particular asserted that in the process of adjusting to the social change associated with the new experience of freedom, African-American women drew upon their experiences in slavery as the source of a militant solidarity evinced by African-American women of all backgrounds, and particularly privileged ones. Often that solidarity was expressed in the language of religious covenant and Christian mission.

Literary, historical, and social-scientific perspectives point to the emergence of a role model in which African-American women were perceived as autonomous, independent, strong, and self-reliant. This model was identified by Dill (1979) as a contradiction to the expectations of the dominant (white) culture. It has been stereotyped and trivialized in popular culture, creating powerful conflicts and tensions within African-American women themselves and within their communities. Nevertheless, it embodies features of the individual lives and organizational careers that are distinctive to the African-American religious tradition.

Alongside the experience of oppression in the United States, another cultural tension stems from the religious imaginations that Africans brought with them to the New World. In West Africa, women were recognized as competent religious leaders. They were priestesses and cult leaders, and they were responsible, as wives and mothers, for the socialization of their children into the diverse and sometimes competing demands of household and family cults. Furthermore, African religions contained within them female deities and feminine imagery of the creator deity. Mbiti (1969) and others have argued persuasively that these African understandings of God the Creator stand squarely within the canons of monotheism and Judeo-Christian understandings. Cultic service in West African cultures was never restricted to men. Moreover, women also maintained their own independent cults, which reinforced their autonomous economic roles. The importance of West African women to production and markets was reflected in the religious life, and the religious life exalted the roles of women in a way that Europeans, particularly the English, would find unthinkable. This prominence (not dominance) of women in a context of patriarchy has led some, particularly Cheikh Anta Diop ([1958] 1978), to argue that African societies should not be viewed through the same lenses with which we examine European traditions and societies.

The emergence, then, of an independent network of slave women was a function, according to Deborah Gray White (1985), of both African cultural foundations and American oppression. Within this world, which enabled women to support one another in sickness, childrearing, childbearing, and work, enslaved women also conducted a religious life with one another. This autonomous world, relatively impenetrable, provided a basis for women's leadership and authority in the larger slave community. According to Webber (1978), there is considerable evidence for women's leadership within the slave quarters community, and that leadership extended occasionally to the role of preacher. Observations in missionaries' accounts and biographies document that women were accomplished leaders of worship and teachers of religious tradition coming out of slavery (Litwack, 1979). Women's commitment to their religious life and the larger community continued in the aftermath of slavery and remains a source of tension between black women and their employers (Jones, 1985). Their prominence in the slave community and their commitment to the religious life guaranteed that women would emerge as part of the leadership class—particularly as educators, who are so essential to the development of a stable post-Emancipation black community.

The tensions surrounding the historical roles of black women in the United States—their work roles and their political roles—have contributed to the contemporary organizational shape of historically black denominations and congregations. At the same time, the churches that black women made together with black men became effective normative, social, and psychological resources for black women in their economic and political roles. Like other areas of African-American life, the black religious experience exhibits apparently contradictory characteristics. These characteristics stem from the historical, social, and cultural dilemmas related to the intersection of race oppression and gender oppression. One aspect of the intersection of gender and race in the shaping of black religion is the existence of diverse expressions of a dual-sex political system in historically black churches, stemming from black women's traditions of autonomy, independence, and self-reliance. A second aspect is the existence of a tradition of conflict stemming from black women's consciousness concerning their special history, their political activism and community work, and their resistance to the imposition of Euro-American patriarchy. These two aspects of African-American women's religious experience are not the only distinctive ones, but they point to the depth of the historical and cultural roots that have shaped the black religious experience in America and the centrality of "the woman question" to the dynamics of that experience.

Although African-American life in contemporary society is diverse and complex, religion has been a diffuse phenomenon that has helped to shape and to organize orientations to family, work, politics, economic behavior, and education. The problems of race and gender have been and continue to be salient in all of these as well as part of larger religious questions and of an understanding that black women and men have both suffered (Davis, 1981). While black religion is patriarchal, it sometimes exhibits an ambivalent patriarchy. In the history of sociological analysis and of American racist ideologies, the failures of black people to conform precisely to the norms of Euro-American patriarchy in their family lives and labor histories have been the cause of much victim blaming and innumerable cultural assaults. As Giddings (1984: 33–39) points out, the status of African-American women is a foundation for the status of the entire community. An understanding of the dynamics of gender

relations in the black community is essential, but remains incomplete
because of the failure to analyze those relations in the religious experience.

The contested gender relations of black religion are obscured because
of the exaggerated focus on the preacher and the edifices. While important, the role of the preacher has unfortunately overshadowed other
forms of religious leadership. By reading the dynamics of the civil rights
movement back into black religious and political history, the complexities, multiple traditions, and alternative models of power, authority, and
leadership have been ignored. In addition, the elevation of the edifice
of the church to a sociological concept (with the storefront church im-
aged only as an isolated sect and cult) has obscured the linkages between
institutionalized religion and women's experience. (One sociologist told
me that he had noticed the little storefront churches pastored by
women, but it had never occurred to anyone to ask whence they came.)
Equating the male preacher with the black church and the edifice with
the sociological reality has also diminished our capacity to appreciate the
historical and evolutionary processes contributing to the emergence of
national church networks. The additional failure to account for tradition has limited our view of religion as a cultural force. All these failures
of perspective have combined to intensify the practice of ignoring and
minimizing the importance of women. To correct these failures, it is
important to focus on those aspects of gender relations which give the
religious experience a distinctive character. Analysis of the role of
women highlights the ways in which black women and men manipulated
elements of two cultures and their respective social organizations to
fashion a distinctive pillar of American Protestantism. The duality and
conflict associated with women's roles point to the dynamic complexity
and "multiple consciousness" underlying issues of gender, race, and
their intersection.

THE ROOTS OF CONTRADICTION AND PARADOX: AFRICAN CULTURE AND AMERICAN SLAVERY

The organization of gender in the black community has been influenced
by the manner in which black people extracted meaning from their experience as slaves in the antebellum South. This extracted meaning was
brought to bear on such questions as the proper role of women in black
social life. Answers to the questions that arose during and after slavery
took into account black women's capabilities, the needs of the race, and
the ways black people were expected to adopt in order to become acceptable members of the dominant culture. It is easy to ignore the conflict
and tension over the woman question because the conflict transpired in

the privacy of black churches and of community organizations that often met in black churches. Such an intersection of settings in sacred space meant that questions pertaining to the spiritual were deeply political and, among women and men who were both political and religious leaders (preachers and teachers), the political issues were also spiritual.

Whatever the Euro-American religious forms appropriated by the slaves, the content of these forms was not appropriated without extensive critical reflection on the source: their oppressors. Black Christians share every denomination label of white Christians, as well as many of their own. In spite of these shared labels and affiliations, black denominations and congregations embody unique aspects of the African-American experience. As slaves, Africans arrived with a religious perspective that did not exclude women from cult service. Indeed, African religious systems, regardless of how patriarchal they were, exalted both the male and the female in their various collective expressions of the holy (the cult). There was a tradition of religious independence as well as of leadership among African women. According to Letitia Woods Brown (1975: 5), "in religious ceremonies, women were priests, even leaders of some cults. Women also maintained their own secret societies." Furthermore, religions centering on goddesses and female ancestors thrived in the African context. The survival of these religions, such as Cuban Santeria and Haitian Vodun, in the Catholic societies of the New World attest to the fact that women's cult service and the veneration of both male and female ancestors were not forgotten during the Middle Passage. In the United States, the African-American expression of Christianity during slavery was largely Afro-Baptist (Sobel, 1979) and African Methodist. In the slave and Reconstruction South, the Baptist / Methodist division was not always meaningful, although in terms of cultural influence and numbers, Baptists dominated.

Another influential element in the African perspective was the relationship of the cult servant to the larger community. The cult servant (priest or priestess) embodied culturally constructed differences between the sacred and the profane. However, the role was not necessarily an elite one. It did not carry with it an aura of professionalism that implied social distance, deference, or autonomy. Although there was the understanding that the role required specialized knowledge, the structure of social relationships between priest / priestess and community was akin to the relationships of the Israelites to their prophets than to their relationships to their priests. Later on, with the coming of European missionaries to West Africa, this tension between the African and European notions of the cult servant contributed to the religious rebellions that gave rise to the African prophet movements and the independent churches. African communities believed that the cult servant was a specialized religious role that was subject to the authority of the community. In contrast, European priests and preachers believed that their cult service was a specialized religious role with authority to which the community was subject. The polity (but not necessarily the theology or doctrine) that matched the African model most closely was the Baptist polity. Furthermore, Baptist churches provided a certain degree of autonomy to slave communities under the most oppressive—and, after 1820, repressive—circumstances. Raboteau (1978) and Sobel (1979) both suggest that the slave response to missionary preaching was a reasoned choice among diverse Christian polities.

Africans confronted Europeans at a point when European religion was becoming increasingly specialized, compartmentalized, and segregated from everyday public life. Religion was increasingly the product of evangelical enterprise. The lack of an established religion was one of the features of antebellum life that prompted Stanley Elkins (1959) to introduce the concept of unopposed capitalism into his analysis of American slavery. In contrast, every aspect of African social organization involved religious ceremony. The segregation of the cult from everyday life that characterized Euro-American society was alien to African religious practice. Since women's societies and other collective enterprises were important components of African culture and social organization, women's experience carried with it a set of independent religious traditions. In addition to their performance as cult servants for entire African communities, women possessed their own ceremonies and cults. Their work and political roles varied from culture to culture, but all of these roles carried with them some type of religious ceremony. Furthermore, women's roles were not remanded to a sphere of social life that could be labeled "private" as they are in the public-private dichotomy of contemporary social life.

In the context of African patriarchy, the African woman's role as an individual political person could be severely limited. However, particularly in those cultures that contributed heavily to the British and American slave trades, African women effectively imposed themselves on the political process as a collective body. African women's response to New World slavery was influenced not only by the distinctive nature of cult service and the religious foundations of their everyday life, but also by their traditions of collective politics. African women's effective collective politics stemmed from their economic roles. The economic impact of women on their cultures was (and still is) considerable. According to LaFrances Rodgers Rose (1980: 16),

> the African woman was more than a mother. . . . She was instrumental in the economic marketplace. She controlled certain industries—the making

and selling of cloth, pottery, spinning, and the sale of goods of various kinds. The economic position of the African woman was high. The women were traders, and what they earned [often] belonged to them. Some women became independently wealthy. The West African woman was also responsible for raising the food for her family—she planted the crops and maintained them.

It was this independent economic base that paved the way for the collective political participation that was institutionalized in West African societies.

West African women developed their own political institutions, according to Judith van Allen (1976: 68), through which they were able to "express their disapproval and secure their demands by collective public demonstrations, including ridicule, satirical singing and dancing, and group strikes." Okonjo (1976: 45) highlights the importance of dual-sex political systems, "in which the major interest groups are defined and represented by sex [gender]." She suggests:

> Dual sex organization contrasts with the "single-sex" system that obtains in most of the Western world, where political status-bearing roles are predominantly the preserve of men. In the single-sex system, women can achieve distinction and recognition only by taking on the roles of men in public life and performing them well.

Okonjo (53) points out that African organizations of the daughters of a lineage and of the wives of a lineage represented women's collective interests in the problems of mutual aid, violations of domestic law, decisions concerning agricultural labor, and the social control of men. Such collective power was related to the salience of women's title societies, in which membership was based upon economic advantage and which in turn led to even more economic as well as political advantage, since status in other groups was often influenced by titles. Women's organizations were based upon age as well as family relationships. African women existed in societies of women their own age and status; their peers were called "sisters," and their elders were called "mothers."

Occasionally, these collective politics led to institutionalized authority as well. The roles of the *omu* (loosely translated "queen," but meaning a female king or head of the women's world) and the *ilogo* ("women's cabinet") held real power and represented important sources of authority for women. Eva Meyerowitz (1960) points out that in spite of the English translation of *omu* as "queen mother," these women were not wives of kings but rather were the important points of contact between the men's and the women's worlds within the context of decision making. During the struggle against European colonialism, some of these women emerged as leaders of entire African communities (Wilson, 1980).

The West African women who came to the New World came with a highly developed sense of their importance to a polity and an economy. Slavery, then, was a loss of authority for women as well as men. Any struggle to gain autonomy and regain authority over their lives, from an African perspective, was a struggle for both female and male authority. The organizational and sexual politics of historically black denominations contain evidence of this struggle for autonomy and of dual-sex political systems. The exigencies of survival and the imposition of sexualized racism reinforced the collective political consciousness of black women. The failure of these collective politics in the contexts of European colonialism, such as in the Ibo Women's War, highlight the differences between European and African patriarchies.

The paradoxes introduced by the African perspective were intensified by the material conditions and gender relations of slavery. This process was aided by the visible and invisible slave churches. These congregations consisted of women and men who shared a world of work, a reality which shaped a conscious egalitarian ethos within the slave community. As Angela Davis (1981: 23) reminds us,

> Black women were equal to their men in the oppression they suffered. They were their men's social equals within the slave community; and they resisted slavery with a passion equal to their men's. This was one of the greatest ironies of the slave system, for in subjecting women to the most ruthless exploitation conceivable, exploitation which knew no sex distinctions, the groundwork was created not only for Black women to assert their equality through their social relations, but also to express it through their acts of resistance.

Davis (1981), Dill (1979), and White (1985) argue persuasively that what emerged from this political economy of slavery and the counterculture of the slave community was a distinctive (in the context of Euro-American patriarchy) model of womanhood. Davis (1981: 29) insists that it was slave women "who passed on to their nominally free female descendants a legacy of hard work, perseverance and self-reliance, a legacy of tenacity, resistance and insistence on sexual equality—in short, a legacy spelling out standards for a new womanhood." Dill (1979) suggests that this model of womanhood, with its constituent elements of independence, autonomy, self-reliance, and strength, was a contradiction and a source of dialectical opposition to the female role model dictated by Euro-American patriarchy. Emerging as it did from strength through community, this model of womanhood was derided in the Jezebel and Mammy stereotypes (White, 1985) and in the racist imagery labeling black women as dangerous and deviant mothers (Gilkes, 1983b) and "bad black women" (Lerner, 1971).

Black men evaluated black women's experience in both positive and negative terms. Regardless of the degree to which they agreed or disagreed with the dominant culture's model of gender organization, black men have never been free (from the influence of women) to impose either equality or total male domination. Since northern and southern antebellum churches were political as well as spiritual centers of their communities, women were an integral part of emergent black political organizations. Black women argued persuasively that they should be included, and a comparison (by both men and women) between racial oppression and white male behavior toward women was often raised in these arguments (Perkins, 1981: 321). As a result, black male political discourse acquired some feminist content through such spokesmen as Frederick Douglass, W. E. B. Du Bois, and Martin Delany. Roslyn Terborg-Penn (1978: 29–34) demonstrates that as early as 1789, black men and women participated together in organizations devoted to abolition and racial uplift. Although there was some resistance by black men to full participation of women, for the most part they accepted women's participation in their conventions, elected black women to office, invited them to speak publicly, defended their right to an education, and recognized their role in the workplace. In 1848 a resolution was proposed at the National Convention of Colored Freemen that, according to Terborg-Penn (1978: 34), invited "females hereafter to take part in our deliberations"; after some debate, the convention ruled that since "all colored persons" could be delegates, "that the word 'person' be understood to include 'women'." Women's inclusion in deliberative bodies carried over to religious bodies such as the American National Baptist Convention and the A.M.E. Church. Any refusals that arose surrounding the right of women to preach had to be addressed directly to them. It is this process that made possible the emergence of women such as Maria Stewart, Sojourner Truth, and Frances Ellen Watkins Harper as public lecturers and as role models, enabling other black women as well as white women to become activists and lecturers.

Vestiges of African tradition combined with the political economy and the gender relations of slavery to produce tensions within both slave and free churches. Yet, according to Thomas Webber's (1978) analysis, the shared suffering and oppression of slavery produced a slave community characterized by a remarkable lack of sexism. Although the black male *preacher* was the leader recognized by whites and their religious institutions, black women emerged as worship leaders, preachers, catechizers, exhorters, prayer warriors, singers, teachers, and storytellers— all authoritative agents of the black religious tradition. Many slave churches existed without a black pastor (male preacher) of its own choosing in the last decades of slavery. The tasks of worship were not dependent on "his" presence. Shared notions of "real" religion were not dependent upon a properly built edifice, special training in the arts of ministry, or the gender of the worship leader. The various tasks necessary for adequate worship—expounding upon a scripture, praying, raising a song, teaching religious doctrine and practice—were broken down and distributed among the members of a congregation according to their talents. The essence of black religious tradition was completely portable. Whereas the integrity of slave families was dependent upon having its members present in an enduring household, the "household of faith," or one's "church home," was dependent only upon the gathering of "two or three who touch and agree." In order for the free black church to conform to its counterpart in the dominant culture, it was necessary to suppress the freedom with which black church women had exercised their roles in the churches of the antebellum South and in the evangelical campaigns of both the North and the South. When the invisible institution of slave religion went public, the woman question was one of considerable debate. These debates and conflicts gave rise to practices and institutions that reflected a range of opinions on the roles of women, and to a complex set of women's organizations which exercised considerable power and influence and nurtured a tradition of feminist / womanist biblical exegesis and theological discourse. Although the dual-sex politics of black church women and their unyielding tradition of conflict concerning the proper place of women have not toppled patriarchy, they have profoundly influenced the institutional expressions of sexism and the content of male ideology. If this interpretation of these two aspects of black women's religious experience is correct, the strategies of black male preachers to maintain the traditional exclusion of black female clergy from the National Baptist Convention will differ in content from those used recently in the Southern Baptist Convention.

THE DUAL-SEX POLITICS OF BLACK CHURCHES

The institutional expression of gender-based politics in black churches varies from congregation to congregation and from denomination to denomination. Recent observations and comparative analyses of contemporary African and black American church traditions have acknowledged parallels between the prayer leadership of black women in all variations of black Protestantism and the African Queen Mother (H. A. Carter, 1976), and between the distinctive role of black pastors' wives and African female leadership (W. W. Carter, 1976). In addition, the roles to which the labels "teacher," "missionary," "evangelist," and "deaconess" are affixed are wide-ranging in their rights, duties, obligations, authority, and structural relationships within a congregation or a denomination. For those black denominations formed after the end of Reconstruction, conflict over the role of women contributed to the reorganization and of churches and the founding of new ones. The end of Reconstruction was a time of violently imposed changes and community reorganization, and, of the many denominations that emerged from that period of community reorganization, those that continued to grow after the deaths of their founders seem to have been the ones that contained the strongest "women's departments" or that ordained women to pastoral roles (Gilkes, 1983a).

The most distinctive aspect of dual-sex church politics is the role of the Church Mother. While most black churches in the Baptist, Methodist, and "Sanctified" (Pentecostal, Holiness, Apostolic) denominations have a woman to whom members refer as the "church mother," her position varies. In almost all cases, she is an older woman, often elderly, who is considered an example of spiritual maturity and morality to the rest of her congregation. Her career as a Christian is usually exemplary and long, and most members know of her various activities in the missionary unit or on the deaconess board. Perhaps she is the widow of a pastor or a bishop or a deacon, but not necessarily. She is one of the few people whose seat in the congregation is formally or informally reserved. When she dies, her seat may be draped in black. Most important, she is publicly addressed by the pastor, the bishops, and the members of the congregation as "Mother."

As a spiritual and moral leader, she is expected to know her Bible. Since most black churches are "Bible-believing" churches, she exemplifies the tradition of personal devotion through the reading and knowing of one's Bible. While she may not teach Sunday School, she may also be the leader of the adult class. She is the type of person that one pastor described as someone "who offers you spiritual advice that you learn to take." However, she can also be a source of exhortation for the congregation. When she speaks, she speaks in little sermons. On one occasion, the official church mother of a Baptist church gave a rousing and spirit-filled exhortation at a special occasion. Later, the nationally known male preacher from another denomination rose to speak and mentioned that his decision to "preach" rather than simply to "speak" was based upon the divine "direction" that he had received through the church mother. One church mother, Mother Pollard, is famous for her participation in the Montgomery bus boycott and her remarking that, although her feet were tired, her soul was rested.

Occasionally, the church mother performs the role of a stage manager or director of public worship. Where tension exists concerning certain practices, her opinion may prevail. In one Baptist congregation, the insistence by the church mother that "this is not a Sanctified Church!"

moved the deacon board to call an emergency meeting with the pastor in order to persuade him to withdraw his permission for drums to be used during the morning service: the church mother prevailed. Other members of the congregation may walk out when they disagree with the pastor, but their actions will be ignored. The church mother is never ignored.

In the Baptist and African Methodist traditions, her role is largely one of influence. Although she may be formally installed in her office, she does not have formal authority. Yet her influence may grant her considerable power, even an effective veto, in church politics and affairs. Her role as church mother may on occasion reach beyond the congregation if she is active in public politics. Her force as a role model may also affect the tradition of activism in her community. Not only her personal religious history but also her labor force participation and her political career become informal models for others to follow. As a community activist, she may be the first woman to break some of the sexist barriers in black pulpits, or she may be given a permanent seat on the board of directors or the executive board of a community organization. Her stature in the overall politics of the community may occasionally modify the operation of oppressive political structures, such as the police department and the mayor's office. Sarah Evans (1980) and Paula Giddings (1984) observed fragments of this tradition in the Southern rural wing of the civil rights movement. The southern "mama," according to Evans's corrupted description of church and community mothers (1980), served as a role model to white women whose experience in the civil rights movement motivated them to become the nucleus of the contemporary women's movement and to insist on the right to participate equally in the anti-war movement with radical men. According to one activist (Giddings, 1984: 301), those white women observed that women such as Fannie Lou Hamer and Ella Baker had not internalized a sense of female inferiority.

While space does not permit discussion of the importance of music to the black worship tradition, being able to "raise a song" is counted as an important spiritual skill. Howard Thurman (1979) remembered that the congregation of his childhood was highly concerned about this ability. New members were adopted by older members and were carefully taught public prayer and raising a song. Thus, the role of such women as Bernice Johnson Reagon and Fannie Lou Hamer in revitalizing the civil rights movement using traditional sacred music was consistent with expectations placed upon church and community mothers. "Singing was the tool that helped to forge that unity—and the strength to deal with the consequences of Black resistance" (Giddings, 1984: 283); women were crucial to that process (King, 1987).

Although Church Mothers have no fixed structural power in Baptist and African Methodist traditions,* they do have such power within churches organized in the late nineteenth-century South. Collectively referred to as the Sanctified Church, black Holiness, Pentecostal, and Apostolic denominations institutionalized the role of the church mother, and she became the basis for woman-centered church politics affecting entire denominations. The largest of these, the Church of God in Christ (COGIC), treated the role as that of an overseer or bishop of women during the early days of the denomination. In every geographic jurisdiction, a man was appointed overseer, along with a woman overseer of the "women's work."

These overseers, or "state mothers," were charged with the task of "organizing" the women. As a result, mothers' boards were formed in the various congregations which affiliated with similar state and regional structures. One woman overseer was appointed for every male overseer. In the COGIC, the founder, Charles Harrison Mason (who was a widower), believed that only women should instruct other women in proper religious and moral behavior. Mason and many of the other church founders of this period (male and female) were the children of slaves who had been raised in the independent slave Baptist churches of the rural South. In these churches, male deacons governed the behavior of church men, and female deaconesses governed the behavior of the church women; the boards of deacons were also organized according to the status of slave or free (Gutman, 1976; Sobel, 1979). The women's departments and their Sanctified churches survived in part because of the earlier female slave network, which had prepared southern religious leaders to be comfortable with such expressions of collective autonomy. Dual-sex politics were part of their childhood experience.

The organizational politics of black women in the local and national black community also influenced the models of women's participation in churches. When conflicts erupted among black Baptists and Methodists during this late nineteenth-century period concerning traditions such as the "ring shout" or "holy dance," black women were beginning to make an impression on the community as activists and educators. By the end of the nineteenth century, women who were prominent activists in their denominations carried that activism into a movement for racial uplift, which culminated in the formation of the National Association of Colored Women. At the same time, the importance placed on education meant that educated men and women were recruited as teachers in the South, and within the community the emerging leadership class consisted largely of "preachers and teachers." The insistence by Baptists that women (who were as well-trained in theology and biblical studies as the men) could not "preach" but could only "teach" meant that these labels came less to define different activities and more to define male and female versions of the same activity.

As founders of Holiness and Pentecostal denominations sought to improve the status and the educational levels of these churches, they recruited educated Baptist and African Methodist women to join in their work. The women who responded had been frustrated in their attempts to exercise their gifts in Baptist and Methodist congregations. In the new denominations they not only established schools and educated members of the clergy, but also preached revivals, founded churches, and maintained charge of those churches until a pastor was assigned by the bishops. These educated professional women, full of gospel zeal, were also the women chosen by founders, bishops, and pastors as wives. An interesting cultural contradiction emerged when the most prominent role model married to the "best catch" in a church was an educated, professional woman. Usually she was a school teacher or community activist. Occasionally, she was a "superwoman," in the person of someone like Dr. Susan McKinney. A physician and pastor's wife who managed two medical practices in Brooklyn, New York, in the late nineteenth century, Dr. McKinney was also a community activist, an organizer in the National Association of Colored Women, and organist in her husband's church. When she was widowed, Dr. McKinney married another preacher, Theophilus Steward (Davis, 1981; Giddings, 1984; Ploski and Brown, 1967).

Within the COGIC, it is not unusual for male church leaders to testify to the fact that their salvation was preached by a woman revivalist. It was on the foundation of the role of the church mother that the infrastructure of the women's department was built. Within these structures, the roles of missionary and evangelist evolved in response to the prohibition on women's ordination to the roles of pastor, elder, and bishop. In my research, I have not met a church mother who is not a licensed missionary or evangelist. However, missionaries and evangelists are not necessarily church mothers. In order for missionaries and evangelists to "teach" (actually, preach), they must have the signatures of both their pastor and their church mother on their license. In order to teach within the jurisdiction, they must have the signatures of both the bishop (formerly the overseer) and the jurisdictional supervisor (the state or jurisdictional mother, formerly also the overseer) of the women's work. These signatures and a letter of recommendation from the jurisdictional supervisor are necessary for a woman to move to another jurisdiction as a missionary or an evangelist. Finally, it is the jurisdictional mothers or supervisors who determine whether a woman can become a national evangelist.

In some jurisdictions, the general category of "missionary" includes all of the various women's roles, and the term "minister" encompasses all pastors, elders, bishops, and male evangelists. These groups meet, first separately and then together, on specified days of the month. After their separate meetings, the missionaries and ministers meet in the same room, with women sitting on one side and men on the other. In those congregations within the COGIC that enforce the "double pulpit"—the lectern for women and the *real* pulpit for men—church mothers and evangelists sit on one side at the front of the church, and the pastor and other elders sit on the other. Some evangelists have informed me that older pastors in smaller and more traditional churches do not enforce the double pulpit, and women speak from the same place as men *preach*. In these smaller churches, evangelists have the opportunity to become "pastors in truth" when an elderly pastor dies or ceases to preach regularly. A number of COGIC congregations are "pastored" by widows of elders and bishops who were previously well-known missionaries, evangelists, or church mothers and who administered the church and did the teaching each Sunday after their husbands became ill and incapacitated. One evangelist implied that there was a certain incentive for young evangelists and missionaries to marry elderly pastors and bishops since doing so might present the opportunity to inherit a pastorate.

Some dualism also exists in black Baptist churches. In these congregations, the missionary has the same role as the missionary in the COGIC. She may "teach" and lead worship from the floor, but she may not "preach" from the pulpit. Many elderly Baptist women hear the term "missionary" as a euphemism for a woman minister. The organization of a Women's Auxiliary within the National Baptist Convention antedated and paralleled the growth of women's departments in the Sanctified church. There was much borrowing and interaction between women across denominations and within women's community and political organizations. Nationally known leaders such as Mary McLeod Bethune, a Methodist, preached from the pulpits in Baptist and Sanctified churches.

Not only are these dual-sex politics reflected in the role of the church mother, thus providing a basis for autonomous woman-centered organizations, but such politics are also evident in the evolution of the missionary role in home and foreign mission societies. Black women manipulated these positions in creative ways to generate autonomy and power for themselves in denominational affairs. Such a position also provided a base for addressing larger social issues and questions concerning women's roles in the larger society. While the women disagreed over the role of women in the pulpit, they were consistent in pressuring male church leaders to support women's rights to education and labor force protection. When men resisted such ideas, women could persist by turning to their organizations outside church structures for support and political leverage. Evelyn Brooks Barnett's (1978) analysis of the role of Nannie Helen Burroughs in the organization of Baptist women and the maintenance of the National Training School is instructive in this regard.

Fragments of the dual-sex political system are evident in the role of the deaconess in black churches. In Baptist churches, the board of deaconesses is often the organization (along with the missionary board) from which women are elevated to the status of church mother. In some churches, the missionary board is open to any woman with the appropriate calling and evangelistic zeal, while the deaconess board is reserved for the wives of deacons. In other churches, the congregation elects women to the deaconess board on the basis of their perceived spirituality. Some churches actually ordain deaconesses along with deacons—usually those boards that elect deaconesses because they are deacons' wives or elect deaconesses who feel "called" to the position. The diverse traditions among Baptist churches illustrate how different Baptist communities resolved questions of the role of women in church and society. While the context is clearly patriarchal, black women have constructed a wide variety of leadership roles that provide opportunities for both married and single women to perceive and to be role models for other black women. These positions of leadership and their histories are also the contexts in which the alternative models of womanhood that have their roots in slavery, black women's education, community activism, and labor force participation are affirmed in spite of patriarchy. Although the male preacher is the clearly acknowledged authority in the public sphere, failure to examine women's roles has obscured the varieties of shared power that the collective politics of black women have in fact produced. When one examines the Sanctified church as a cultural phenomenon, it is clear that it has retained a great deal of antebellum egalitarianism within the patriarchal Euro-American polities which have become the organizational contexts of black church culture.

TRADITIONS OF CONFLICT

Dual-sex politics alone do not make black women's experience distinctive. The fragments of African gender organization contribute to a more persistent and prominent thread of tradition: conflict. Conflict did not always take the form of assertive, direct action; rather, it was acted out through traditions enacted to resist marginalization and silencing. The dominant culture's pressure to regularize had a devastating effect on African-American Christian women. They fought back by establishing traditions which reflected the importance they attached to strength and self-reliance.

The patriarchy of the black church has never been peaceful. The content of that patriarchy—a patriarchy that can be labeled ambivalent in its expressions—has been severely modified by the persistent tradition of conflict that black women have maintained within black religious structures. Although women remain subordinate persons in structures where males hold nearly all the highest positions, the ideologies advanced by these men in defense of their domination reflect the embattled nature of their position. Simply stated, there are certain arguments that black preachers dare not advance in public regardless of how much they believe them; for instance, those arguments assailing women's competence were lost in the debates of the nineteenth century. In interpreting any conflict within African-American religious traditions, however, it is critically important to remember that they take place in organizational settings where the operating metaphor and ideology for human relations is family. They take place between "brothers" and "sisters," between "fathers" and "mothers" and "daughters."

To understand fully this tradition of conflict would require a comprehensive sociohistorical analysis of women's roles in all of the historically black denominations. However, even a cursory examination highlights the importance of two examples: an aggressively articulated biblical feminism, and a persistent reminder of women's material through the annual "Women's Day." In addition, black women have been known to oppose the sexism of black preachers by ostentatiously changing churches and occasionally even by founding their own churches. Throughout the history of black church women, one can find significant expressions of their opposition to total patriarchy. Even among those women who sincerely believe that preaching is a man's province (and sometimes even more among such women), there is a tradition of a militant assertion of personhood and a sincere belief in their own competence and capabilities in the larger society.

The Church of God in Christ (COGIC) insists that women are not called to preach. However, the church's manual contains the biblical argument for women's ordination, clearly stated although militantly opposed. Rather than elaborate arguments for women's inferiority or sinful nature, or the reasons they should be silent, the manual simply states that it does not recognize certain scriptures as constituting a mandate to ordain women to the offices of elder, pastor, or bishop. Having been reminded innumerable times by the women of the church (both pro-preaching and anti-preaching) of the importance of women to the founding of congregations and to the salvation, education, and financial support of ministers and bishops, the COGIC does allow women to oversee congregations when there is no pastor. Since the women's "teaching" is indistinguishable from the men's "preaching," there are no tasks of ministry that are the monopoly of elders. There are, however, tasks that are the monopoly of bishops.

The COGIC is the largest and one of the oldest of the Pentecostal churches founded by the children of former slaves, and it represents a continuous expression of slave religious tradition. When one examines all of the debates in various black denominations and the positions taken by other early churches on the woman question, it is clear that the position of the COGIC carries the scars of a protracted conflict. The effectiveness of the women's arguments is reflected in the arguments of men who are equally able to argue the positions of the biblical feminists.

The origins of black biblical feminism probably lie in the African Methodist Episcopal (A.M.E.) Church, whose founder, Richard Allen, was faced with the question of licensing Jarena Lee to preach (Dodson, 1982). Black women did not argue in isolation from the biblical arguments that took place among white feminists. In order to continue participating in the variety of leadership roles they had held during slavery, they had to learn to justify these roles when, after emancipation, black and white missionaries attempted to "regularize" black churches and their practices (Litwack, 1979). Both black men and black women argued in defense of their more ecstatic worship practices (Litwack, 1979; Woodson, 1972); some ex-slaves, like Howard Thurman's grandmother, even insisted that the Pauline Epistles were not inspired scripture meant to govern their lives (Thurman, 1979).

As early as the 1830s, black women orators refuted biblical arguments demanding their silence as public speakers. Giddings (1984: 52) suggests that "the moral urgency of their being black and female . . . suffused black women with a tenacious feminism." She argues that black women "bypassed the barrier of religious thought that circumscribed even radical White activists until the late 1830's (53)." She presents the arguments black women advanced for their right to public participation, especially as orators. One such woman, Maria Stewart, insisted:

> What if I am a woman? . . . Did [God] not raise up Deborah to be mother and a judge in Israel? Did not Queen Esther save the lives of the Jews? And Mary Magdalene first declare the resurrection of Christ from the dead? (Sterling, 1984: 157)

When it came to the arguments that stemmed from the Pauline scriptures, Giddings (1984: 53) demonstrates that Stewart rejected their use to "justify slavery and sexism." Stewart in her speeches (Richardson, 1987; Sterling, 1984) did what biblical critics before her had done: give priority to the statements and actions of Jesus, so that they became arguments for the limited nature of Pauline injunctions. Her biblical feminism was also informed by an argument based on world religions, which took into account the roles of women as cult servants and deities in non-Christian religions. In addition, she appealed to the roles of women in early Catholicism, and to their histories of militance, as a source of legitimacy. Finally, the biblical record that described God as deliverer led her to declare that in "light of the role of women in the past, 'God at this eventful period should raise up your females to strive . . . both in public and private, to assist those who are endeavoring to stop the strong current of prejudice that flows so profusely against us at present!' " (53). Concerning the public role of black women, Stewart admonished: "No longer ridicule their efforts. . . . It will be counted as sin" (quoted in Giddings, 1984: 53).

Although Sojourner Truth is the most famous of black women orators, her role as a biblically grounded preacher is often ignored. The change of her name from Isabella Baumfree came through her divine calling. On a road on Long Island, God called her to *sojourn* over the land and (because she then asked for a last name) to preach the *truth* concerning slavery. Her famous speech at the Seneca Falls women's rights convention was not only a very personal feminist argument but also solid biblical theology: she appealed to women's role in the redemption of humankind from the consequences of the Fall. In discussing an abolitionist heroine, it is important also to note that the denomination of Harriet Tubman never waged an effective biblical argument against the ordination of women; in fact, the African Methodist Episcopal Zion (A.M.E.Z.) Church was one of the earliest black denominations to ordain women.

It was in the Afro-Baptist tradition that arguments surrounding women's roles proved most troublesome. Between 1880 and 1900—the end of Reconstruction and a time of reorganization among constituencies in the black community—an intensive struggle surrounding women's roles occurred. The issues were leadership and conformity to dominant group patriarchy. It was then that the institutional basis for black feminism and organizational autonomy was established. Evelyn Brooks ([1980] 1983) has examined the feminist theology of the black Baptist Church within the American National Baptist Convention (A.N.B.C.), which was the forerunner of the now dominant National Baptist Convention (Incorporated) and the smaller conventions with which it coexists: the National Baptist Convention (unincorporated) and the Progressive National Baptist Convention. After one hundred years, these conventions differ in their official policy toward women clergy, yet all of them contain member churches pastored by women. In spite of the overwhelming sexism among black Baptist men, even the content of their arguments against women's ordination has been shaped by the tradition of biblical debate established by the women theologians of the A.N.B.C.

Since black women educators were often educated in the same settings as black men, they were quite competent to argue theology and biblical interpretation in public. Like African-Americans during the time of slavery, they saw the Bible as an instrument of liberation. Evelyn Brooks (1980) points out that unlike Frances Willard and Susan B. Anthony, women such as Virginia Broughton, Olive Clanton, Mary Cook, and Lucy Wilmot Smith accepted the Bible as a whole and perceived it as a valid basis for religious life. Thus, their arguments revolved around questions of interpretation. Brooks's analysis sees the emergence of the Women's Auxiliary Convention in the National Baptist Convention (Inc.) as a direct result of the feminist biblical tradition. It was probably the loyal opposition of these black women that deposited a fund of arguments supporting black female leadership roles into the oral tradition of the black Baptist community and the black women's club movement.

Although Brooks's analysis focuses on the women's speeches at meetings of the A.N.B.C., she reminds us that such women also engaged in public lectures, house-to-house visitations, and prolific amounts of correspondence. Virginia Broughton capped this twenty-year period (1880–1900) with the publication of a 1904 work called *Women's Work As Gleaned from the Women of the Bible.* In addition, both Mary Cook and Lucy Smith, like Mary McLeod Bethune, Ida Wells Barnett, and Nannie Helen Burroughs, wrote extensively in the black press. Along with others in the A.N.B.C., these

> Baptist interpreters of the Bible perceived themselves as part of the vanguard of the movement to present the theological discussion of woman's place. They used the Bible to sanction both domestic and public roles for women. While each of the feminist theologians had her own unique style and emphasis, the basic arguments resembled each other closely on four essential roles for women: in the home, in the church, in social reform, and in the labor force. In every case, the Baptist women emphasized biblical passages that portrayed women positively (Brooks 1980: 33).

Sometimes these women expressed the opinion that women had a revolutionary role to play in the reformation of the Church; at other times they lifted up the importance of the home as having primacy over the institutional church. Even in the context of biblical feminism, these Baptist women never agreed upon the role of women in "establishing new churches, baptizing, or administering the eucharist" since there were no recorded precedents for such activities in the Bible.

The women did find biblical sanction for some independence from their husbands and for the pursuit of professional careers. Brooks (1980: 39) states:

> Depicting Deborah as a woman with a spirit independent of her husband, Cook asserted: Her work was distinct from her husband's who, it seems, took no part whatever in the work of God while Deborah was inspired by the Eternal expressly to do his will and to testify to her country men that He recognizes in His follower neither male nor female, heeding neither the "weakness" of one, nor the strength of the other, but strictly calling those who are perfect at heart and willing to do His bidding.

According to Brooks, "Biblical examples had revealed that God used women in every capacity and thus proved to Cook that there could be no issue of propriety despite the reluctance of men." It was biblical feminism that insisted that women had a right to engage in "all honest labor." Thus, what began as women's insistence concerning their right to participate fully in their churches emerged as full-blown support for an alternative model of womanhood based on black women's historical experience and for black women's full participation in society. All of the elements of the role model that Dill (1979) describes as being in dialectical opposition to the role prescribed for women by the dominant culture were more than adequately defended by these women.

One of the outcomes of this stream of argument was the emergence of the uplift movement at the end of the nineteenth century (Davis, 1933). The same missionary energy that prompted Baptist women in the A.N.B.C. to write their articles and deliver their speeches was applied to the problem of racial oppression and social uplift. The development of an autonomous black women's movement was a logical outcome of their feminism, and this movement provided an alternative to fighting with black preachers over their monopoly on congregational leadership. The club movement was also an alternative avenue to public leadership. Whereas the dominant culture ignored the black women leaders, members of the black community did not. The women's commitment to the advancement of "the Race" was placed alongside their interest in developing their role as leaders. In 1892, Josephine St. Pierre Ruffin stated the goals of the black women's movement:

> Our women's movement is a woman's movement in that it is led and directed by women for the good of women and men, for the benefit of all humanity. . . . We want, we ask the active interest of our men; . . . we are not alienating or withdrawing, we are only coming to the front, willing to join any others in the same work. (Davis, 1933: 19)

The creation of this independent avenue to community leadership coincided with the formation of Holiness and Pentecostal denominations. The Baptist and Methodist women who joined these new black denominations brought with them the biblical justification for their leadership roles. Both the Holiness and Pentecostal movements provided black Baptist and A.M.E. women the opportunities to expound on the gospel (and, in many cases, to preach, pastor, conduct revival, and found churches) that they were denied in the older denominations.

With a fully developed women's agenda, other black women continued their organizing within their denominations. The reorganization of church constituencies that came with the growth of the Sanctified Church often addressed directly conflicts over the roles of women. As previously stated, the largest group, the C.O.G.I.C., did not ordain women to be elders, pastors, or bishops. Women who could not compromise on this issue found or created other alternatives. Several other smaller denominations ordained women to be elders. Some of these, however, would not ordain women to be bishops. The Presiding Bishop of the Fire Baptized Holiness (F.B.H.) Church of God of the Americas, a black denomination with interracial origins, incurred the ire of other presiding bishops when he consecrated a woman to be bishop in a denomination that she herself had founded. (The F.B.H. Church is an egalitarian church that has always ordained women to full ministry; in theory, women may be bishops, but no woman has ever stood for election.) In the Church of the Living God, Christian Workers for Fellowship, women had difficulties even though they were ordained and assigned to pastorates. Their careers took longer to advance than those of men, although men used the same career ladder: tours of duty as missionaries. A conflict that challenged the authority of pastors erupted in the Alabama District, and women left the church to form a new denomination. Conflicts among Baptists and their Sanctified relatives were so numerous and intense that W. E. B. Du Bois complained about the fractiousness of the Baptists (meaning the men) and lauded black women as "the intellectual leadership of the race" (Walden, 1972: 340). The conflicts over women's roles in church leadership and their proper place in society continued to fuel the politics of congregational and denominational reorganization throughout the first half of the twentieth century.

Black women never ceased to maintain an organized resistance to patriarchy within the black religious experience. The tradition of biblical feminism was maintained in two ways. Women in the Sanctified Church expanded upon the foundations laid by the Baptist women. They expanded their analysis of women's roles to the point that women's issues are articulated in the sermons of the men, and the arguments surrounding scriptural prohibitions have become more finely tuned and elaborated. Using their woman-centered imaginations to expand upon the biblical texts, COGIC evangelists have established traditions that even name the unnamed women of the Bible. In one COGIC congregation I observed, a National Evangelist was preaching on the biblical woman with "the issue of blood." As she developed her sermon (or "teaching"), when she came to the point of calling the woman's name, the entire congregation chimed in with her: "Safronia." I turned to my informant and asked, "Where did she get that name?" My informant replied, "We have a book that names all the women!" It was their own book, in which they had elaborated on women in the Bible in ways similar to earlier perspectives advanced by Virginia Broughton and Nannie Helen Burroughs (Brooks, 1980; Dodson and Gilkes, 1986). Thus, the first way in which the tradition of biblical feminism was maintained was by extending women's arguments begun in the nineteenth century and refining these arguments to answer new questions and repel new assaults on women's leadership.

The second and more universal way in which the tradition of biblical feminism was maintained was through the establishment of Woman's Day. According to Evelyn Brooks Barnett (1978), Nannie Helen Burroughs was a pivotal leader in the maintenance of black women's feminism in the National Baptist Convention (Inc.) as well as in the larger community. She continued the tradition of prolific journalism and lecturing begun by her foremothers. In the convention of 1906, she presented the idea of Women's Day, a Sunday when women would lead and speak in the worship service, as a national event. According to Evelyn Brooks, in Burroughs's travels to visit other Baptist women in their state conventions, she had observed the celebration of the day in their communities. She urged black women Baptists to observe it nationally. Although Woman's Day would advance the goal of raising money for foreign missions, Burroughs's feminist imagination saw the day as a way "the Convention could discover and develop public speakers for church programs. . . . This day was not thought up as a scheme for raising money, but primarily for raising women" (Dodson and Gilkes, 1986). In an undated pamphlet that criticized the appropriation of the day by local churches for fund-raising, Burroughs described the breadth of her vision:

> A million women praying? A million women singing? A million women desiring? A million women laboring for the coming of the kingdom in the hearts of all men, would be a power that would move God on his throne to immediately answer the petitions. It would mean spiritual dynamite that would blast Satan's greatest strong hold and drive sin to its native hearth. (Dodson and Gilkes, 1986)

Burroughs went on to describe the practical considerations that her spiritual vision entailed. She wrote:

We are in desperate need of women learning to become public speakers, and dedicated to a definite cause for which to speak. . . . Women's Day was intended to raise the women themselves—training them for public speaking and informed leadership through authentic, prepared, challenging speeches. . . . The day offers a glorious opportunity for women to learn to speak for themselves. (Dodson and Gilkes, 1986)

In spite of her lamentations about its misuse, Burroughs lived to see Women's Day spread to every segment of the black religious experience. Even black congregations in predominantly white denominations celebrate it. Regardless of the sexism a pastor may harbor, once each year he is obliged to sit in the congregation and listen to a sermon or "teaching" delivered by a woman community leader, missionary, evangelist, denominational executive, educator, minister, or professional. Occasionally these speakers are women who have left for college and are returning home as successful professionals. It is rare that a black church woman with a graduate or professional degree escapes such an invitation and responsibility. Although the day may represent a form of tokenism, it is important to remember that tokenism is an attempt to resist more revolutionary change and thus an indirect acknowledgment of pressure to effect meaningful change. Moreover, over the years of Women's Day, a Sunday which often involves morning and afternoon services and a meal served by the men of the church, black women have been exposed to a wide variety of female professional role models who are accorded honor and prestige. Finally, Women's Day is the link between the dual-sex politics of the black church and the tradition of conflict that has maintained black women's loyal opposition to the patriarchy that characterizes their religious experience. The positive presentation of diverse female images who are also successful in the dominant culture represents the kind of hope that the black religious experience has provided women over the years. At the same time, the practice sidesteps the issue of permanent pastoral and denominational leadership within the institutions in which black women have invested so much time and money. Nevertheless, the final result is to ensure the presence of a woman-centered perspective in the life of the church; that perspective has occasionally even converted a pastor to the position of feminist advocacy.

THE DILEMMAS OF COMMITMENT

Recent research on the historical and contemporary experience of the black woman demonstrate that her experience diverges from that of the white woman. The intersection of gender and race oppression has generated a number of paradoxes which are evident in political and economic roles within the community. As we begin to examine her religious experience, the black woman of radical tradition seems to disappear. However, when one ceases to equate the black church with its pastor and its edifice, the black woman's religious experience emerges as both complex and connected to her other experiences.

In spite of male domination, the black church functions for women as a women's institution. Dual-sex politics mean that women have the autonomy necessary to provide their own leadership training. While their access to authority within the church is limited, women occupy roles which are authoritative within the scope of the entire tradition. Although they are rarely pastors, black women have negotiated a wide variety of expressions in the roles reserved for them and have managed to impose themselves on the political process of their churches through collective strategies. As a result, they have established veto power in the context of black worship and congregational management, and they have restricted the content of black male sexist ideology.

The dual-sex framework has enabled black women to maintain a persistent tradition of conflict in the post-emancipation churches. The maintenance of a loyal opposition has created important alternatives for women aspiring to religious leadership. In spite of their opposing views, most black women who participate in the dynamics of conflict are proud of their commitment to the structures they are trying to change. This apparent paradox becomes intelligible in the context of the overall cultural role of black women. Black women's feminism is an antiracist feminism. Furthermore, throughout their history they have experienced two kinds of patriarchy. The patriarchal racism they have experienced in the United States has been the most destructive, in terms of their own experience and the experiences they observe among their men. The high levels of commitment exhibited by black women to the black church can be understood when one recognizes the historical evolution of their role in maintaining the organizational integrity of the black community. In spite of the problems their pastors may present, black women clearly see the survival of their churches as their responsibility.

The consciousness of black women is informed by their historical role as agents of black community survival. Both dual-sex politics and the tradition of conflict permit black women to communicate this aspect of their historical role to black men. Occasionally, such as on Women's Day, black women's feminism becomes a statement of their primary functional importance to the church and, by extension, to the community. Black women have been assigned their places in the social structure because they are black *and* female. Furthermore, the structures of exploitation and oppression have involved a politics of death, physical destruction, and social disruption. As Angela Davis (1981) has pointed out, the preservation of life and the maintenance of a domestic reality in the lives

of black people have been revolutionary acts in the context of slavery—
and often I would add, in the contexts of later periods.

What is simply an assignment to preserve life in other social contexts
has been a more complex task for black women. Their role has become
focused upon the maintenance of community integrity in the face of
pressures which would divide and atomize it. The failure to examine the
ways in which black women have fulfilled this role in their churches has
created a vast gap in our understanding of the foundations from which
black women construct an antiracist feminism. Furthermore, we have
missed the ways in which black women have asserted their personhood
while maintaining the integrity and continuity of a diverse and pluralis-
tic religious experience. While the organizational shape of the black religious experience, with its wide range of denominations and orientations
toward women's leadership roles, exhibits a complexity that is difficult
to grasp, the continuities that exist across the various segments of that
experience are largely the results of the work of the women. Women's
Day is just one example; many others still need to be explored.

James Harvey Robinson (1927) has reminded us that "history books
are a poor place to look for history." They are an even poorer place
to search for African-American history and African-American women's
history. The religious experience of black women, in spite of their
strong commitment to their churches, has offered a persistent challenge
to the European model of church order and to the technologies and
biblical interpretations which defend oppression and exploitation. In
the process of maintaining that challenge, black church women have asserted their spiritual independence and have explored alternative models of power and authority. Their various experiences represent an important contribution to the current discourse surrounding women,
religion, and social change.

In her survey of black women's experience, Paula Giddings (1984)
suggests that the role of the black woman is of "utmost importance" because of the pivotal link between race and sex that she represents. Giddings is quite correct in her insistence that the transformation of a sexist
and a racist society will not be effected without the guidance of black
women's experience in social change and intellectual revision. When one
examines the course of the black church in both its slave and free histories, it becomes apparent that beyond the prevailing images of preacher
and edifice exists a complex set of politicized networks of women whose
resistance to the masculinization of the churches they themselves helped
to build has institutionalized a feminist perspective and a progressive
female role model. Perhaps their persistent commitment to the institution is the most revolutionary stance of all. One nationally known
preacher and civil rights veteran is reputed to have stated that if women

ever leave the movement, "I am going where the women go, because nothing will ever happen without the women." The need for many things to happen still tends to pull members of the black community together, in spite of their disagreements. This is true in their religious communities as well. The dual-sex politics and tradition of conflict maintained by black women have enabled them to resolve their dilemmas of commitment while building a rich religious experience that remains one of the most important social, psychological, and spiritual resources they possess.

REFERENCES

Blackwell, James E. 1982. *The Black Community: Diversity and Unity.* New York: William Morrow.

Brooks, Evelyn. [1980] 1983. "The Feminist Theology of the Black Baptist Church, 1880–1900." In *Class, Race, and Sex: The Dynamics of Control,* ed. Amy Swerdlow and Hannah Lessinger, 31–59. Boston: G. K. Hall.

Brooks Barnett, Evelyn. 1978. "Nannie Helen Burroughs and the Education of Black Women." In *The Afro-American Woman: Struggles and Images,* ed. Sharon Harley and Rosalyn Terborg-Penn, 97–108. Port Washington, N.Y.: Kennikat Press.

Brown, Letitia Woods. 1975. "Battles Won and Evil Overcome." In *The Black Woman: Myths, Images, and Realities,* ed. Doris J. Mitchell and Jewell H. Bell, 4–7. Cambridge, Mass.: Radcliffe College.

Carter, Harold A. 1976. *The Prayer Tradition of Black People.* Valley Forge, Penn.: Judson Press.

Carter, Weptonomah W. 1976. *The Black Minister's Wife.* Elgin, Ill.: Progressive Baptist Publishing House.

Davis, Angela Y. 1981. *Women, Race, and Class.* New York: Random House.

Davis, Elizabeth L. 1933. *Lifting As They Climb: A History of the National Association of Colored Women.* Washington, D.C.: Moorland-Spingarn Research Center, Howard University.

Dill, Bonnie Thornton. 1979. "The Dialectics of Black Womanhood: Toward a New Model of American Femininity." *Signs: Journal of Women in Culture and Society* 4 (Spring): 543–55.

Diop, Cheikh Anta. [1958] 1978. *The Cultural Unity of Black Africa: The Domains of Patriarchy and Matriarchy in Classical Antiquity.* Chicago: Third World Press.

Dodson, Jualyne. 1982. "Preaching Women in the AME Church." Unpublished typescript paper, Union Theological Seminary, New York.

Dodson, Jualyne E., and Cheryl Townsend Gilkes. 1986. "Something Within: Social Change and Collective Endurance in the Sacred World of Black Christian Women." In *Women and Religion in America,* ed. Rosemary Radford Ruether and Rosemary Skinner Keller. Volume 3, *The Twentieth Century,* 80–128. San Francisco: Harper and Row.

Elkins, Stanley. 1959. *Slavery: A Problem in American Institutional and Intellectual Life*. Chicago: University of Chicago Press.

Evans, Sarah. 1980. *Personal Politics: The Roots of Women's Liberation in the Civil Rights Movement and the New Left*. New York: Vintage.

Giddings, Paula. 1984. *When and Where I Enter: The Impact of Black Women on Race and Sex in America*. New York: William Morrow.

Gilkes, Cheryl Townsend. 1981. "Institutional Motherhood in Black Churches and Communities: Ambivalent American Sexism or Fragmented African Familyhood." Unpublished manuscript, Boston, Mass.

―――― 1983a. "Cultural Constituencies in Conflict: The Sanctified Church and the Reorganization of Community, 1890–1950." Paper presented to a joint session of the Association of Black Sociologists and the Society for the Study of Social Problems, Detroit, Michigan.

―――― 1983b. "From Slavery to Social Welfare: Racism and the Control of Black Women." In *Class, Race, and Sex: The Dynamics of Control*, ed. Amy Swerdlow and Hannah Lessinger, 288–300. Boston: G. K. Hall.

Gutman, Herbert. 1976. *The Black Family in Slavery and Freedom, 1750–1925*. New York: Random House.

Jones, Jacqueline. 1985. *Labor of Love, Labor of Sorrow: Black Women, Work, and the Family from Slavery to the Present*. New York: Basic Books.

King, Deborah K. 1988. "Multiple Jeopardy, Multiple Consciousness: The Context of a Black Feminist Ideology." *Signs: Journal of Women in Culture and Society* 14 (1), 42–73.

King, Mary. 1987. *Freedom Song: A Personal Story of the 1960s Civil Rights Movement*. New York: William Morrow.

Lerner, Gerda. 1971. *Black Women in White America: A Documentary History*. New York: Random House.

Litwack, Leon F. 1979. *Been in the Storm So Long: The Aftermath of Slavery*. New York: Vintage Books.

Mbiti, John S. 1969. *African Religions and Philosophy*. Garden City, N.Y.: Doubleday/Anchor.

Meyerowitz, Eva L. R. 1960. *The Divine Kingship in Ghana and Ancient Egypt*. London: Faber and Faber.

Okonjo, Kamene. 1976. "The Dual Sex Political System in Operation: Igbo Women and Community Politics in Midwestern Nigeria." In *Women in Africa: Studies in Social and Economic Change*, ed. Nancy J. Hafkin and Edna G. Bay, 45–58. Stanford, Calif.: Stanford University Press.

Perkins, Linda. 1981. "Black Women and Racial 'Uplift' Prior to Emancipation." In *The Black Woman Cross-Culturally*, ed. Filomena Chioma Steady, 317–334. Cambridge, Mass.: Schenkman.

Ploski, Harry A., and Roscoe C. Brown. 1967. *The Negro Almanac*. New York: Bellwether Publishing.

Raboteau, Albert J. 1978. *Slave Religion: The Invisible Institution in the Ante-bellum South*. Oxford: Oxford University Press.

Richardson, Marilyn, ed. 1987. *Maria W. Stewart, America's First Black Woman Political Writer*. Bloomington: Indiana University Press.

Robinson, James Harvey. 1927. "Some of the Fruits of Historical Study." In *Readings in Sociology,* ed. Jerome Davis and Harry Elmer Barnes, 3–6. Boston: D.C. Heath.

Rose, LaFrances Rodgers. 1980. *The Black Woman.* Beverly Hills, Calif.: Sage Publications.

Sobel, Mechal. 1979. *Trabelin' On: The Slave's Journey to an Afro-Baptist Faith.* Westport, Conn.: Greenwood Press.

Sterling, Dorothy. 1984. *We Are Your Sisters: Black Women in the Nineteenth Century.* New York: W. W. Norton.

Terborg-Penn, Rosalyn. 1978. "Discrimination against Afro-American Women in the Woman's Movement, 1830–1920." In *The Black Woman: Struggles and Images,* ed. Sharon Harley and Rosalyn Terborg-Penn, 17–27. Port Washington, N.Y.: Kennikat Press.

Thurman, Howard. 1979. *With Head and Heart: The Autobiography of Howard Thurman.* New York: Harcourt Brace Jovanovich.

van Allen, Judith. 1976. " 'Aba Riots' or Igbo 'Women's War'? Ideology, Stratification, and the Invisibility of Women." In *Women in Africa: Studies in Social and Economic Change,* ed. Nancy Hafkin and Edna Bay, 59–85. Stanford, Calif.: Stanford University Press.

Walden, Daniel, ed. 1972. *W. E. B. Du Bois: The Crisis Writings.* Greenwich, Conn.: Fawcett Publications.

Webber, Thomas L. 1978. *Deep Like the Rivers: Education in the Slave Quarter Community, 1831–1865.* New York: W. W. Norton.

White, Deborah Gray. 1985. *Ar'n't I A Woman: Female Slaves in the Plantation South.* New York: W. W. Norton.

Wilson, Geraldine. 1980. "The Self-Group Actualization of Black Women." In *The Black Woman,* ed. LaFrances Rodgers Rose, 301–314. Beverly Hills, Calif.: Sage Publications.

Woodson, Carter G. [1921] 1972. *The History of the Negro Church.* Washington, D.C.: Associated Publishers.

CHAPTER FIVE

The Politics of African-American Ministerial Autobiography from Reconstruction to the 1920s

William L. Andrews

One of the striking differences between nineteenth-century African-American autobiographies published before and after Emancipation is their attitude toward institutions. In the classic antebellum slave narrative, the individual is usually pictured as at odds with institutions, in particular the institution of slavery, which robs individuals of personal power and social identity. Frederick Douglass's censure of "those bodies, north and south, calling themselves Christian churches and yet in union with slaveholders" stems from the antebellum slave narrator's conviction that the institutional framework of American life, from politics to religion, had been fundamentally corrupted by slavery. Attacking the institutionalized church for its "Pharisaical strictness to the outward forms of religion," Douglass allied himself in his *Narrative* with "the pure, peaceable, and impartial Christianity of Christ," which, he implies, inspires an individual to take a stand against the instituted authority of the church.[1] Douglass was equally suspicious of black as well as white religious institutions. Soon after his escape from slavery, he joined an African Methodist Episcopal Zion (A.M.E. Zion) church in New Bedford, Massachusetts, committing himself to its polity by accepting a license to preach there in 1839. Yet once he decided that the A.M.E. Zion denomination was insufficiently militant against slavery, Douglass informed his parishioners in New Bedford that he would have nothing further to do with the church.[2]

In contrast, in many black men's autobiographies of the late nineteenth and early twentieth centuries the moral priority of individual over institution is reversed, particularly among those autobiographers who identify themselves as founders or leaders of institutions. The collapse of Reconstruction and the gradual realization among blacks, especially in the South, that they would have to rely on their own resources in their social and economic struggle for justice convinced many that racial solidarity, grounded in black institutions, would have to become their bulwark against racism. Thus, beginning with the missionaries of the African Methodist Episcopal (A.M.E.) church, who went south in 1864 to help the free black community organize itself,[3] late nineteenth- and early twentieth-century black Americans, in search of collective empowerment, embraced institution-building, particularly in the areas of religion and education. Bishop Daniel A. Payne of the A.M.E. church, whose role in the institutionalization of the black Methodist church can hardly be overestimated, spoke for many of his cohorts in stressing duty and discipline over freedom and individualism in his postbellum autobiography. Taking the official line of the church hierarchy, Payne dismissed those in the church who insist " 'I am no slave'; 'I will not be gagged' " and then proclaim their "liberty to assail everything and every person . . . no matter how sacred the thing" or "how exalted the office." To Payne, freedom of self-expression—which had been the hallmark of a fully liberated black person in antebellum African-American autobiography—could never supercede the discipline of the institutionalized church. "Liberty must be regulated and controlled by the Church of the living God," Payne concluded in a manner typical of those who might be called "the institutional men" of African-American autobiography.[4]

These men,[5] many of whom had been born into slavery, did not see their orientation toward an institutional, rather than individual, agenda as a radical break with the past. Their autobiographies picture them as leaders of a communal effort to *realize* in concrete form—a church or a school, most often—the *ideal* of freedom articulated by the prophetic black American writers of the antebellum era. Preaching a gospel of power through concrete deeds, not ephemeral words, the institutional men of late nineteenth- and early twentieth-century black autobiography image themselves as pragmatic doers who will bring to fruition the promise of the past. Constructing a viable future did require recognizing the obsolescence of certain tactics associated with black agitators of the abolition era, however. In *From Log Cabin to the Pulpit* (1903), Rev. William H. Robinson spoke for most black institutional men when he recounted his decision to turn away from the kind of public persona and mode of discourse that had distinguished antebellum leaders like Frederick Douglass. Before his conversion, Robinson states, "it was the height of my ambition to be a political orator, for I had in me that retaliating spirit and thought there was no better way to vent my feelings towards the Southern people than to tongue-lash them in politics." He soon learned, however, that "if I wanted to be a useful man to my people and country," lashing whites through vengeful words would have to be forsaken, along with the whips and chains of slavery itself, in favor of a more productive means of rebuilding the South.[6] For most institutional men, true progress demands self-forgetfulness, indifference to individual desires, restraints on feelings that inhibit action, and enough skepticism about politics to distinguish the show from the substance. Not surprisingly, the autobiographies of black institutional men differ markedly from the famous antebellum slave narratives in the relative importance attached to matters relating to the self and its desires, feelings, and fulfillment, particularly as the self is revealed through language.

To the institutional men, actions literally speak louder than words, which is one reason why they generally write externally directed memoirs of what they accomplished rather than internally focused confessions of how they developed in consciousness. This does not mean that speeches and position papers of various kinds have no place in their narratives; in fact, many an institutional man portrays speech-making on behalf of an institution as a useful way of extending its influence. When one finds a speech or a sermon in the autobiographies of institutional men, however, its status is not intended to be that of a rival discourse to the narration. Because lecturing or preaching can enact an institutional agenda or, better yet, inform others of an action already accomplished by or for the institution, the autobiographies of institutional men suggest that speech can be a kind of action, even as action can be the most powerful kind of speech.[7]

The most prominent institutional man in black autobiography between Reconstruction and the Depression was Booker T. Washington, who epitomizes the many educators, school-builders, and practitioners of secular uplift who made their contribution to African-American autobiography in the late nineteenth century. The fame of Washington, the influence of *Up from Slavery* in white and black America, and the hope among those who adopted his educational program that they too might publicize themselves as successfully through their autobiographies all provide ready insight into the politics of black educators' autobiographies from Reconstruction to the 1920s.[8] On the other hand, Washington's autobiography generally frustrates those who wish to peer behind his apolitical but studiedly politic mask to discover the man himself. To most of Washington's more recent readers, the identity of the Tuskegeean tends to become "lost in a cause" (as one of his critics has paraphrased Washington). Washington seems both effaced by the institution he so insistently identifies with and displaced by the myth of self-sacrificing success that at first he appropriates, but which eventually appropriates him. Though Washington seems intent on aggrandizing himself by subscribing to the myth of the self-made man, a sense of self-diminution is what impresses many readers of his autobiography.[9] Repelled by the wall that the conventions of Washington's narrative build around him and within which his selfhood seems imprisoned, critics have taken to tapping on small blocks of incidents in the Tuskegeean's autobiographical monolith. Listening intently to a single Washington anecdote, such as a flashback to his boyhood in slavery during some moment of great self-celebration in his adult life, these critics hope to find a key to the elusiveness of tone, the ambiguity of meaning, and the ambivalence of purpose that lurk behind the stolid exterior of Washington's "inertial" narration.[10]

The problems that critics have had in getting behind Washington's institutionalized facade are similar to those that confront a reader of black men's ministerial autobiographies of the late nineteenth and early twentieth centuries. This difficulty is certainly one reason why recent criticism has paid so much attention to the more self-expressive spiritual narratives of black women.[11] Because of their marginalization by the male-dominated church, black women have had to rely on their own "traditions of autonomy, independence, and self-reliance," which, as Cheryl Townsend Gilkes explains, have informed African-American religious life since the antebellum era.[12] While their male counterparts had access to public institutional justification for their ministerial careers, black "sisters of the spirit" in the nineteenth and early twentieth centuries have claimed more personal sanction for their religious inspirations and careers, a fact that has given their narratives a self-revelatory dimension often lacking in the autobiographies of their male contemporaries. Unquestionably, black women's ministerial autobiographies of the nineteenth and early twentieth centuries are valuable sources of what would be called today "subjugated knowledges."[13] There is nevertheless good reason for studying the autobiographies of those who, in the aggregate, have long represented the "legitimate" tradition, the heroic history of the church, even though we are now wary of their hegemonic status and their pretense to a totalized discourse.

Between the fall of Reconstruction and the rise of the New Negro in the 1920s, the black male minister enjoyed more of a presence, in numerical terms alone, among the ranks of African-American autobiographers than ever before or since. This essay is based on a reading of approximately thirty-five male-authored ministerial autobiographies published between 1875 and 1925. Neither the previous half-century nor the fifty years following this crucial period in the evolution of black American autobiography saw the black ministry so extensively self-portrayed.[14] Just as the male fugitive slave held discursive sway over black autobiography during the antebellum era, the male minister welcomed the responsibility of representing the race in autobiography throughout the postbellum era and well into the twentieth century.

Though we may question these men's claim to this prerogative, many of their contemporaries—even those unsympathetic to their leadership—could not but grant the ministers' cultural prominence. For instance, the first "who's who" of black men in the United States, William J. Simmons's *Men of Mark* (1887), includes sketches of 71 ministers among the 177 brief biographies that make up his book. The ratio of ministers to educators, politicians, or businessmen represented in *Men of Mark* is almost three to one. In *The New Man* (1895), the autobiography of Henry Clay Bruce, a black businessman and early admirer of Booker T. Washington, the black ministry is described as wielding "a greater influence over the people than any other class of men." Washington's biographer, Louis Harlan, argues that Washington himself made his first bid for national recognition by attacking the moral fitness and educational preparedness of the black clergy in the South, primarily because he saw the undermining of this group's authority as crucial to the ascension of his own leadership. Carter G. Woodson's *History of the Negro Church* makes a case for the black ministry's consistent sociopolitical, as well as religious, leadership of black America throughout the nineteenth century and well into the increasingly secular twentieth. In 1945 he observed that the ministry "will doubtless continue, as it has since the Reconstruction, a sort of avenue through which the ambitious youth [of the race] must pass to secure a hearing and become a man of influence among his people."[15]

Through their autobiographies, black ministers of the late nineteenth and early twentieth centuries promoted themselves as new leaders for a new time. Rev. Alexander Newton spoke for many of his brethren of the cloth when he wrote in his autobiography that from his earliest church training, "I was deeply impressed with the importance of making my life a means of serving God in the uplifting of my people."[16] This idea that a servant of God would be fully engaged in racial uplift allowed black ministers like Tunis Campbell and Thomas O. Fuller to recount proudly their careers as political officeholders without feeling obliged to defend themselves against the charge of worldly ambition.[17] Ever since early Reconstruction, as Leon Litwack has noted, the black political leadership and black religious leadership in the South had been composed of the same men.[18]

The conviction that their calling granted them the right to monitor not only the religious but also the political life of black America emboldened the post–Civil War ministry to attack the leading spokesman of the race, Frederick Douglass, when he challenged the authority of the church by publicly questioning the central agency of God in African-American history. Suggesting that blacks had achieved emancipation primarily through human rather than divine power, Douglass first ran afoul of the black church in 1870. The clergy not only censured Douglass, it also capitalized on his vulnerability by asserting itself as a model for the kind of leadership black America needed in the postbellum era. In "Frederick Douglass, Not Our Leader," the *Christian Recorder,* the official organ of the A.M.E. Church, argued that black America needed to be represented not by a secular man like Douglass but rather by "the man who acknowledges his accountability to God for his actions, who looks up to Him for wisdom to know the right, for strength to do the right, and who will boldly take this position before the world."[19] In their bid for the social as well as spiritual leadership of post-Emancipation black America, many black ministers not only took this position but claimed as well that it sanctioned their attempts to arbitrate political issues affecting the black community.

The political significance of the black preacher during the time of slavery, the period of Reconstruction, the turn-of-the-century era of the nadir of black civil rights, and much of the twentieth century has been extensively debated.[20] But the politics of black ministerial autobiography—perhaps the major subgenre of African-American autobiography for at least fifty years, spanning the last quarter of the nineteenth and the first quarter of the twentieth century—has hardly been explored. In undertaking such an exploration, we must remember that divisions between secular and sacramental leadership are never easy to demarcate in discussing the black preacher of the nineteenth century. W. E. B. Du Bois's classic portrait of the preacher in *The Souls of Black Folk* (1903) acknowledges the complexity of the preacher's status as a leader of his people. "The Preacher is the most unique personality developed by the Negro on American soil," Du Bois announces. "A leader, a politician, an orator, a 'boss,' an intriguer, an idealist—all these he is, and ever, too, the centre of a group of men, now twenty, now a thousand in number. The combination of a certain adroitness with deep-seated earnestness, of tact with consummate ability, gave him his preeminence, and helps him maintain it." Under the leadership of such ministers as Alexander Crummell, Daniel A. Payne, and J. C. Price, Du Bois continues, the nineteenth-century black church successfully promulgated a social gospel of "self-development" and racial "self-assertion," pioneered in the political arena by the likes of Douglass and John Mercer Langston, that carried black America forward through the darkest days of post-Reconstruction reactionism in the United States.[21] That the black ministry deserved credit for making self-assertion a communally constructive ideal is an inescapable conclusion to be drawn from Du Bois's brief analysis of the political significance of the work of Crummell, Payne, and Price.

Bishop Payne would have been pleased to have been credited with inspiring the collective self-assertion of black Americans and progress toward his own lofty ideals of spiritual and social respectability. It is much less likely, however, that as an autobiographer he aimed at evoking the kind of self-assertion that permeates the post–Civil War autobiographies of a Douglass or a Langston and at times even threatens to overwhelm them in self-congratulation. For the most part, black ministers contemporary with Douglass and Langston seem to have disallowed themselves the luxury of conventional self-assertion in their autobiographies. Telling the story of the self's development toward its fulfillment in God and the church was one thing; asserting the self as an end in itself was quite another. Institutional constraints within the black church, as we have noted, together with literary traditions that depreciate the role and value of the self in Protestant spiritual autobiography helped rein in any black minister disposed to make his own individuality and his own voice the locus of significance and signification in his personal narrative.[22] James D. Corrothers spoke for many of his fellow clerics when he wrote in his autobiography, *In Spite of the Handicap* (1916), "the Almighty THOUGHT moves calmly toward the desired end: bending our wills to meet the General Plan, and moulding *our* thought, IT wills our way. Our *Thoughts!*—what are *they?*"[23]

This question, "Our thoughts—what are they?" is for Rev. Corrothers a rhetorical question that invites a self-abnegating answer. Nevertheless, although Corrothers pays tribute in his autobiography to the priority and plenitude of "the General Plan" for his individual life, the bulk of his book (and of any other ministerial autobiography) is still devoted to the particulars of *his* story, not to the generalities of the Almighty Plan. "Our thoughts" may be of little consequence in comparison to those of God, but within the purview of his autobiographical recollections, Corrothers's thoughts receive detailed articulation. While it was politic for a man like Corrothers to sound the conventional note of self-deprecation, what is *shown* in his autobiography—the process by which Corrothers discovered himself in and through the ministry—greatly outweighs in sheer narrative bulk what is *told* us in the autobiography about the slightness of the self or the magnificence of God. In short, the act of narrating—through which individual his-story takes on dramatic character in these ministerial autobiographies—may be seen as vying with official, institutional rhetoric—in all its self-denying, Other-affirming manifestations—for the attention of the reader and for the implicit authority that comes with it. Because the act of storytelling has borne political significance in African-American autobiography since its origins,[24] there is ample reason to investigate the impetus of an individual narrative against the institutionalized design of "the General Plan" in autobiographies that are as apparently anti–self-conscious as those of black ministers.

An investigation of the politics of black ministerial autobiography may proceed, therefore, from perceived disjunctions between the text's function as a promulgation of the church and its significance as a presentation of a self. Instead of coding this disjunction as individual versus institution, however—which would assign a simple opposition to these entities, when in fact the line between their agendas is often hard to draw—I suggest that the disjunction should be read in terms of a competition of discourses for precedence and authority in a given text. On the one hand, I will identify what might be called a discourse of preaching, in which, put as simply as possible, a minister tells his reader about his views on a given subject. This discourse of preaching in ministerial autobiography should not be confused with the black sermon as a distinctive oral or written genre, in which, as Hortense Spillers has pointed out, personal as well as communal "narratives of insurgence" often emerge "between the lines of Scripture" on which the sermon itself is based and patterned.[25] In black ministerial autobiography, a similar tension arises between insurgent narrative and the regulating lines of received wisdom, when what I am calling the discourse of preaching appears in juxtaposition with what I will term a discourse of storytelling. Put, again, in its simplest form, in a discourse of storytelling a ministerial autobiographer shows his reader what he did or thought. Although it is never easy to make the familiar distinction between "telling" and "showing" in an autobiography, since argumentation and narration so readily dovetail, I maintain that there is a perceptible though not absolute difference between preaching and storytelling in the autobiographies I discuss. This difference manifests itself politically in the unstable sense of authority that emerges from the interplay of the two discourses in representative autobiographies.

In the discourse of preaching, a minister appears to be about the business of taking positions, making arguments, and drawing conclusions—in other words, consolidating the ideational and/or ideological stratum of his text. The discourse of preaching has a number of the characteristics of what M. M. Bakhtin has called "authoritative discourse." Preaching evokes its authority by citing "the authoritative word," namely, *the* Word, whose privileged status is reinforced by its assumed historical priority and by its traditional legalistic recognition as "the word of the fathers" (handed down, in the case of Christian authoritative discourse, from *the* Father). As in other forms of authoritative discourse, preaching, by virtue of its utterance of "generally acknowledged truths" and "the official line," invites no analysis, admits no challenge, and grants no "free appropriation" or "assimilation" of itself. The discourse of preaching is in this sense inert, monolithic, set apart from the discourse of storytelling.[26] From one perspective, preacherly discourse in ministerial autobiographies seems to place narrative in its service by demanding of it a chronological line on which to string instances from which homiletic value may be gleaned. Many ministerial autobiographies are so punctuated with reprinted sermons, speeches, prayers, and other official church documents—all of them variations on the discourse of preaching—that the actual storytelling seems little more than a plot to convey the reader, willy-nilly, from sermon to sermon—from one officially edifying instance to the next. One may speak of ministerial narratives as plotting against the reader in this sense. Their overall plot formalizes the official church line, "the General Plan," and may be seen as having an implicit policing function in reinforcing the authority of the discourse of preaching.

By the discourse of storytelling, however, I do not mean the emplotted story taken as a whole in a given autobiography. Instead, I refer to the narration of an individual event or a succession of interrelated events. Not just any event in an autobiography will qualify as the kind of storytelling I am pointing to, however. The event cannot be an isolated or singular occurrence; it must bear some relationship to—it must enter into some sort of dialogue, or even dialectic, with—what I have been terming the "plot" of the autobiography.[27] In the narration of certain events in an autobiography we discover what Bakhtin calls "internally persuasive discourse"—that is, expression that has no inherent privilege and must claim its own authority in its own way. This kind of discourse "is frequently not even acknowledged in society," but it is widespread nevertheless, and the tensions generated by its struggle with "authoritative discourse" are "what usually determine the history of an individual ideological consciousness."[28] By examining some of the tensions between the officially authorized discourse of preaching and the internally persuasive discourse of narrated events in several ministerial autobiographies, I do not pretend to offer a history of anyone's individual ideological consciousness. But I do think that such an examination can reveal ideological consciousness in dynamic process in texts as apparently ideologically inert and totalized as are the autobiographies of black ministers in the late nineteenth and early twentieth centuries. This dynamic is facilitated by and contingent on what the act of narrating does to the unitary voice and universalizing ideology of ministerial autobiography.[29]

Here is an example of this dynamic, taken from William H. Robinson's *From Log Cabin to the Pulpit,* in which the narrating of an event seems designed simply to serve the ends of preaching. At this point Robinson is recalling his conversion experience:

> One day the preacher persuaded me to stay at the house, saying I was too weak to go with him to the woods. He knew what was ailing me, I could tell that in his morning and evening devotion, as he would offer me to the throne of grace, with so much fervor. After he was gone I took the shot

gun, saying to his wife that I would go hunting. I had gone but a short distance when something seemed to say to me, "you had as well take that gun and blow your brains out." Of course this was the reasoning of the devil making his last great effort to decoy me and destroy my soul. But God has promised in His word that He would be a help in every time of need, and this great truth demonstrated itself to me in this great hour of peril, for when my foot had almost slipped and my soul almost into eternity—where hope is a stranger and mercy could never reach my undone condition, the great spirit of God whispered in my soul, saying "woe be unto your damnation" (111–12).

In this passage, storytelling proposes to narrate an individual event, but preaching soon disposes of the personal reference and appropriates it to the purposes of God. Beginning with the phrase "But God has promised in His word," the narration is suspended in favor of the enunciation of God's authoritative "word." Through biblical paraphrases like "He would be a help in every time of need" (recalling Psalms 46:1—"God is our refuge and strength, / A very present help in trouble") and eventually the quoting of God Himself, such preaching converts the narration into a pretext for the reciting of the official line of the church. One is not surprised to learn that, after hearing God's warning, Robinson found his mind was "fully made up" to be converted, and "in less time than it will take me to tell it I was happily converted to Christ" (112). Once the authoritative word of God enters into the narration, the episode must come to closure; the action is now "fully made up," and William Robinson's story is converted to God's.

This, at least, is the conclusion intended by most ministers when they resort to this fairly standard technique of preaching on a narrated event in their autobiographies. It is worth noting, however, that while the episode closes with God's having the last word, He does not speak the only word in the narration. The devil has a speaking part, too. Indeed, the voice of the devil is given a distinctive status in the narration, comparable to that of God, by virtue of the fact that both Satan and God speak in direct discourse—unlike Robinson himself, whose narration is retrospective and in that sense indirect. It is also striking that the word of the devil forms the transition between the narrating of an event and the preaching on that event. The word of the devil, in effect, precipitates a crisis in the narrated action that can only be resolved by the evocation of the authoritative word through preaching. Against the threat of the devil's "reasoning," which would carry the narration into nihilistic chaos—blowing Robinson's brains out—comes the conserving promise of God, which brings the narration back to order and leaves Robinson "with my mind fully made up" to accept God's plan for his life. In the devil is figured the unplanned, unruly, and unauthorized impetus in narration toward some other end, apocalyptically imagined here as entropic dissolution, which in turn necessitates and justifies reclamation and closure by an authorized discourse. While it is the ideological purpose of the discourse of preaching to thwart this devilish turn of narration at every pass, it is also true, as I will show, that narration can and does expose—if not thwart—preaching's purposes. In the process, narration reveals itself as an internally persuasive discourse, capable of demystifying and even overriding preaching's claim to the last word.

In the *Life of the Rev. Elisha W. Green* (1888), an ex-slave from Kentucky posits early in his story his intention of recounting "how and by what movements I came to be a preacher."[30] While a slave in the early 1840s, Elisha Green became sexton of the white Baptist Church of his hometown and thus began to worship regularly among the white Baptists. Soon a few of the deacons in the church saw in him the makings of a preacher. They went to "John P. Dobbyns, my master, and got the authority to license me" (5). Green then enters into the narrative of his life a copy of the license the white Baptists gave him to preach:

> At a regular meeting of the Maysville Baptist Church, May 10, 1845, the following resolution was unanimously adopted: Be it
> *Resolved,* That Elisha Green, the property of John P. Dobbyns, of this city, has full liberty and permission from this day to exercise his gifts in the public before the colored population of this city or any others before whom in the providence of God he may be cast. E. F. Metcalf, *Church Clerk* (5)

Green enters this license, word for word, into his memoir, not just because it is part of the record of his life, but also to authorize himself as a preacher, one who was justified in adopting the discourse of the preacher.[31] Green exercises the authority of preacherly discourse when speaking, for example, of the fate of his first church, in Paris, Kentucky: "I will say here, that while in this age of freedom and intellectual progress, looking back to those days of infancy of the Paris church, seeing how God has guided and blessed her and wiped from the country the stain of slavery which kept us from worshiping according to the Bible, in the midst of this great change in the affairs of church and State, I can say that 'the people that sat in darkness have seen a great light' " (13). In this statement, Green looks back over the passage of many decades and, aided by scriptural precedent, summarizes the fruits of his ministry, first in slavery and then in freedom. His theme is progress, in particular institutional progress, as reflected in the evolution of the church he founded—which, he pointedly notes, has outlived the rude stable in which it began in slavery and has erected two successively larger buildings in which to house its increasing numbers.

While Green consistently preaches the corporate progress of black Christians in his book in a manner typical of black ministerial autobiography, one cannot help noticing some disparities between what happens to the people of God and what happens to Green, their pastor, in his *Life.* From the first to the last personal anecdote in the *Life,* the path of Green's individual career as a black minister defies pattern or plotting. There is no "general plan," no trajectory of progress, for Green's own life. Many of his personal anecdotes are recounted without an attempt to bring them to an edifying conclusion. This inconclusiveness is particularly notable in his recollections of his experience as a preacher during the time of slavery. Here is how Green resumes his narrative after quoting his May 10, 1845, license to preach: "On one Lord's day I was called to go up to the mouth of Cabin Creek to preach a funeral, and not knowing [this], Mr. Means, who is the undertaker now in Maysville, got a company and went up there for the purpose of protecting me. When I had gotten through preaching I came out of the door of the schoolhouse and my opponent walked around me and looked as though I was a lion" (5). Here the anecdote ends, with no commentary. Immediately another begins in which Green describes how he was prevented from attending a funeral of a member of his congregation because of the Fugitive Slave Law. The anecdote ends with Green quoting his words to a ferryboat captain to the effect that whites had no reason to fear his running away. Then he launches into a third anecdote:

> In 1855 I went to Lexington, Ky., to assist Bishop George W. Dupee. When I had finished my service in Lexington, I went to Georgetown, about twelve miles from Lexington on the Cincinnati Southern Railroad. Bishop Dupee requested me to go and fill an appointment for him, as he was sick. When I arrived the church was crowded. I went into the pulpit, read a chapter, sang and prayed. I was in the act of taking my text when unexpectedly a white man came in with a stick in his hand. . . . He knocked on the floor and asked if there were any white men there. The answer was "No." He then shook his stick at me and said:
> "You come out of that pulpit, then." Said I: "Very well," and I came out. . . . Early the next morning Elder Larue, pastor of the white Baptist Church of Georgetown, came to see me. . . . He asked me when I was going home. I told him that I was going home to-day, for I was satisfied with Georgetown. When I said this to him, he replied to me, "You can stay here and preach as long as you wish" (6).

Green's only conclusion is to remark, "I think I staid there and preached three nights after this." Then another anecdote follows in which Green recalls having been denied a ticket for a train back to Paris, having boarded the train nonetheless, and having been allowed by the conductor to remain on the train to his destination even though he had no ticket. Only some years later did Green learn from the conductor that he had not put Green off the train because "my face satisfied him" (7).

This series of anecdotes brings the first chapter of the *Life of the Rev. Elisha W. Green* to an end, although not to a clear conclusion. It is clear enough, however, that this particular series of recollections does not explain to the reader "how and by what movements I came to be a preacher." They seem more to illustrate how Green's preaching was hampered and how sometimes he was prevented from acting on the "full liberty" granted to him in his license. This tension between what is explicitly granted by the authoritative discourse of the license and the challenge to it implicit in the internally persuasive discourse of the subsequent narrations gives Green's autobiography its political character. Because of this tension, the language of the license is destabilized; its wording is brought into what Bakhtin would call a "zone of contact" created by the anecdotes. Its authority comes under scrutiny as a reader tries to reconcile it with the significance of the anecdotes. The meaning of a phrase like "full liberty" undergoes reconsideration in light of the evidence that Green's preaching had to be "protected" by Mr. Means, that Green was prevented from attending a parishioner's funeral, and that he was forbidden from preaching in Lexington until Elder Larue stepped in to support him. Yet nowhere in the narrative does Green explain what sort of liberty he actually *did* have "to exercise his gifts in the public." For whatever reason, the first chapter of Green's *Life* ends inconclusively, with the experience of the preacher severely qualifying, if not downright contradicting, the license from which he claims his authority to write *as* a preacher in the first place.

The strain between the license and the anecdotes in the *Life*'s opening chapter points to a fundamental disjunction in Green's political identity in the antebellum South. The white men who authored his license conferred on Green the status of a preacher while maintaining his identity as a piece of chattel, "the property of John P. Dobbyns." How can a piece of property be possessed of "gifts" and be rewarded with "full liberty" to use them? Doubtless the Baptist elders who licensed Green did not ponder this paradox. Would the ironies inherent in the paradox have occurred to the readers of Green's self-published and probably locally distributed 1888 autobiography? Perhaps, but there is at least a reasonable doubt as to whether his white readers would have recognized the irony without the illustrations that emerge from the subsequent anecdotes.

Why, then, after narrating the anecdotes, did Green not pause to preach on the meaning of what happened to him as a preacher in slavery? Possibly because he could not, or would not, reduce his condition as a slave preacher to a conclusive, authoritative statement. To do so would have taken the white Baptists off the hook, in a sense. It would have suggested that there *was* a way to resolve the paradox of Elisha Green's condition as property at full liberty; it would have implied that the paradox was itself a normal and normalizing way of defining Green (as the white Baptists assumed) rather than an inherently *in*definite, *un*-finished identity. Thus, it is not surprising that Green's narrative repeatedly shows how his experience defied the attempt by the white Baptists to define him except as a contradiction in terms. The elliptical nature of his anecdotes, their disjointedness, and their inconclusiveness also resist any temptation on the part of a reader to totalize the condition and significance of the black preacher. Even after he obtains his freedom, what Green says of himself as a free black preacher—"I will say that I was more of a slave after I bought myself than before" (14)—reconfirms the ongoing paradoxical character of his identity, a fact that subsequent anecdotes illustrate to the very end of the *Life*.

The contradiction of discourses in the first chapter of the autobiography of Elisha Green represents a complex form of double-voicing which, in its most mechanical expression, may be found throughout black ministerial autobiographies of the late nineteenth and early twentieth centuries. Whenever an autobiographer quotes an authoritative discourse from a source—most often the Bible, or else some popular poem or officially recognized religious or political authority (Lincoln, for instance)—and then makes those words his or her own by translating them into contemporary idiom or applying them to a contemporary situation, we have an instance of double-voiced discourse.[32] In Green's *Life* it is the language of the white churchmen, with its pretense to definitiveness and authority over the black preacher's identity, that is double-voiced and rendered problematic by the narrations that follow it.

The politics of this sort of destabilization of "white" declaration by "black" narration is not hard to recognize. What is harder to reckon with is another form of double-voicing in black ministerial autobiography, in which storytelling contradicts and subverts the autobiographer's own preacherly pronouncements, thereby creating an apparently *self*-contradictory discourse. An example of this sort of double-voicing may be found in one of the most widely read black autobiographies of the World War I era, *My Life and Work* (1917) by Alexander Walters, a bishop in the A.M.E. Zion Church.

Alexander Walters was the black-minister-as-political-activist *par excellence*. August Meier treats Walters as the bellwether of the Afro-American Council, which originated in the 1890s as a cog in the Tuskegee machine but which by 1906, with Walters as its president, was taking a distinctly militant tone in its approach to black civil and political rights. Walters was also prominent in the Constitution League, a civil rights organization that helped pave the way for the National Association for the Advancement of Colored People (NAACP). During the presidential campaigns of 1908 and 1912, Walters actively campaigned through the offices of the National Negro American Political League and the Colored National Democratic League in an effort to get out the black vote for the Democratic party, in response to Republican complacency and paternalism.[33] Yet he was no mere Democratic party lackey, as he demonstrated by refusing to accept Woodrow Wilson's appointment as Minister to Liberia in 1915.

The first one-third of Walters's autobiography offers his reader a narrative of his successes, from his humble birth as a slave in Bardstown, Kentucky, to his election as a bishop in the A.M.E. Zion church in 1892, when he was not quite thirty-four years old. Thereafter, the book is given over almost entirely to the reprinting of his sermons, speeches, and positions papers as bishop; he arranges these in chapters that chronicle his leadership positions in various religious and political organizations and the accomplishments of those organizations under his leadership. Because of Walters's decision to devote the greater part of his book to the history of his public life and pronouncements, the discourse of preaching crowds out the discourse of storytelling in the latter two-thirds of his book. The official voice of the institutional spokesman is ceded the authority and the space in the autobiography to address (quite literally) the problems of black advancement in the social, economic, and political realm that become the thematic burden of the latter half of *My Life and Work*.

Walters's speech to the 1895 National Convention of Christian Endeavorers, entitled "The Responsibility of the Afro-American in America," epitomizes the politicized preaching highlighted in the latter chapters of *My Life and Work*. In this address, Walters urges that black people take responsibility for their own "civil and political rights" by cultivating "intelligence, character, wealth, and wise agitation."[34] Espousing intellectual achievement, high standards of character, and economic success, Walters allies himself with the verities that his colleagues had been preaching in the African-American church since before the Civil War. His championing of "agitation," on the other hand, is a more individual and riskier tack for a church leader to take, especially in 1895, the year in which Booker T. Washington's Atlanta Exposition address seemed to establish a counter-orthodoxy in politics. Preaching "wise agitation" reflects Walters's characteristic way of steering a moderate course between activism and conservatism. The wise agitator, Walters counsels his audience, would be known by "an intelligent, reasonable, yet manly presentation of the discriminations and outrages to which we are subjected" (209). Through his institutional voice, Walters offers his audience a model of the agitator who tempers his denunciations of racism with a wisdom borne of the conviction that "with character, intelligence and wealth we will not have to go out of our way to demand respect, for we will *command* it, especially if we exercise good judgment" (210).

A reading of the last two-thirds of *My Life and Work* leaves one with the impression that the personal storytelling of the first part of the autobiography is intended primarily to explain how Walters earned the right and the authority to adopt the discourse of black spokesman and exemplar that dominates so much of his book. Walters's narrative of his boyhood and young manhood is essentially an outline of the steps by which he became prepared for and then rose in the ministry. The plot is propelled by a sense of the inevitability of what Walters calls "the promise of God that I would succeed" (45). Seldom is there a pause for a personal anecdote of any sort. The only hiatus in what reads like an extended and detailed resume appears in the eighth and ninth chapters of *My Life and Work*, when Walters takes time out to recount a journey he took to Europe and the Holy Land in 1889. For the most part, Walters's narrative of this journey is conventional, containing the usual descriptions of and reactions to the guidebooks' recommended points of interest. However, while discussing his activities at the World Sunday School Convention, Walters interrupts the pace and focus of his narrative to record the longest and most self-revealing anecdote of his entire autobiography.

The anecdote has to do with Walters's first visit to London in 1889, to attend, along with a sizable biracial group, the World Sunday School Convention. Upon arrival, Walters had the good fortune to become the houseguest of Samuel Cole, dubbed "one of the elite of London" in *My Life and Work*. Admitting that he had not expected to receive the royal treatment that was lavished on him at the Coles' house, Walter assures his readers that he assiduously played the part of "a gentleman of leisure and luxury," since "of course I did not wish to have it known that I was not accustomed to all the luxuries of life and acquainted with all the rules of etiquette" (61). Besides, for a black American, the pleasure of being treated so deferentially in London by high- and low-born whites alike was truly tonic, as Walters makes clear. He acknowledges that he enjoyed acting as though he were to the manor born, but what he *really* enjoyed—and what he savors the most through the telling of the longest anecdote in his autobiography—is how he converted his private play into a highly public performance, stage-managed expressly to compel white American bigots to witness a black man in the role of their social equal.

The opportunity that Walters recalls with such relish came one Saturday afternoon when Cole informed his guest that as he would not be present on the Sabbath to take Mrs. Cole and a lady friend from Scotland to church, he would be grateful if Walters would accompany them. Walters accepts, and then he goes on:

> A thought occurred to me (I know not whence it came) to take advantage of the occasion to have some fun with our white American brethren and let them see how a colored man was respected and honored in England. The whole [American] delegation had been invited to worship at Mr. Spurgeon's church. . . . and I knew they were all likely to be present. I went to a gents' furnishing store and instructed the salesman to fit my hand with a pair of kid gloves of the latest, and told him not to regard the cost, as I wanted a neat fit. . . . Believe me, when I tell you he gave me the neatest fit I ever had in my life; I had not cared for gloves very much, heretofore, but I was especially anxious to have the best in the market on this occasion. I had purchased a new suit before leaving home for the convention. With my new suit, kid gloves and low quartered shoes, I was prepared to escort the ladies to church (61–62).

"I could not sleep well on Saturday night for thinking of my approaching triumph" (62), Walters interjects before finishing his anecdote. When the magic hour arrives, Walters assists the ladies into the family carriage and then tells the driver, "If you see a great many carriages in front of the church when we arrive, you saunter about until the way is cleared." Thus Walters contrives an arrival that no one in the American delegation could possibly ignore. Only when the way to the curb is cleared of other carriages does he allow his conveyance to approach the entrance to the church. When the footman opens the carriage door, "I stepped out and with my neatly-gloved hand assisted Mrs. Cole and her friend to alight. With all the grace imaginable, and in full view of the assembled multitude, who stood gazing on with amazement, I escorted the ladies into the church, much to the astonishment of my deeply prejudiced Southern brethren" (63). Walters concludes, "I don't know when I have gotten so much real enjoyment out of an occasion, furnished ready to hand by unreasonable prejudice" (63).

The voice that recounts this anecdote does not speak in the same tone or seem motivated by the same idea of "wise agitation" as Walters espouses later in his autobiography. Only six years separate the Walters who goes out of his way to needle whites in London from the Walters who preaches that with intelligence, character, and wealth, blacks will not have to "go out of [their] way to demand white respect," since by using "good judgment," they will *"command"* it (210). Nothing in the later chapters of *My Life and Work* indicates that Walters repudiated his earlier behavior, or even that he saw a contradiction between what he practiced in London and what he preached to the Christian Endeavorers of Worcester, Massachusetts. Telling the London anecdote in such detail, and then letting his preaching on "wise agitation" override the earlier anecdote, suggests that although Walters would give prominence of position to the preaching in his text, in accordance with the orthodoxy of ministerial autobiography, he nevertheless relished a storytelling opportunity when he found it, whether or not he was sure how it would fit into the general plan and program of his text.

The stress placed in the early chapters of *My Life and Work* on Alexander Walters's single-minded pursuit of success in the religious sphere of the black community gives no hint that he was also a man who, given the chance, would enjoy nothing better than to taunt southern bigots by flaunting his social equality with whites in England. Moreover, after Walters returns from his travels abroad, is elected bishop, and preaches "wise agitation" as a means of gaining white respect, he abandons any talk of having "fun" with white racists at their own expense. From the perspective of the exponent of "wise agitation" in securing white respect, it was probably not "good judgment" for Alexander Walters to have gone "out of his way" to aggravate white bigots in London by showing them a black man consorting with white women under circumstances of social equality. Similarly, from the perspective of a bishop in the A.M.E. Zion church, Walters could be accused of behavior unbecoming of a Christian for allowing himself to get so caught up in what he termed "my approaching triumph" at the very doorstep of a house of God. Given the many professional, social, and political triumphs that punctuate *My Life and Work,* a reader may be more than a little surprised that Walters could think of no time in his life when he had "gotten so much real enjoyment out of an occasion" as he had during this episode in London.

What was the source of this unique enjoyment that so gratified Walters that he was willing to allow it so much freedom in his text, even at the risk of sounding self-contradictory, hypocritical, or simply petty in comparison to his later pronouncements? Interestingly, Walters does not offer any motive for his bit of London play other than a desire "to have some fun" with white racists by letting them see how he, "a colored man," was "respected and honored in England." As for the origin of this "thought that occurred to me," Walters will only state, archly and in language that parodies the Bible, "I know not whence it came." Yet in the very tone and parodic nature of this disclaimer, the storyteller invites his reader to conclude that a certain kind of devilment was at the bottom of the preacher's desire to "have some fun" in the manner he chose. Clearly, Reverend Walters did not expect his actions to convert any of "our American brethren" from their racism; he was out simply to rub their noses in it. His goal was certainly agitation, but it was not agitation designed to enhance the respect accorded black people in America. Walters's plan was simply to force his "brethren" to see how he, Walters, "was respected and honored in Europe." Although this sort of agitation may seem self-indulgent and even counterproductive, the fact that the narration calls attention to the preacher's achievement of social respect and honor abroad "in Europe," not at home, takes on a telling irony. Walters's moment of "fun" comes both at his own *and* others' expense: the anecdote mocks the powerlessness of the racists to block Walters in Europe, while it subtly reminds the reader of the black minister's lack of social self-determination in the United States. Thus, the London anecdote cuts, rather diabolically, two ways—and in so doing makes of Walters's apparently impolitic action a fundamentally political recollection.

It is appropriate that only during the European hiatus from the larger record of his success story does Walters divagate from his ministerial purpose, in order to recount his devilish, decidedly *un*saintly, behavior. In Europe Walters felt himself for the first time liberated from the usual pastoral role he played in the United States. He felt free to play the secular gentleman; he felt empowered to play a trick on his "brethren"; and, when recalling this interlude in his life, he felt entitled to play with his own story and style of self-presentation and to profess "enjoyment," not moral or spiritual gain, in doing so. This sort of enjoyment, which carries over from the memory to the act of narrating it, is the sort of "pleasure of the text" that rarely emerges from a black ministerial autobiography.[35] Yet the fact that it turns up at all, and in a plainly out-of-the-way place in this autobiography, testifies to its unprogrammed significance. The desire for self-gratification, though inhibited and even implicitly denied by the preacher's sense of institutional responsibility, asserts itself willy-nilly through the act of storytelling. In the process, the programmed expectations and responses of readers of autobiographies like Walters's are surprised by the "real enjoyment" that occurs when a plot is diverted from its course and is prevented, at least momentarily, from resolving itself in the official mode and manner. Recounting this episode in his European travels may have taken Walters "out of his way" with respect to the preacher's sense of how African-Americans should "demand respect." But following the way opened up in his story by the unsanctioned pleasure of this European recollection enables Walters to "command respect" from present-day, resisting readers who seek in narratives like his the key to the *un*resolving of the public self-deportment of respectable black institutional men in late nineteenth- and early twentieth-century America. Perhaps more attention to what is rhetorically "out of the way" in the life-narrations of black institutional men from Booker T. Washington to Alexander Walters can help us reassess the cultural import, as well as the human complexity, of black autobiographers whose heretofore successful attempts to monumentalize themselves in writing ought no longer to be taken at face value.

NOTES

I would like to thank Robert Caserio for his suggestions and criticism of an early draft of this essay.

1. *Narrative of the Life of Frederick Douglass,* ed. Houston A. Baker (New York: Viking Penguin, 1982), 156–57.

2. In *The Autobiography of Rev. Thomas James* (Rochester, N.Y.: Author, 1886), the author recounts the story of Douglass's relationship to the New Bedford A.M.E. Zion Church in the late 1830s. See also William L. Andrews, "Frederick Douglass, Preacher," *American Literature* 54 (December 1982): 592–97.

3. See Clarence E. Walker's *A Rock in a Weary Land: The African Methodist Episcopal Church during the Civil War and Reconstruction* (Baton Rouge: Louisiana State University Press, 1982).

4. Daniel A. Payne, *Recollections of Seventy Years,* ed. C. S. Smith (Nashville: A.M.E. Sunday School Union, 1888), 285–86.

5. What is described in this essay as the institutional mentality of African-American autobiography in the late nineteenth and early twentieth centuries is represented almost entirely by male narratives. The power wielded by women in major black religious and educational institutions during this era tended to come from distaff organizations—"women's departments"—within the institutions, not from positions of leadership over the institution as a whole. For a sociological analysis of the "dual-sex politics" of post-Emancipation black churches, with an emphasis on institutionalized leadership roles for women, see Cheryl Townsend Gilkes's contribution to this volume (chapter 4). Tension between assertive women and male institutionalized authority in the late nineteenth- and early twentieth-century black church is attested by two autobiographies: Julia A. J. Foote's *A Brand Plucked from the Fire* (Cleveland, Ohio: Author, 1879) and Virginia Broughton's *Twenty Year's Experience of a Missionary* (Chicago: Pony Press, 1907). Foote's narrative records continual conflicts between her individualistic sense of spiritual sanction and the instituted authority of a male-dominated church. Broughton's narrative deemphasizes conflict between women and male authority and shows how women brought men to an acceptance of women's missionary work to and for women among the black Baptists of the South.

6. William H. Robinson, *From Log Cabin to the Pulpit* (Eau Claire, Wisc.: James H. Tifft, 1903), 105–7.

7. For a discussion of other general characteristics of institutional men's autobiographies, see William L. Andrews, "Forgotten Voices of Afro-American Autobiography, 1865–1930," *A/B: Auto/Biography Studies* 2 (1986): 21–27.

8. For a representative selection of the autobiographies of black educators, see besides Washington's *Up from Slavery* (New York: Doubleday, Page, 1901), Laurence Jones's *Up through Difficulties* (Braxton, Miss.: Pine Torch, 1913), William H. Holtzclaw's *The Black Man's Burden* (New York: Neale, 1915), William James Edwards's *Twenty-Five Years in the Black Belt* (Boston: Cornhill, 1918), and Robert Russa Moton's *Finding a Way Out* (Garden City, NY: Doubleday, Page, 1920).

9. For representative criticisms of *Up from Slavery* along these lines, see Robert B. Stepto's chapter, "Lost in a Cause: Booker T. Washington's *Up from Slavery*," in *From behind the Veil* (Urbana: University of Illinois Press, 1979), 32–51; and Houston A. Baker, *The Journey Back* (Chicago: University of Chicago Press, 1980), 46–52.

10. See, for instance, the discussions of the same flashback in *Up from Slavery* in James M. Cox's "Autobiography and Washington" in *Recovering Literature's Lost Ground* (Baton Rouge: Louisiana State University Press, 1989), 121–43, and in William E. Cain's *The Crisis in Criticism* (Baltimore, Md.: Johns Hopkins University Press, 1984), 264–74.

11. That black religious women's autobiographies have captured the interest of many is evident from the new editions of their work: William L. Andrews, ed., *Sisters of the Spirit* (Bloomington: Indiana University Press, 1986); Sue E. Houchins, ed., *Spiritual Narratives* (New York: Oxford University Press, 1988); and Jean McMahon Humez, ed., *Gifts of Power: The Writings of Rebecca Jackson, Black Visionary, Shaker Eldress* (Amherst: University of Massachusetts Press, 1981).

12. See Gilkes's contribution to this volume, "The Politics of 'Silence': Dual-Sex Political Systems and Women's Traditions of Conflict in African-American Religion" (chapter 4).

13. The concept of "subjugated knowledge" is taken from Michel Foucault, *Power/Knowledge*, ed. Colin Gordon (New York: Pantheon, 1980), 81–84.

14. Using primarily Russell C. Brignano's *Black Americans in Autobiography* (Durham, N.C.: Duke University Press, 1984), I find that between 1925 and 1975, approximately twenty-five male *and* female ministers and preachers published autobiographies. Using, in addition to Brignano's work, the bibliography of black autobiography that appends my own *To Tell a Free Story* (Urbana: University of Illinois Press, 1986), I judge that between 1820 and 1875 approximately twenty-five male and female black ministers and preachers dictated or wrote autobiographies. Thus, the central fifty-year period in the history of African-American autobiography on which this essay is centered is remarkable for its unusual outpouring of ministerial autobiographies—approximately forty, of which all were male-authored except five: those by Rebecca G. Stewart (1877), Julia A. J. Foote (1879), Elizabeth (1889), Amanda Berry Smith (1893), and Virginia W. Broughton (1907).

15. William J. Simmons, *Men of Mark* (Cleveland, Ohio: George M. Rewell, 1887); Henry Clay Bruce, *The New Man* (York, Penn.: P. Anstadt & Sons, 1895), 148; Louis R. Harlan, *Booker T. Washington: The Making of a Black Leader, 1856–1901* (New York: Oxford University Press, 1972), 191–94; Carter G. Woodson, *The History of the Negro Church* (Washington, D.C.: Associated Publishers, 1945), 276.

16. Alexander Herritage Newton, *Out of the Briars* (Philadelphia: A.M.E. Book Concern, 1910), 27.

17. See Tunis G. Campbell, *Sufferings of the Rev. T. G. Campbell and His Family, in Georgia* (Washington, D.C.: Enterprise, 1877) and Thomas O. Fuller, *Twenty Years in Public Life, 1890–1910* (Nashville: National Baptist Publishing Board,

1910). Rev. Elisha W. Green's observation "Politics and I are not related, only so far as it becomes my duty to advise my people to look to their own interests" typifies the sense of communal, if not specifically political, responsibility that many black ministers evince in their autobiographies. See *Life of the Rev. Elisha W. Green* (Maysville, Ky.: Republican Printing Office, 1888), 33.

18. Leon Litwack, *Been in the Storm So Long: The Aftermath of Slavery* (New York: Knopf, 1979), 470–71.

19. Waldo E. Martin, *The Mind of Frederick Douglass* (Chapel Hill: University of North Carolina Press, 1984), 179.

20. In addition to Woodson's *History of the Negro Church,* see Charles V. Hamilton, *The Black Preacher in America* (New York: William Morrow, 1972); Gayraud S. Wilmore, *Black Religion and Black Radicalism* (Garden City, N.Y.: Doubleday, 1972); Albert Raboteau, *Slave Religion* (New York: Oxford University Press, 1978); Lawrence Levine, *Black Culture and Black Consciousness* (New York: Oxford University Press, 1977); and Sterling Stuckey, *Slave Culture* (New York: Oxford University Press, 1987). See also Cheryl Townsend Gilkes's challenge to what she terms "the exaggerated focus" on the role of the preacher in black religious history—to the virtual exclusion of other forms of religious leadership in the church—in her "The Politics of 'Silence': Dual-Sex Political Systems and Women's Traditions of Conflict in African-American Religion" in this volume.

21. W. E. B. Du Bois, *Writings* (New York: Library of America, 1986), 494, 397.

22. The personal literature of the Puritans, from which the conversion narrative and the ministerial autobiography emanate, teaches that selfhood is a state to be overcome and obliterated in favor of "an act of submission to a transcendent absolute." See Sacvan Bercovitch, *The Puritan Origins of the American Self* (New Haven, Conn.: Yale University Press, 1975), 13. Thus, God, the "transcendent absolute" of all spiritual autobiography, black and white, becomes the real protagonist, the essential initiator of all the spiritual action, while the self, when not an obstacle to oneness with God and God's plan, at best reacts and conforms to providential designs on the individual.

23. James D. Corrothers, *In Spite of the Handicap* (New York: George H. Doran, 1916), 173.

24. See William L. Andrews, *To Tell a Free Story: The First Century of Afro-American Autobiography, 1760–1865* (Urbana: University of Illinois Press, 1986).

25. Hortense Spillers, "Moving On Down the Line: Variations on the African-American Sermon," in *The Bounds of Race,* ed. Dominick La Capra (Ithaca, N.Y.: Cornell University Press, 1991), 41.

26. M. M. Bakhtin, *The Dialogic Imagination,* ed. Michael Holquist, trans. Caryl Emerson and Michael Holquist (Austin: University of Texas Press, 1981), 342–44.

27. For the notion of "events" here, I am indebted to Paul Ricoeur, *Time and Narrative* (Chicago: University of Chicago Press, 1984), 1:65.

28. Bakhtin, *Dialogic Imagination,* 342–45.

29. For a similar kind of study, which emphasizes the difference between the "disembodied episcopal voice" of the narrator of Saint Augustine's *Confessions*

and the individuated, historicized, sinful protagonist of that book, a distinction that has as much to do with the necessities of autobiographical narration as with the theology of conversion itself, see John Freccero, "Autobiography and Narrative," in *Reconstructing Individualism*, ed. Thomas C. Heller, et al. (Stanford: Stanford University Press, 1986), 16–29. In a different but parallel vein, Sau-ling Cynthia Wong concludes an analysis of Maxine Hong Kingston's *The Woman Warrior* by stressing how narrative "extravagance" insinuates itself into the talk-stories of Kingston's mother, Brave Orchid, despite the latter's announced intention of offering her daughter only grimly didactic tales. See "Necessity and Extravagance in Maxine Hong Kingston's *The Woman Warrior:* Art and the Ethnic Experience," *MELUS* 15 (1988): 3–26.

30. See Elisha Green, *Life of the Rev. Elisha W. Green* (Maysville, Ky.: Republican Printing Office, 1888), 5. Subsequent quotations from Green's *Life* are from this edition.

31. It is significant that Green offers no subsequent information in his autobiography concerning his right to entitle himself "Reverend."

32. "Double-voiced discourse" is Bakhtin's general term for a wide variety of representations of another's words in a text. See *The Dialogic Imagination*, 347–55.

33. August Meier, *Negro Thought in America, 1880–1915* (Ann Arbor: University of Michigan Press, 1963), 172–82, 186–87.

34. Alexander Walters, *My Life and Work* (New York: Fleming H. Revell, 1917), 207. Subsequent quotations from *My Life and Work* are from this edition.

35. By the "pleasure of the text," I refer to notions having to do with the playful engagement of reader and text articulated in Roland Barthes, *The Pleasure of the Text*, trans. Richard Miller (New York: Hill and Wang, 1975).

CHAPTER SIX

The Baptist Church in the
Years of Crisis
J. C. Austin and Pilgrim Baptist Church,
1926-1950

Randall K. Burkett

Afro-American religious life in the urban North, especially during the second quarter of the twentieth century, has often been described as the "era of sects and cults." It is generally argued that, in the face of a dramatic population increase resulting from the influx of southern migrants, coupled with economic dislocation and eventual massive unemployment that culminated in the Great Depression, the mainline Black denominations were unable to respond effectively to the spiritual and social needs of the Black community. Unable to cope with urbanization and its attendant secularization, the established churches are seen to have yielded center stage to myriad smaller religious institutions, which blended a sense of intimacy with an emphasis on religious ecstasy.[1]

Gayraud Wilmore, one of the most provocative and astute observers of Afro-American religious history, essentially takes this position in his book *Black Religion and Black Radicalism*.[2] The chapter that he devotes to this period is entitled "The Deradicalization of the Black Church," clearly reflecting his perspective. Wilmore posits, in effect, the "fall" of the Black church in the interwar years. He is especially harsh on the clergy, whom he characterizes as having adopted Booker T. Washington's gradualism and as having bought into a white Christian notion of a self-effacing white Christ. To the extent that the clergy became involved in civil rights organizations at all, Wilmore charges, they did so primarily as a way of entering the mainstream of American society, reflecting their growing identification with dominant white cultural norms. As a consequence, he concludes, the clergy served as a restraining influence on the potential militancy of certain civil rights organizations, keeping them on an accommodationist path. At the same time, the mainline churches themselves, in their search for respectability, "succumbed to the cajolery and bribery of the white power structure and became its foil."[3]

While the mainline denominations were moving toward the periphery of Black cultural life, through their own internal dynamics, according to Wilmore's analysis they were also being driven toward marginalization by external creative energies both from "below" and from "above." On the one hand, lower-class movements, typified by the storefront churches and the "sects and cults," were growing by leaps and bounds. Wilmore cites the traditional litany of these organizations—the Holiness and Pentecostal churches; the de-Christianized groups such as the Black Jews, the Moorish Science Temple, and the Nation of Islam; and the deific groups such as Daddy Grace's United House of Prayer for All People and Father Divine's Peace Mission Movement—as examples of the rich diversity of Black religious institutional life in this period.[4]

On the other hand, among the Black middle and upper classes, the mainline churches met with a growing indifference, if not outright hostility. Whether measured by the movement of upwardly mobile Blacks from Baptist and Methodist to Congregational, Presbyterian, and Episcopal denominations, or by the emergence of the predominately secular Harlem Renaissance, the traditionally Black denominations, according to conventional wisdom, were being abandoned as relics of a past age— that is, as institutions once useful but now essentially a drain and a restraining influence on future progress, especially as that progress was measured by full integration into the dominant white American society.[5]

It certainly is clear that Afro-American religious life was going through a period of extraordinary change in the interwar years. The religious vitality of the so-called sects and cults and of the storefront churches is a phenomenon well deserving of the attention it has received in the literature. Another important factor contributing to major change was the increasing differentiation of the Black community; specifically, a range of voluntary associations grew to prominence, removing from the mainline churches some of the responsibility they had borne in an earlier period as political, social, fraternal, and benevolent institutions, and antireligious and secular elements emerged among a portion of the Black community. However, there was much more vitality in the mainline institutional churches during the post–World War I era—especially among the Baptists—than researchers have recognized. A comparison of the *Census of Religious Bodies* for the years 1926 and 1936, the last year such a census was conducted by the federal government, shows a nearly 9 percent increase in Black membership among all denominations, from 5.2 million to 5.7 million. Black Baptists alone, however, showed an even larger gain, from 3.2 million in 1926 to nearly 3.8 million a decade later. Literally all of this gain was registered among urban churches, whose rolls swelled from 1.2 million to 1.9 million in the period, and enabled the Baptists to claim fully two-thirds (67 percent) of all Black church members in 1936, up from 61.6 percent a decade earlier.[6]

While it is true that the Census Bureau undercounted smaller religious organizations and ignored others altogether (for example, Father Divine's Peace Mission Movement is not enumerated), this fact does not discount the striking increase in the number of Black Baptists. This increase is particularly noteworthy in light of the significant drop during the same period in the number of church members in other denominations (including not only the African Methodists but also smaller groups such as the Churches of Christ and the Churches of the Living God). In what follows, I redress the neglect of the historical Black denominations in general, and of Baptists in particular, in the interwar years by focusing on the life of one highly influential Baptist minister, Junius Caesar Austin, whose ability, eloquence, and wide-ranging interests in preaching, politics, music, aviation, education, civil rights, and foreign missions placed him in the forefront of progressive clergy in urban America.

J. C. AUSTIN: EARLY YEARS

J. C. Austin (1887–1968) was born in the upper South, in New Canton, a rural village in Buckingham County, Virginia. He received the call to the ministry at the age of eleven and served in the Baptist pastorate for just a few months short of seventy years. His early theological and social outlook were shaped by his educational experience at the Virginia Seminary and College at Lynchburg, one of the oldest independent Black Baptist seminaries in the country.

Virginia Seminary was organized in 1887 by the Virginia Baptist State Convention.[7] From its earliest days, the school was staffed by a leadership that George Shepperson and Thomas Price describe as "highly independent in spirit, believing . . . that the Negro peoples were perfectly capable of carrying on with their work without the white man always at their elbows."[8] Its president, Gregory W. Hayes, was once chastised by white Baptists for his spirit of "foolish independence and self-assertion," which had turned Lynchburg into "a sort of hotbed of racism."[9] The school was one of a number of Black educational institutions formed in the late nineteenth century that "taught doctrines and inculcated attitudes which some call politely 'racial radicalism,' and others, more bluntly, 'sedition.' "[10]

J. C. Austin imbibed this aggressive and independent spirit as a student during the first decade of the twentieth century. Virginia Seminary awarded him a B.A. degree in 1905, a Bachelor of Divinity degree in 1908, and a Doctorate of Divinity in 1910. He later studied for several summers at Temple University.[11] In 1915, he was called to Ebenezer Baptist Church in Pittsburgh, where he served until 1926. His ministry in Pittsburgh was auspicious; before he had reached his fortieth birthday, Austin had already made his mark as one of the leading clergymen of the National Baptist Convention of the U.S.A., Incorporated.

By this time also, the fundamental themes and style of his ministry were set. First, his magnetic preaching style and creative organizational skills enabled him to build a congregation of more than five thousand members in Pittsburgh by 1926. Second, his strong denominational leadership was evidenced by his election in 1924 as president of the Pennsylvania State Baptist Convention and by his frequent speaking engagements at the most prestigious Black Baptist churches throughout the country. Third, he was actively involved in the political, economic, and social life of Pittsburgh, as demonstrated by his election as president of the Pittsburgh chapter of the NAACP, his encouragement of the exodus of the southern Blacks to the North, and his founding of such organizations as the Home Finder's League and the Steele City National Bank.[12] Fourth, he participated in protest and Black nationalist organizations such as the International League of Darker Peoples, the National Race Congress, and the Universal Negro Improvement Association.[13] Fifth, he was firmly committed to the religious and political redemption of Africa, as both the American Negro's special destiny in the Divine Scheme and the sine qua non for Black America's own liberation from white oppression.[14] J. C. Austin would continue and expand his involvement in these five arenas during the period we turn to next: the first quarter century of his activities in Chicago, from 1926 to 1950.

PILGRIM BAPTIST CHURCH

The starting point for an appreciation of Austin's independence in all the arenas of his activity must be Pilgrim Baptist Church in Chicago and the close-knit ties that bound Austin and his congregation together. Pilgrim Church was a classic "Black Diaspora" church,[15] organized during the period when European migration to the United States was being curtailed and when the massive internal migration of Afro-Americans from rural to urban and from southern to northern America was cresting. Pilgrim Baptist Church had begun as a prayer meeting of five individuals who first met in a private home on January 6, 1915. In 1919, the growing congregation called the Reverend Samuel E. J. Watson as its first pastor. Under Watson's leadership, church membership skyrocketed to several thousand. In 1921, the congregation moved to its present location at Thirty-third Street and Indiana Avenue, the former home of the synagogue built by the architects Dankmar Adler and Louis Sullivan.

When Watson died unexpectedly in 1925, the congregation called as its pastor the Reverend Junius Caesar Austin.[16]

Austin was first and foremost an extraordinary preacher. The testimony from friends and foes alike is unanimous: in his day, Austin was one of the three or four greatest preachers of the National Baptist Convention. Frequently people came two or three hours before the service in order to get a seat. The church, which held 2,500, was filled two and occasionally three times each Sunday. According to one source, Austin's sermon notes could not be left untended on the pulpit after the service, or some aspiring preacher was likely to pocket them.[17]

The sermons themselves were sometimes topical and direct, in the Black nationalist tradition by which Austin had been molded in the crucible of Lynchburg Seminary. Illustrative of his sermon topics is one that he preached in Pittsburgh shortly before he came to Chicago, based on the theme "Slavery! Slavery! Economic Slavery, Peonage, and race injustice . . . must go."[18] A published sermon from 1937, entitled "Advancing the Kingdom of God in Business," demonstrates that in Chicago Austin did not abandon his sharp critique of contemporary American society, and that his sermons were well-researched, thoughtful, and eloquent. In this sermon, Austin insists that "economics is inextricably interwoven with the issues of the good life which is the aim of the Kingdom of God." He characterizes the United States industrial system of laissez-faire capitalism as "a relic of 1776," and declares that the capitalist social order, which "clings to the moribund platitude that all men have equal opportunities to acquire and achieve," is predicated upon a "mistaken idea."[19]

Austin also preached powerful exegetical and devotional sermons. By 1930, Pilgrim was the third largest church in the National Baptist Convention, and one of the ten largest churches in the United States.[20] Austin's sermons were carried over radio both regionally and, on occasion, nationally, on programs such as "Wings over Jordan."

In addition to his potent oratorical skills, Austin had the organizational and financial acumen to take control of a very large church with an enormous debt—nearly $150,000. In the face of the ever-worsening Depression, he liquidated the debt within ten years and placed the church on a solid fiscal foundation that permitted a steady expansion of its programs. By 1950, more than $125,000 in building repairs and renovations had been completed, a parsonage had been acquired, $28,000 had been expended toward the development of a community center, and $17,000 had been raised toward construction of a gymnasium and housing project.

The church itself was organized into approximately one hundred auxiliary units, to assure that every member of the congregation had a "home" in Pilgrim's vast community. Austin was particularly effective in organizing groups of church women, who, among their other roles, functioned as social workers, "missionary women whose job it was to go out . . . into these tenements and hovels those folks were living in and teach them hygiene and how to care for their babies and make sure they had food."[21] With the aid of five assistant ministers and a deacon board of fifty-eight, Austin turned Pilgrim into a seven-day-a-week center for welfare, education, health care, job training and placement, youth activity, culture, and religion.[22]

The arena of musical programming provides an excellent window into Austin's aggressive and entrepreneurial style in bringing the best talent to Pilgrim. One of his first moves upon arriving in Chicago was to hire as musical director the renowned Edward H. Boatner, a prominent classically trained church musician. Boatner developed an array of musical programs that included a wide range of choral and instrumental presentations for Sunday mornings and other occasions throughout the year. In spite of the popularity of these programs, Austin was aware that classical religious music did not have the widespread appeal to attract newer migrants to the city. On the sixth anniversary of his pastorate at Pilgrim, he invited the Reverend J. H. L. Smith, from Ebenezer Baptist Church in Chicago, to bring his newly formed gospel chorus to perform under the direction of its founder, Thomas A. Dorsey. Austin immediately recognized the tremendous popular appeal of the jazz rhythm at the heart of gospel sound, and within one month (and over Boatner's objections) he had induced Dorsey to move to Pilgrim Church.

Dorsey remained at Pilgrim Church throughout his long career, and both he and Austin benefited immensely from their mutual association. As Michael W. Harris has concluded, Austin's embrace of this new musical form was pivotal to its acceptance in the church at large. "One can assume," Harris writes, "that had Austin not organized a chorus at Pilgrim, the advent of gospel blues in old-line churches would have stagnated in derision and for want of serious regard from the old-line establishment. . . . Only an old-line preacher and church of the stature of Austin and Pilgrim could have imparted respect to gospel blues' notoriety. From this perspective, the February 1932 meeting between Dorsey and Austin marked a turning point in the emergence of gospel blues. . . ."[23]

The point to underscore in reflecting on Austin's work at Pilgrim is one that has been made succinctly by St. Clair Drake and Horace Clayton in summarizing a discussion of the place of the churches in Black Chicago:

Despite the dependence of Negro congregations upon the occasional friendly aid of white co-religionists, the Negro church is largely free of white control. Negro preachers have the greatest "freedom" of any Race Leaders. Politicians must fit themselves into machine politics. Most "civic" leaders are dependent upon white Philanthropy. Most of Bronzeville's preachers are answerable to no one except their congregations. They can say what they please about current affairs and race relations; there are no church superiors to discipline them and no white people to take economic reprisals. Because they are so largely free of the political and economic controls of the white community, Bronzeville expects them to be *real* Race Men.[24]

If, in fact, J. C. Austin was able—in several areas of political, social, and denominational activity—to operate according to his own perception of the needs of his church, race, and nation, he was permitted to do so because of the secure foundation he had built at Pilgrim Church. His eloquent preaching and his organizational and financial skills gave him a power base in the burgeoning Black populace of Chicago that was substantially independent of the white community, and—given Baptist polity—independent of denominational control as well. This left him free to act essentially as he saw fit across a wide horizon of the political landscape before him.

THE NATIONAL BAPTIST CONVENTION

A second arena of Austin's activity was his denomination, the National Baptist Convention of the U.S.A., Incorporated (NBC). It is impossible to describe in any detail the Byzantine complexity of the politics that characterized the National Baptist Convention during this period. What I would like to offer is a tentative outline concerning the pattern of politics within the NBC, insofar as one can do so, from the perspective of J. C. Austin, one of the pivotal figures in that denomination in the interwar years.

First, one must recognize that, excluding the Woman's Convention, the National Baptist Convention for most of the twentieth century was dominated by the powerful pastors of Pilgrim Church's cross-town rival, Olivet Baptist Church. The fact that for nearly fifty of the last seventy-five years the president of the Convention has also been pastor of Olivet is an indication of this control. Olivet is the oldest Baptist church in Chicago, founded in 1853. Like Pilgrim, it benefited enormously from the flood of Black migrants who poured out of the South after Reconstruction. Its ranks swelled from 4 thousand members in 1915 to more than 12 thousand in the 1930s, when it became the largest Protestant congregation in America.[25]

In 1915, Olivet Church called as its minister Lacey Kirk Williams, a Texan who had been educated at Arkansas Baptist College and Bishop

College in Bishop, Texas. He ascended to the presidency of the National Baptist Convention in 1923 and held that post until his death in 1940.[26] In the early years of their association, Austin and Williams were apparently able to work together. In 1924, while still in Pittsburgh, Austin was elected to the influential position of chairman of the Foreign Mission Board, presumably with Williams's support or at least his acquiescence. However, Austin's first move upon reaching Chicago—hiring Edward Boatner as musical director—could only be interpreted as a direct challenge to Williams's leadership. Boatner had previously been employed at Olivet, and Williams had even installed him as musical director of the National Baptist Convention in order to keep him happily ensconced at Olivet. Austin's offer to double Boatner's salary in order to secure his services demonstrates not only Austin's confidence in being able to raise funds, but also his intention to compete head-on with the most powerful figure in the denomination. As Michael Harris points out, clergy in this period were fiercely competitive; this competition affected all aspects of their church programs and was by no means restricted to interdenominational rivalries.[27]

Austin's action undoubtedly infuriated Williams, who did not hesitate to respond. In 1929, at the annual meeting of the National Baptist Convention in Kansas City, Missouri, Williams publicly forced Austin out of the chairmanship of the Foreign Mission Board. Austin later described this action in a letter to his lifelong friend and ally, Nannie H. Burroughs. Written in mid-September 1929, the letter began:

Dear Sister Nannie,

I have buckled on my war shoes, at least since war has been declared on me, and I am standing now right on the firing line facing the enemy with the sword of truth in hand determined to contend for every inch of the ground while counting upon the promises of God, and following no tricks, clicks, nor schemes but principles of righteousness.

Our man here [William] has pledged himself to the Devil to crush me for no other purpose than the fact that the National Baptist forces make a little too much noise over me, and I have been too successful at the head of the Foreign Mission Board. Whenever I appeared in Kansas, the demonstration was greater than when the President himself appeared, and my offerings surpassed any effort he put on. So determined was he to remove me from chairmanship, and realizing that he could not do it while I was on the ground, he waited until the messengers were gone and with only thirty-seven people in the hall late Monday afternoon, when I was near St. Louis. He with his tricksters ruled me out of office on the grounds that I didn't live in Philadelphia, and elected C. C. Scott.

I am receiving letters of protest every day from outstanding men also very firm invitations from the *other side of the* Baptist family.[28]

Nannie Burroughs's response to Austin was prompt, firm, and supportive:

> I am absolutely disgusted with tricksters, hypocrites, and sycophants. You are altogether right to demand a public performance and square deal.
>
> I heard of your matchless address and tremendous carrying power. Keep your head and keep your tongue. Someone asked a woman how to make a rabbit pie. She said "First catch your rabbit." Don't start your war until you have your implements with which to fight, then go to it. I am with you world without end.[29]

The breach between the two men was widened a few months later, following the murder of the auditor of the National Baptist Convention, Edward D. Pierson. Pierson had apparently uncovered instances of fraud among some chief officers of the convention, and was en route from Nashville to Chicago in mid-April 1930 to present his charges when he was abducted, bound, and shot, and then tossed into a river in southern Indiana. His body was discovered the next day, and eventually several high officials of the NBC, including the secretary of the Sunday School Publishing Board, the Reverend A. M. Townsend, Sr., and his son were indicted for murder. Although no one was ever brought to trial, some Baptists insinuated that Williams himself was responsible for having Pierson eliminated.[30]

In a tumultuous convention in Chicago a few months after the murder, Williams was clearly on the defensive, and Austin sought to press his advantage by having his own name placed in nomination for the presidency. When his nomination was ruled ineligible, on the grounds (later proved to be false) that Austin had not registered his church or his delegates for the convention, pandemonium broke out, and Williams supporters quickly engineered his reelection by acclamation. At the end of the chaotic ten-day meeting, Austin publicly pledged his support to Williams, pointedly stating that he "was not contemplating a split from the convention."[31]

By the next year, however, newspaper reports described the creation of a "militant group led by the resourceful Dr. J. C. Austin of the Windy City"[32] which was opposing Williams and the NBC establishment. One of Austin's allies wrote in an open letter to him, printed in the *Pittsburgh Courier:* "Progressive Baptist leaders feel that the Baptist Church, now claiming millions, must lose its hold on these people, unless it can offer an intelligent, educated and honest leadership. . . . They want to see the various Baptist boards relieved of absentee bossism and to have insinuations of dishonesty against leaders, such as [A. M.] Townsend, either proved or disproved."[33] This was probably the first reference in print to an identifiable group of "progressive" Baptists who had formed in opposition to convention leadership. These progressives included J. C. Jackson, president of the New England Baptist Missionary Society; Lewis G. Jordan of Philadelphia, former chairman of the Foreign Mission Board and historiographer of the convention; William H. Jernagin of Washington, D.C., president of the Baptist Sunday School Union and Baptist Teachers Union; Nannie H. Burroughs, founder of the National Training School for Women and Girls and one of the most powerful and dynamic women in the NBC; J. Raymond Henderson of the Second Baptist Church in Los Angeles; and William H. Moses of New York. The group also included younger men such as Adam Clayton Powell, Jr., Gardner C. Taylor, and many others.

Austin repeatedly sought the presidency of the convention during the next three decades, although he never succeeded in wresting control from the establishment. His best opportunity for victory probably came in 1941, when an open convention was held to elect a successor to L. K. Williams, who had died the previous year in a plane crash. When Austin lost that election to the "steam roller" tactics of the opposition,[34] there were widespread rumors of a denominational split, and the newspapers carried stories about the imminent creation of a "Progressive Baptist" convention. One article, appearing in September 1941, reported: "Dissatisfied with the outcome of the election, Dr. Austin called a meeting ... Friday morning where more than 1,000 Baptist leaders became members of a newly formed organization to be known as the Progressive Baptists of the National Baptist Convention."[35] However, Austin and others apparently later decided that the eve of the entry of the United States into world war was not the time to divide their denomination, and the creation of the Progressive Baptist Convention did not come for another twenty years.

AUSTIN AND POLITICS

Austin's involvement in local Chicago as well as national politics merits an essay in itself, but two or three examples of his activities illustrate his vigorous participation. One of the first organizations that Austin created at Pilgrim Baptist Church was the Cooperative Business, Professional, and Labor League. As stated in a broadside describing its purposes, the league was predicated upon the belief "that there is a great community of interest existing among our business, professional, and laboring classes, which community of interest is so inseparable that none can make substantial progress without the support of the other. Our business people, our professional people, and our laboring people must go forward together or there will not be much going forward by any of us."[36]

The league's goal was to foster Black employment through the support of Black business. Austin was an advocate of the "Double-Duty dollar," and he clearly believed in "mixing" religion and business. He repeatedly admonished his parishioners, "Don't spend your money with a dealer who does not in turn provide some opportunity for us to live by labor." The league also sought to foster Black pride by teaching youth to be "proud of themselves and the accomplishments of Negro people." It sought, for example, to help secure education for talented young people; it supported the work of Carter G. Woodson and the Association for the Study of Negro Life and History; it recognized the accomplishments of Black leaders in all fields (such as commemorating the "pioneer aviatrix" Bessie Coleman); and it served as a forum for debate by inviting political figures to speak at Pilgrim Church.

To illustrate Austin's participation in local Chicago politics, one can cite the testimony of Harold Gosnell in his still-useful book *Negro Politicians: The Rise of Negro Politics in Chicago* (1935). Gosnell states that following the death of African Methodist Episcopal bishop Archibald J. Carey in 1931, Austin became a prominent clerical supporter of "Big Bill" Thompson, the old Republican political boss and Chicago mayor. Gosnell quotes an Austin campaign speech in which he declared:

> Let us follow the leadership of a man who knows nothing but forward and upward in the person of William Hale Thompson. . . . We saw Big Bill go down out of the confidence of the people, out of the love of the people. . . . He struggled in the grave. . . . The *Tribune* wrote an obituary. I went back again and looked upon the grave. . . . But thank God, before the primary I heard the grave crack, the tombstone fall and saw William Hale Thompson rise (applause) and stand over his enemies and say "I am on the side of truth, of right, of justice." (Big applause.)[37]

Thompson was a Republican political boss of the old order who, as mayor, had weathered the crisis of the infamous Chicago race riot of 1919 and had still retained the overwhelming loyalty of the Black community. While a few clergy (including Lacey K. Williams) opposed Thompson for having "turned over the Negro communities of Chicago to the vice lords, policy kings, bootleggers and racketeers,"[38] Austin was more interested in the political gains to be made for the Black community by supporting the Thompson machine. As Alan Spear has pointed out, the Chicago Black political leadership was deeply suspicious of the reformist agenda of the "progressive" Republicans, who were led by Illinois governor Charles S. Deneen. These Black leaders saw political reform as the end of Black access to party bosses and patronage and the reinstitution of Blacks' subservience to a predominately white electorate.[39]

We should not be surprised, then, that Thompson was praised by Austin in the most grandiloquent terms. Austin declared at one political rally: "God made just one William Hale Thompson and forgot the mold. Truth, courage, consecration, ideas of right, ideas of justice, let there be right, righteousness. Let it come to earth. Call it William Hale Thompson. . . . I would call him Napoleon, I would call him Abraham Lincoln. When history is written, they will write in the blue sky high above all of them the name of William Hale Thompson."[40] One suspects that although he may have accepted the analogy of Thompson to Napoleon, Gosnell personally must have had trouble with Austin's comparison of Thompson to Lincoln. Nevertheless, Gosnell concluded his chapter, entitled "The Second Lincoln," with the observation that "by furnishing Negroes with new jobs, by protecting them against mishandling by the police, by recognizing them as citizens, by fitting its appeals to the various groups found within the Negro community, the faction created a situation in which colored preachers could refer to Thompson as the 'Second Lincoln' and win applause."[41]

Austin was also active on the national political scene. Austin and his Cooperative Business, Professional, and Labor League hosted a debate on the fourth of July, 1931, between Benjamin J. Davis, a former Republican National Committeeman from Georgia, and Oscar DePriest, the Republican congressman from the South Side of Chicago who was the first Afro-American to be elected to the United States Congress in the twentieth century. The debate centered on Mr. DePriest's urging that Blacks in the South consider breaking their near-total allegiance to the Republican party, since the "lily white Republicans in the south . . . did not want to help [Negroes] and could not help them if they wanted to."[42]

In fact, six weeks prior to the debate, DePriest had called for creation of a "Non-Partisan Negro Conference," the goal of which would be "to determine the needs and grievances of colored citizens in America and formulate a plan for their amelioration."[43] The meeting was eventually held in Washington, D.C., on December 2–4, 1931. Some 179 delegates from twenty-five states plus the District of Columbia attended the meeting to debate such topics as disenfranchisement, lynching, civil service, economic opportunities, religion and politics, women in public life, and the distribution of federal educational funds. Austin, along with Kelly Miller, Judge W. C. Hueston, Bishop E. D. W. Jones, Nannie H. Burroughs, and publisher Robert L. Vann, were members of the Findings Committee. This committee concluded:

We regard political parties as an instrument to be used and not as a fetish to be worshipped. Tools may wear out and grow blunt. They may be resharpened or cast aside for different or better ones. The ballot was given the Negro as a weapon of defense. The effectiveness of the ballot is appreciated and recognized mainly when the voter has the potentiality and evidences the disposition to change the result. . . . At this time of a wavering balance between the two parties, the Negro vote can easily be utilized for what it is most worth—political and civil equality and economic opportunity. One can always make a better bargain, when there are two bidders instead of one.[44]

One of the most fundamental and far-reaching political realignments in the first half of the twentieth century proved to be the shift of Black voters from the Republican to the Democratic party. Although there were isolated cases of Republican defections as early as the turn of the century, the move did not gather popular support until the Depression. The greatest shift to the Democrats was accomplished during the presidency of Franklin D. Roosevelt. While it is difficult to assess the effect of the Non-Partisan Negro Conference on this pivotal change in party affiliation, it is typical that Austin was centrally involved in the early debate.[45]

AUSTIN AND VOLUNTARY ASSOCIATIONS

J. C. Austin was involved with a wide range of voluntary associations organized for cultural, social, political, fraternal, and religious ends. He was a member of the Elks, the Masons, the Knights of Pythias, and the Independent Order of St. Luke. We have already noted that he was an avid supporter of the Association for the Study of Negro Life and History. His activities and interests were eclectic. He was early fascinated with air travel, and in May 1935 he founded one of the first organizations of Negro aviators in the United States, at Pilgrim Baptist Church. Many of its charter members were good friends and members of his congregation. He was founder and president of the Inter-Church Good Will Conference of Chicago, an interdenominational and interracial association of clergy. He was a key member (along with Chandler Owen, George Cleveland Hall, Irene McCoy Gaines, and others) of the Citizen's Committee organized in 1928 to support the Brotherhood of Sleeping Car Porters, and he took an active role on behalf of the Chicago Scottsboro Defense Committee in the mid–1930s. The list of organizations, associations, and committees to which he belonged is considerable.[46]

An episode in the mid–1930s involving Austin, the National Office of the NAACP, and the local Chicago Branch of the NAACP may serve to illustrate both the degree of Austin's activity and the complexity of his involvement (and that of other clergy) in voluntary associations. Austin had hosted a number of prominent national officers of the NAACP as speakers at Pilgrim Church in the early 1930s, including Daisy E. Lampkin, regional field secretary, and Robert W. Bagnall, director of branches. In late 1935, Austin agreed to devote an entire Sunday service to the NAACP, and the Chicago Branch president, A. C. MacNeal, wrote to many of Chicago's largest churches calling their attention to the "splendid type of co-operation on the part of Reverend Austin" and inviting them to follow Austin's example by setting aside a Sunday morning in their churches to speak about the work of the association.

Two years later, NAACP secretary Walter White wrote to MacNeal, informing him of an initiative that Austin had recently put forth. In a speech at a conference in Washington, D.C., Austin had urged that "instead of sitting down passing resolution[s,] the conference should get behind the N.A.A.C.P., which is the one organization which could make a fight for the Association." At the close of the conference, Austin had offered a resolution to establish an NAACP lobby in Washington. Delighted with this show of support, White urged MacNeal to follow up on Austin's suggestions, and he himself agreed to Austin's invitation to speak at a "great anti-lynching meeting" at Pilgrim Church, where Austin foresaw "5,000 Negroes with buttons on and upturned faces and open hearts and receptive minds to receive your message." White and Austin had already agreed on a date for this meeting when the Chicago branch chief wired that the arrangements were acceptable only if the branch bore one-fourth of the traveling expenses and received three-fourths of the net proceeds. These terms were unacceptable to the national office, and the meeting had to be canceled.[47]

As this episode illustrates, the long history of hostility and jealousy between the NAACP national office and the Chicago branch often made cooperation between the two nearly impossible. In 1939, E. Frederick Morrow, coordinator of branches, wrote to national headquarters from Chicago that the situation was desperate:

> The branch too long has been dominated by a few individuals who run it as they see fit. There is little democracy. There is a distinct "class-caste" atmosphere. This militates against securing the membership of the man in the street. This has been told me so many times, it haunts me. There is a feeling that it is run by the lawyers, for the lawyers. No effort has been made to reach out and get new blood, or new contacts.
>
> You are already familiar with the rabid anti-national office attitude here. I do not know all the history of this, but it harms the program, for there cannot be harmony where distrust exists, and one has to explain every move and intention. Some have even warmly threaten[ed] rebellion against the N[ational] O[ffice], and running things to suit themselves.[48]

Austin was caught in this cross fire. With a small group of well-entrenched individuals controlling the local chapter, it was difficult for him or any other clergy to exert influence over local NAACP affairs in Chicago. They found it much easier to develop cordial relations with national officers; one can well imagine that this was a solution satisfactory to local officials as well, who did not want powerful clergy threatening their control of the branch.

AUSTIN AND AFRICA

J. C. Austin's commitment to Africa and to the redemption of Africa through the missionary efforts of Black Christians was at the core of his theology. From his college days at Lynchburg Seminary until his death more than a half-century later, African missions were a matter of central concern to him. It was this concern, more than any other single factor, that had attracted Austin to the Garvey movement, to which he spoke at the International Convention of Negro Peoples of the World in 1922, in a speech entitled "Representing the Negro Clergy." His first major denominational responsibility in the NBC was that of chairman of the Foreign Mission Board, a position to which he had been elected in 1924. Missions were a top priority at Pilgrim Baptist Church, and by the end of his first year as minister there, the church was already ranked as the denomination's third largest contributor to foreign missions, giving more than $1,200 to support their work. For years, Pilgrim Church paid the salary of Dr. Samuel W. Martin, a missionary in Issele-Uku, Nigeria.[49]

In February 1950, Austin was selected, along with nine of the National Baptist Convention's most prominent advocates of foreign missions, to review the denomination's work in Africa. This fact-finding and study commission, known among Baptists as the "Tall Pines," traveled throughout West Africa for more than a month. The group met with government officials as well as their own missionaries and congregations. The secretary of the Foreign Mission Board, C. C. Adams, described in his journal a visit to the Issele-Uku mission station:

Thursday, February 23, was a long-looked-for day at the Pilgrim Mission. The occasion: the formal dedication of the Teacher's Training College, known as the Austin Building, in honor of Dr. J. C. Austin, of Chicago, Illinois. Brother [Samuel] Martin had prepared a wonderful program that called together people from far and wide—chiefs, civilian and educational authorities from the highest levels. Some of them were British of rare culture, all of whom were loud in praise of Brother Martin and his work and leadership. The impressive program of dedication was followed by colorful demonstrations of calisthenics by the student body on the campus. These were simply dazzling and beyond my power of description.[50]

Austin was also specially honored by ten African chiefs of the Benin region, who bestowed on him a royal chiefhood and a magnificent robe and cap. Typically, Austin sought to use this special status to advance a scheme that he hoped would benefit both Africans and Afro-Americans. On his return to the United States, he created an "African Exports and Imports N.B.C., U.S.A." and took the role of executive secretary in it. The goal of this organization was to provide a direct outlet in the United States for the cultural, artistic, and other products of West Africans, with the National Baptist Convention serving as intermediary in fostering trade between the two continents.

Austin's reports upon his return to the United States demonstrate that he was acutely sensitive to the powerful political forces that were taking shape in West Africa. "I found Lagos quite tense and ready to fight for freedom," he wrote to Claude Barnett of the Associated Negro Press. "The same spirit I found in the Gold Coast at Accra. I also met the governor who gave us a grand reception in the opening of his court session. On the morning of our appearance, Gov. [Charles Noble Arden] Clarke of Nigeria delivered his address in favor of a new constitution which offers freedom and independence to the people of the Gold Coast." He saw in these political developments a potent message for Afro-Americans as well: "I saw and counselled with a black president and a black secretary of State. . . . I saw black engineers and conductors running speeding express trains. I saw black clerks and managers working in stores and black officials high in government everywhere I went. I went to Africa only to be convinced that not only the hope of the black man, but the hope of peace and the hope of the world rests in Africa."[51]

J. C. Austin's perennial refrain that "the Negro in America will never be free until Africa gets her clothes on" reflected one of the most venerable traditions in Black religious nationalist thought. This was essentially the belief that the freedom of Africa and the freedom of Afro-America—indeed, of all Africa-in-Diaspora—were inextricably linked to one another and to an understanding of God's scrutable plan, epitomized in the biblical prophecy of Psalm 68:31: "Princes shall come out of Egypt, Ethiopia shall soon stretch forth her hands unto God."

CONCLUSION

In his provocative essay "Political Change in the Negro Ghetto, 1900–1940," the political scientist Martin Kilson describes several patterns of political adaptation that were available to Afro-Americans in the early twentieth century. He characterizes one of these patterns as "interest group articulation," in which cliques or interest groups seek to advance their own needs. Particularly intriguing among varieties of group formation, Kilson writes, "is the political movement based on the aggregation of voluntary associations." He explains:

> In this situation, a skillful and often charismatic leader first maximizes the politicization of his own voluntary association and then, having secured this initial base, branches out, penetrating first ideologically and then organizationally other nonpoliticized voluntary associations. The penetration or aggregation process was pursued by a highly politicized voluntary agency of the leader, and invariably ideology (usually racialist or black nationalist) proved the most important political resources.[52]

Kilson had in mind the political organization developed by Adam Clayton Powell, Jr., in the late 1930s, but he might have easily taken the work of J. C. Austin as his example. Coming to Chicago in the mid-1920s, well-grounded in the Black religious nationalism that he had learned at Lynchburg Seminary and refined during his association with the Garvey movement during his Pittsburgh years, Austin first set about to establish a firm base for activism at Pilgrim Baptist Church. He soon found himself increasingly at odds with the established leadership of his denomination and began a lifelong campaign to reform it along "progressive" lines.

At the same time, he immersed himself in local and national political activity. Through the formation of the Cooperative, Business, Professional, and Labor League, Austin sought to politicize and mobilize both the burgeoning Black middle class in Chicago (which, Kilson reminds us, was probably larger than the Black elite in any other city in the country, including New York City) as well as the lower-middle-class and poor laborers who constituted the majority of the Black population in Chicago. He became for a brief time a leading clerical supporter of William Hale Thompson, head of one of the few city political machines in America open to the idea of Black participation on terms of relative equality with other ethnic groups. Again, Kilson is instructive:

> Thompson's mode of organizing Negroes in Chicago in order to guarantee their support was even more important to the eventual inclusion of blacks in Chicago machine politics than the voting pattern. . . . Unlike those in any other major city in this period, the Republican leaders in Chicago cultivated the independent-minded Negro middle class leaders rather than those Negro political leaders inclined to neoclientage linkages with white power structures. Equally important, the Negro leaders who organized Big Bill Thompson's Negro support insisted upon something other than neoclientage ties to the Chicago machine.[53]

Austin recognized and capitalized on the unique opportunity Thompson presented, and he utilized his connections to secure jobs, economic opportunity, and political clout. Whether in helping to organize the Non-Partisan Negro Conference in 1931, in seeking to penetrate special interest groups like the Chicago NAACP, or in attempting to form an export / import association to benefit both Africans and Afro-Americans, Austin was a highly astute and effective preacher-politician. Although he chose not to seek elective political office himself, Austin understood the uses of political power, and he always believed that the church had a responsibility to address political, social, and economic issues as part of its mission.

In the *Intercollegian Wonder Book of the Negro in Chicago 1779–1927,* Pilgrim Baptist Church was described as "a great forum for race uplift and general interest. It is the business man's Clearing House, and a soul saving station for the sinful city. It is truly a church with a program, led on by a minister with a vision."[54] Whether or not it is appropriate to characterize Pilgrim Church and its pastor as among the "wonders" of the world of Black Chicago, Austin was certainly one of a number of clergy who responded creatively and effectively to the crisis of the interwar years. The independent, pan-Africanist, and Black religious nationalist spirit that Austin espoused epitomizes precisely the tradition in the historic Black denominations that Wilmore has identified as constituting the genius of the historic Black church. Its roots are deep in the nineteenth-century protest tradition of Richard Allen and Henry Turner, Nathaniel Paul and William Simmons, James Pennington and Henry Garnet, and Alexander Crummell and James Holly, about whom much is already known. The exemplars of this tradition in the twentieth century—not only both Powells and both Kings, but also Reverdy C. Ransom and R. R. Wright, Jr., Nannie Burroughs and Gardner C. Taylor, Mary McLeod Bethune and William Y. Bell, Anna Julia Cooper and George Freeman Bragg, Jr., and many others—deserve our attention. With careful study of their lives and work, we will have a much fairer view of the richness of Black religious life in the second quarter of the twentieth century. We may come to see that for a number of men and for a growing number of women, these critical years offered unparalleled opportunity for the creation of new institutional structures, both within the historic Black denominations and among newly formed groups known as "sects and cults," and that many of these individuals maintained a critical and even prophetic stance against the pervasive racism of the period.

NOTES

1. The classic articulation of the theme of the failure of the Black Church in the interwar years is found in E. Franklin Frazier, *The Negro Church in America*

(New York: Shocken Books, 1963), particularly chapter 4, "Negro Religion in the City." See also Arthur H. Fauset, *Black Gods of the Metropolis* (Philadelphia: University of Pennsylvania Press, 1944), and Raymond J. Jones, *A Comparative Study of Religious Cult Behavior Among Negroes, with Special Reference to Emotional Group Conditioning Factors* (Washington, D.C.: Howard University Graduate School, 1939).

2. Gayraud S. Wilmore, *Black Religion and Black Radicalism: An Interpretation of the Religious History of Afro-American People*, 2d ed. (New York: Orbis Books, 1983), 144.

3. Wilmore, in *Black Religion and Black Radicalism*, 144, cites with approval a statement made by Joseph R. Washington in *Black Religion* (Boston: Beacon Press, 1964), 35.

4. Wilmore, *Black Religion and Black Radicalism*, 152–60. Robert Weisbrot, in his study *Father Divine and the Struggle for Racial Equality* (Urbana: University of Illinois Press, 1983), adopts the conventional view that Black clergy in the 1920s and 1930s were preoccupied with an other-worldly spirituality and a this-worldly concern for their own economic aggrandizement. His view of Father Divine as a socially conscious reformer committed to racial equality, who was attempting to instill political awareness among his followers, is a valuable corrective to previous studies. He underestimates, however, the commitment of Black clergy to social Christianity throughout this period, and he ignores the central religious impulse that empowered the Peace Mission Movement. Father Divine's position as a fervent theocrat and self-declared messiah and his demand for absolute celibacy from his followers, for example, are surely more than unfortunate political liabilities in his reformist agenda. See especially Weisbrot, chapter 7, "The Politics of Racial Justice."

5. Wilmore, *Black Religion and Black Radicalism*, 160–66. The most forceful statement concerning the Black Church as a barrier to integration is found in Frazier's *Negro Church*, chap. 5 and conclusion.

6. U.S. Department of Commerce, Bureau of the Census *Census of Religious Bodies: 1936*, (Washington, D.C.: U.S. Government Printing Office, 1941), 1: 900–3.

7. For a fascinating account of the origins of Virginia Seminary as a racially independent school, see Lester F. Russell, *Black Baptist Secondary Schools in Virginia, 1887–1957* (Metuchen, N.J.: Scarecrow Press, 1981), especially 49–57 and 140–48. The school was actually incorporated in the Commonwealth of Virginia on February 24, 1888.

8. George Shepperson and Thomas Price, *Independent African: John Chilembwe and the Origins, Setting, and Significance of the Nyasaland Native Rising of 1915* (Edinburgh: Edinburgh University Press, 1958), 114.

9. Gregory W. Hayes (1862–1907) became president of the Virginia Seminary in 1891 and was primarily responsible for charting the school's course of racial independence, which resulted in the splitting (in 1899) of the Virginia Black Baptists into two separate organizations, the Virginia Baptist State Convention and the Baptist General Association of Virginia (Colored). The former was composed of "race-men," who stood for racial independence in support of Hayes's philosophy, while the latter were "co-operationists," who were willing to share (or, some would insist, sacrifice) educational control with whites in ex-

change for financial support: see Russell, *Black Baptist Secondary Schools,* 52–56. Charges against Hayes by white Baptists are found in the text of a letter from Dr. M. MacVicar of the American Baptist Home Mission Society to the Reverend Z. D. Lewis, September 27, 1898, reprinted by Russell, ibid., 140–43.

10. Shepperson and Price, *Independent African,* 98. Among Lynchburg's most famous graduates was the African revolutionary leader John Chilembwe, who attended the school from 1898 to 1900. Chilembwe's education at Lynchburg had been financed by the Reverend Willis W. Brown, a close friend and mentor of Junius C. Austin, and the one who sold Marcus Garvey the building that became Garvey's headquarters, known as "Liberty Hall."

11. *Chicago Tribune,* October 19, 1957. *A Testimonial to the Reverend Junius Ceasar [sic] Austin: Pastor of Ebenezer Baptist Church of Pittsburgh, Pennsylvania, 1915–1926* (n.p., n.d.) was a pamphlet published in commemoration of Austin's eleven years at Ebenezer Baptist Church. It states (though we have no independent documentation) that he did postgraduate work at Temple College in Philadelphia. The pamphlet also notes that Austin "did his apprentice work under Dr. W. E. Moore, then pastor of Zion Baptist Church, and later was ordained from this parish with the late Dr. Motts, former Dean of the Temple Theological department as his catechist" (6).

12. The Home Finder's League was organized by Austin to help Southern immigrants to Pittsburgh find housing. This effort was more successful than was the Steele City National Bank, which collapsed in January 1926, just as Austin left Pittsburgh for Chicago. Austin and other bank officers were blamed for the bank's failure and were accused of defrauding depositors of funds. Shareholders eventually recouped forty-two cents on each dollar invested, according to an article in the Chicago *Defender* (February 12, 1927), 1. See also Chicago *Defender* (April 2, 1927), 2.

13. The International League of Darker Peoples was organized in 1919 to ensure that Blacks would present a united front at the Paris Peace Conference. The National Race Congress had been founded in Washington, D.C., three years earlier to oppose lynching and mob violence, with Austin's friend and fellow Baptist clergyman William H. Jernagin as president. Austin's willingness to speak forthrightly on racial issues, in spite of the opposition of his more moderate and cautious colleagues, is evidenced by the sermon "Representing the Negro Ministry," which he gave as the keynote address of Marcus Garvey's Third International Convention of the Negro Peoples of the World on August 1, 1922. Austin was criticized, both by members of his own congregation and by some of his fellow clergy, for his support of the Universal Negro Improvement Association (UNIA). A Department of Justice undercover agent's report states, "I spoke to several of the leading preachers of Harlem during the day regarding the action of Rev. J. C. Austin in taking part in the program of the U.N.I.A. and they all were of the opinion that he should not have done so and was harming both himself and the Baptist cause by dealing with Marcus Garvey." For Austin's involvement in the UNIA, see the brief biographical essay of Austin in Randall K. Burkett, *Black Redemption: Clergymen Speak for the Garvey Movement* (Philadelphia: Temple University Press, 1978), and chapter 4 of Burkett's *Garveyism as a Religious Movement: The Institutionalization of a Black Civil Religion* (Metuchen, N.J.: Scarecrow Press, 1978), especially 114–16.

14. See Burkett, *Black Redemption,* 112–17. For general information about Black churches in Pittsburgh generally during this period, see Dennis Clark Dickerson's essay "Black Workers and Black Churches in Western Pennsylvania, 1915–1950," in *Blacks in Pennsylvania History: Research and Educational Perspectives,* ed. David McBride (Harrisburg: Pennsylvania Historical and Museum Commission, 1983), 51–62. Dickerson has made available to me a substantial amount of primary source material, oral interviews, and other information that he gathered on Austin during his own research. As St. Clair Drake has demonstrated, the image of the redemption of Africa was "one important focus of meaningful activity among New World Negroes," and it served as "an energizing myth in both the New World and in Africa itself for those pre-political movements that arose while the powerless were gathering their strength for realistic and rewarding political activity." St. Clair Drake, *The Redemption of Africa and Black Religion* (Chicago: Third World Press, 1970), 11.

15. St. Clair Drake and Horace R. Cayton, *Black Metropolis: A Study of Negro Life in a Northern City* (New York: Harcourt, Brace and Company, 1945), 58ff.

16. A brief history of the origin of Pilgrim Baptist Church may be found in *Pilgrim Baptist Church Achievement Celebration, 1926–1939* (n.p., n.d., pamphlet), 6, 9. Rev. Samuel E. J. Watson died on June 16, 1925.

17. Interview with Austin's children, Dorothea Austin Brown and Junius C. Austin, Jr., Chicago, June 10 and 12, 1981. Harold Cooper, public relations officer for Lagos, Nigeria, may be taken as representative of the many visitors to Pilgrim Church who never forgot Austin's eloquence. Writing to Claude A. Barnett in 1953, several years after having heard Austin preach, Cooper wrote, "I should also be grateful if you could let me know the exact address of my old friend Dr. Austin, to whom I wish to write about a number of matters. I hope he is still in robust health and still packing the Pilgrim Baptist Church every Sunday morning. One of my most vivid memories is of that remarkable service which you and I attended. I have described it to many of my clerical acquaintances in the United Kingdom, who compared it glumly with their own weekly experience of preaching to almost empty churches." Harold Cooper to Claude A. Barnett, November 1, 1953, in Claude A. Barnett Papers, Chicago Historical Society, Chicago (henceforth cited as CHS). I am deeply grateful to Archie Motley and Linda Evans of the CHS staff, who have provided generous assistance in facilitating my research for this article.

18. *Pittsburgh Courier,* November 22, 1924, 5.

19. This sermon was published in the *Negro Journal of Religion* 3 (1937): 5, 12. Another of Austin's sermons, "Jesus' Idea of Royalty," was published in the *Negro Journal of Religion* 1 (1935): 8–9.

20. Lewis G. Jordan, *Negro Baptist History, U.S.A., 1750–1930* (Nashville, Tenn.: Sunday School Publishing Board, n.d.), 80.

21. Michael Wesley Harris, "The Advent of Gospel Blues in Black Old-Line Churches in Chicago, 1932–33, As Seen through the Life and Mind of Thomas Andrew Dorsey" (Ph.D. diss., Harvard University, 1982), 176. Harris is quoting from an interview that he conducted with Austin's son, the Reverend Junius C. Austin, Jr., on June 24, 1977.

22. See *Pilgrim Baptist Church Achievement Celebration,* cited above, and the

church's commemorative volume *Gold and Silver Anniversary Honoring Dr. J. C. Austin, 1901–1951* (Chicago: Sumar Press, n.d.), 5, 6.

23. Michael Wesley Harris, *The Rise of Gospel Blues: The Music of Thomas Andrew Dorsey in the Urban Church* (New York: Oxford University Press, 1992), 200, and passim. My account of the role of music at Pilgrim is largely drawn from Harris's work. It should be noted that Harris is highly critical of what he views as the crass opportunism in Austin's efforts to adopt crowd-pleasing strategies, whether in his preaching or in his musical styles. He describes, for instance, Edward Boatner's disgust at Austin's decision to welcome Dorsey's music, and recounts Austin's declaration to Boatner that as long as he (Austin) was musical director, the gospel chorus would be acceptable only if it sat in the back of the church. "Only one who was driven by the anticipation of success," Harris concludes, would accept such an ultimatum. See 198 and 196–202.

24. Drake and Cayton, *Black Metropolis*, 427–28.

25. Miles Mark Fisher, "History of Olivet Baptist Church of Chicago" (Master's thesis, University of Chicago, 1922), especially 82–98; "Six Major Negro Churches," in Federal Writers Project Papers, Box 187, Illinois State Historical Library, Springfield. I am grateful to Roger D. Bridges for bringing this and other material concerning Black churches in Chicago to my attention.

26. Lacey Kirk Williams had pastored the largest Baptist churches in Texas and had served as president of the Baptist Missionary and Educational Convention in that state. He was brought to Olivet Church in the hope that he "would sustain relations between the Olivet Church and the white Baptists of Chicago" and would also "unite the Negro Baptists of Chicago." Fisher, "History of Olivet Baptist Church," 84.

27. Harris, "Advent of Gospel Blues," 190–91.

28. Junius C. Austin to Nannie H. Burroughs, September 11, 1929, in Nannie H. Burroughs Papers, Container 1, Library of Congress, Washington, D.C. The "other side" to whom Austin refers is undoubtedly the National Baptist Convention of America, the second largest Black Baptist denomination, formed in 1915.

29. T. C. and N. H. Burroughs to Junius C. Austin, September 24, 1929, in Burroughs Papers, Letters Sent, Box 33, Library of Congress. The feisty Nannie Burroughs, who in 1903 had founded the National Training School for Girls and Women in Washington, D.C., was by this time already having her own troubles with Lacey K. Williams and the establishment leadership of the National Baptist Convention. See Evelyn Brooks Barnett, "Nannie Burroughs and the Education of Black Women," in *The Afro-American Woman: Struggles and Images*, ed. Sharon Harley and Rosalyn Terborg-Penn (Port Washington, N.Y.: Kennikat Press, 1978), 97–108. The problem had to do both with the jealousy of some men in the NBC of the power that Burroughs had acquired as one of the founders of the women's division of the convention and with the independent sources of revenue that she had developed among both Black and white Baptist women. The problem began as early as 1920, intensified in 1928 (see, for example, "Controversy Sidestepped by Williams," *Chicago Defender*, [February 25, 1928], part 1, p. 2; and "Shall We Crucify a Woman?" by J. Pius Barbour, *Baptist Leader* 51, no. 21 [April 20, 1928], p. 1), and came to a head a decade later, when L. K. Williams

took the extraordinary action of cutting off all NBC funds to the National Training School. Barnett, "Nannie Burroughs," 99.

30. See, for example, "Baptists Lead Drive to Solve Slaying," *Chicago Defender,* May 3, 1930, a copy of which, along with other clippings, press releases, and correspondence concerning the Pierson case, may be found in the Barnett Papers, CHS. Suspicion about L. K. Williams's involvement in Pierson's murder apparently lingered in the NBC, as is evident from a banner headline in the *Chicago Defender* more than a decade after the event: "[Adam Clayton] Powell Denies Naming L. K. Williams in Pierson Murder," *Chicago Defender,* December 7, 1940, 1. I am indebted to Matthew McMichael for tracking down, in the Indiana Commission on Public Records, the letter from the governor of Tennessee to the governor of Indiana refusing to extradite the Townsends to Indiana for trial. He also located numerous Indiana newspaper accounts of the murder and directed me to the Scott County, Indiana, Circuit Court records concerning the case. These records are found in "State of Indiana v. George Washington, alias William Moorehead," Scott Circuit Court, file nos. 2469 and 2471, available from the Clerk of Courts, Scottsburg, Indiana. The case was dropped in 1931, when Pierson's widow and children asked that it not be pursued further.

31. See, for example, *Chicago Defender,* August 30, 1930; *Baltimore Afro-American,* August 30, 1930; and *Pittsburgh Courier,* August 30, 1930.

32. *Pittsburgh Courier,* July 18, 1931, sec. 2, p. 10.

33. *Pittsburgh Courier,* June 27, 1931, sec. 3, p. 10.

34. *Philadelphia Afro-American,* September 20, 1941, 10. Another factor that undoubtedly affected the outcome of the NBC election was a visit by J. C. Austin to Father Divine's Peace Mission movement headquarters just prior to the election. Austin insisted that he only consulted Divine "as a student of people and religions. I watch every movement going on in America, whether close to my door or not. Whenever I see a man like Divine who is able to gather great groups about him, I investigate, because I want to see what it is he is offering the people, what it is he has that attracts, which fills some need of the masses." Austin's opponents, of course, had a field day with the episode, and the notorious Rev. Thomas Harten declared that if the Reverend Mr. Austin had been spending time in Father Divine's heavens and associating with the cult leader, he did not believe Austin to be a fit man to be elected president of the National Baptist Convention. *Philadelphia Afro-American,* September 6, 1941, 1, and September 13, 1941, 3. See also *Baltimore Afro-American,* September 6, 1941, 4; September 20, 1941, 8. I am grateful to Robert Weisbrot for calling my attention to this episode.

35. *Chicago Defender,* September 20, 1941, 2.

36. Broadside, "The Cooperative Business, Professional and Labor League," n.d. (ca. 1926), with a photo of Rev. J. C. Austin in the center, Irene McCoy Gaines Papers, CHS.

37. Harold F. Gosnell, *Negro Politicians: The Rise of Negro Politics in Chicago* (Chicago: University of Chicago Press, 1935), 52.

38. Ibid., 60.

39. Allan H. Spear, *Black Chicago: The Making of a Negro Ghetto, 1890–1920* (Chicago: University of Chicago Press, 1967), 121–22.

40. Gosnell, *Negro Politicians,* 52.

41. Ibid., 62. Another useful source is Ralph J. Bunche's contemporaneous analysis of "The Thompson-Negro Alliance," *Opportunity: A Journal of Negro Life* 7 (1929): 78–80.

42. *Pittsburgh Courier,* July 4, 1931, sec. 1, 4.

43. Ibid., 6.

44. "The Non-Partisan Negro Conference, Held in Washington, D.C., December 2, 3, and 4, 1931," Mimeograph, 3 in Burroughs Papers, Box 315, Library of Congress. A copy of the meeting's agenda may be found in the Gaines Papers, CHS.

45. Andrew Buni, in his study *Robert L. Vann of the Pittsburgh Courier: Politics and Black Journalism* (Pittsburgh: University of Pittsburgh Press, 1974), reports that Vann withdrew from the Non-Partisan League during the 1932 presidential election, accusing DePriest of attempting to make it a political arm of the Republican party (373, n. 135). Nancy J. Weiss, in *Farewell to the Party of Lincoln: Black Politics in the Age of FDR* (Princeton, N.J.: Princeton University Press, 1983), makes no mention of the Non-Partisan Negro Conference as a factor in the realignment of Black voting patterns. Weiss, unfortunately, does not deal with the Black church as a factor in the transformation of Black political affiliation, although she acknowledges the role of individual members of the clergy in that process.

The stated goal of the Non-Partisan Negro Conference was not to shift Black voters wholesale into the Democratic party but rather to enable Blacks to stand apart from both parties and use their leverage as a swing vote to achieve political gains for the race. Evidence that Austin took this "balance-of-power" approach seriously is suggested by the fact that although he supported Democratic politicians in the 1940s, he took a leading role in supporting Dwight D. Eisenhower (to the surprise of many) in the 1952 and 1956 presidential campaigns. See Roi Ottley, "Negro Pastor Urges His Race to Back Ike," undated clipping, Barnett Papers, Box 386, CHS.

46. For a partial listing of Austin's membership in voluntary associations, see the brief biographical sketch in Joseph J. Boris, ed., *Who's Who in Colored America* (New York: Who's Who in Colored America Corp., 1927), 1: 7–8. Documents in the Irene McCoy Gaines Papers, CHS, illustrate Austin's involvement with the Brotherhood of Sleeping Car Porters and the Chicago Scottsboro Defense Committee.

47. Archie L. Weaver to Frank M. Turner, December 17, 1931; Broadside, "The National Association for the Advancement of Colored People . . . Hear Robert W. Bagnell at Pilgrim Baptist Church" (n.p., n.d.); Form letter, A. C. MacNeal to "Dear Reverend," December 2, 1935; Walter White to A. C. MacNeal, January 29, 1937; J. C. Austin to Walter White, February 1, 1937. All of these materials are in the NAACP Papers, Branch Files, Group 1, Series G, Boxes 50, 52, and 53, located in the Manuscript Division of the Library of Congress. I am grateful to Michael Homel for calling these and other papers concerning J. C. Austin to my attention.

48. Memorandum, Coordinator of Branches [E. Frederick Morrow] to National Office, November 14, 1939; see also Walter White to E. Frederick Morrow, November 16, 1939; E. Frederick Morrow to Walter White, November 22, 1939; and Memorandum, Mr. Morrow, Subject: Chicago Branch, December 20,

1939. All of these materials may be found in the NAACP Papers, Branch Files, Group 1, Series G, Box 54, Library of Congress.

49. Edward A. Freeman, *The Epoch of Negro Baptists and the Foreign Mission Board* (Kansas City, Kans.: Central Seminary Press, 1953), 160. See also J. H. Jackson, "A Voyage to West Africa and Some Reflections on Modern Missions," in *Proceedings of the Fifty-sixth Annual Session of the National Baptist Convention, September 9–14, 1936* (n.p.), 203.

50. Quoted in Freeman, *Epoch of Negro Baptists,* 269. Baptist missionary Gladys East (daughter of James E. East, Foreign Mission Board corresponding secretary, 1921–1934), who served in Liberia from 1944 until her retirement in 1976, vividly recalled the visit of the "Tall Pines" to West Africa in 1950. She remembered the delegation's visit as an extraordinary event in the history of Black Baptist missions in Africa. Personal interview, July 9, 1982.

51. J. C. Austin to Claud Barnet [sic], March 4, 1950, Barnett Papers, CHS; Associated Negro Press releases entitled "Chicago Welcomes Rev. Austin Back from African Mission," "Mayor Joins Throng at Pilgrim Reception" (dated April 5, 1950), and "Rev. J. C. Austin Reports on Baptist Ministers' Tour of West Africa: Finds Encouragement for Trading Program: Sees Readiness to Fight for Freedom" (dated April 12, 1950), all in Barnett Papers, CHS.

52. Martin Kilson, "Political Change in the Negro Ghetto, 1900–1940," in *Key Issues in the Afro-American Experience,* ed. Nathan I. Huggins, Martin Kilson, and Daniel M. Fox (New York: Harcourt Brace Jovanovich, 1971), 2: 167–92, especially 2: 179. My attention was drawn to this essay by Charles Branham's excellent article "Black Chicago: Accommodationist Politics before the Great Migration," *Ethnic Chicago,* ed. Melvin G. Holli and Peter D'A. Jones, rev. ed. (Grand Rapids, Mich.: William B. Eerdmans Publishing, 1984), 338–79.

53. Kilson, "Political Change in Negro Ghetto," 186.

54. Frederic H. H. Robb, ed., *1927 Intercollegian Wonder Book; or The Negro in Chicago 1779–1927* (Chicago: Washington Intercollegiate Club of Chicago, 1927), 167. This rare but marvellously informative history of Black Chicago is reprinted in Randall K. Burkett, Nancy H. Burkett, and Henry Louis Gates, Jr., eds., *Black Biographical Dictionaries 1790–1950* (Alexandria: Chadwyck-Healey, 1989).

CHAPTER SEVEN

Martin Luther King, Jr., and the African-American Social Gospel

Clayborne Carson

Most recent studies of Martin Luther King, Jr., emphasize the extent to which his ideas were rooted in African-American religious traditions. Departing from King's own autobiographical account and from earlier studies that stressed the importance of King's graduate studies at Crozer Theological Seminary and Boston University,[1] contemporary scholars have focused attention on King's African-American religious roots.[2] The Martin Luther King, Jr., Papers Project has contributed to this scholarly trend by documenting the King family's long-standing ties to Ebenezer Baptist Church and the social gospel ministries of his father and grandfather, both of whom were civil rights leaders as well as pastors.[3] The King project's research also suggests, however, that the current trend in scholarship may understate the extent to which King's African-American religious roots were inextricably intertwined with the European-American intellectual influences of his college years. The initial volumes of the project's fourteen-volume edition of King's papers have contributed to a new understanding of King's graduate school experiences, demonstrating that his academic writings, though flawed by serious instances of plagiarism, were often reliable expressions of his complex, evolving Weltanschauung.[4] Moreover, King's writings make clear that his roots in African-American religion did not necessarily separate him from European-American theological influences, because many of the black religious leaders who were his role models were themselves products of predominantly white seminaries and graduate schools. Rather than being torn between two mutually exclusive religious traditions, King's uniquely effective transracial leadership was based on his ability to combine elements of African-American and European-American religious traditions.

King was deeply influenced by his childhood immersion in African-American religious life, but his years at Crozer and Boston increased his ability to incorporate aspects of academic theology into his sermons and public speeches. His student papers demonstrate that he adopted European-American theological ideas that ultimately reinforced rather than undermined the African-American social gospel tradition epitomized by his father and grandfather. Although King's advanced training in theology set him apart from most African-American clergymen, the documentary evidence regarding his formative years suggests that his graduate studies engendered an increased appreciation for his African-American religious roots. From childhood, King had been uncomfortable with the emotionalism and scriptural literalism that he associated with traditional Baptist liturgy, but he was also familiar with innovative, politically active, and intellectually sophisticated African-American clergymen who had themselves been influenced by European-American theological scholarship. These clergymen served as role models for King as he mined theological scholarship for nuggets of insight that could enrich his preaching. As he sought to resolve religious doubts that had initially prevented him from accepting his calling, King looked upon European-American theological ideas not as alternatives to traditional black Baptist beliefs but as necessary correctives to those beliefs.

Tracing the evolution of his religious beliefs in a sketch written at Crozer entitled "An Autobiography of Religious Development," King recalled that an initial sense of religious estrangement had unexpectedly and abruptly become apparent at a Sunday morning revival meeting he attended at about the age of seven. A guest evangelist from Virginia had come to talk about salvation and to seek recruits for the church. Having grown up in the church, King had never given much thought to joining it formally, but the emotion of the revival and the decision of his sister to step forward prompted an impulsive decision to accept conversion. He reflected, "I had never given this matter a thought, and even at the time of [my] baptism I was unaware of what was taking place." King admitted that he "joined the church not out of any dynamic conviction, but out of a childhood desire to keep up with my sister." In the same sketch, he wrote that, although he accepted the teachings of his Sunday school teachers until he was about twelve,

> this uncritical attitude could not last long, for it was contrary to the very nature of my being. I had always been the questioning and precocious type. At the age of 13 I shocked my Sunday School class by denying the bodily resurrection of Jesus. From the age of thirteen on doubts began to spring forth unrelentingly.[5]

King's recognition that he did not share some of the religious convictions of other family members might have been emotionally devastating, but his inalienable sense of belonging to the church led him toward reconciliation rather than continued rebellion. Although his convictions removed him from the kind of fundamentalist faith that placed great importance on emotionalism and a conversion experience, he never considered abandoning his inherited faith. His early doubts did not interfere with his intense involvement in church life, his love of church music, or his fascination with the art of preaching. His father, Martin Luther King, Sr., noted the way in which his son absorbed attitudes ("he loved church . . . the feeling for ceremonies and ritual, the passionate love of Baptist music") and skills ("a great speaker . . . and he sang, too, in a fine, clear voice") that would prepare him for a preaching career.[6] Letters written to his parents in his early adolescence reveal an intimate knowledge of the details of Baptist church life: congregational governance, ward meetings, church finances, and continual social events.[7]

Moreover, King was aware that the accomplishments of his father's generation of African-American religious leaders represented more than just emotional folk preaching and scriptural literalism. Despite theological differences, King attributed his decision to enter the ministry to the influence of a father who "set forth a noble example that I didn't [mind] following." King's father and grandfather were not only Baptist ministers but also pioneering exponents of a distinctively African-American version of social gospel Christianity. When King's grandfather, the Reverend A. D. Williams, arrived in Atlanta in 1893, social gospel activism was becoming increasingly common among both black and white urban clergymen. After taking over the pastorate of Atlanta's Ebenezer Baptist Church in March 1894, Williams built a large congregation through forceful preaching that addressed the everyday concerns of poor and working-class residents. Baptist denominational practices encouraged ministers such as Williams to retain the support of occasionally rebellious congregations through charismatic leadership that extended beyond purely spiritual matters. Having arrived in Atlanta on the eve of a major period of institutional development among African-American Baptists, Williams joined two thousand other delegates and visitors who met at Atlanta's Friendship Baptist Church in September 1895 to organize the National Baptist Convention, the largest black organization in the United States.

For the remainder of his life, Williams played a leading role in Baptist affairs, both at state and national levels. In addition, he took the lead in responding to W. E. B. Du Bois's call for civil rights activism by joining five hundred other black Georgians in February 1906 to form the Georgia Equal Rights League. In 1917, Williams became one of the founders of the Atlanta branch of the National Association for the Advancement of Colored People (NAACP). After becoming president of the local chapter in 1918, he mobilized newly enfranchised African-American women in a campaign to register black voters. He also led a successful drive to pressure white officials into providing improved educational facilities for black children. This effort resulted in the establishment of a black high school that Martin Luther King, Jr., later attended.

Martin Luther King, Sr., continued this tradition of social gospel activism after he married Williams's only daughter in 1926. Although his son would sometimes depict him as a conservative, King, Sr., identified himself as a social gospel preacher who believed that his ministry should be focused on the everyday needs of his congregation rather than other-worldly concerns. While a theology student at Morehouse College, King, Sr., had been exposed to the liberal theological ideas of C. D. Hubert, who headed the school's theology program. As the two ministers struggled to retain the loyalty of their congregations during the Great Depression, King recalled that Williams insisted, "Whosoever carries the word must make the word flesh." King explained that Williams used church funds to "make food available to the hungry and clothes to those without them. We kept children while mothers worked. The church bought and supplied medicines. Ebenezer tried to be an anchor as the storm rose."[8]

After taking over Ebenezer upon Williams's death in 1931, Martin Luther King, Sr., expanded the scope of his predecessor's politically engaged ministry. Early in 1935, he organized meetings to encourage blacks to register to vote and, despite resistance from more cautious clergyman and lay leaders, organized a march to City Hall. A year later he became chairman of the Committee on the Equalization of Teachers' Salaries, which was formed to protest against discriminatory policies that paid higher salaries to white teachers than to equally qualified blacks. In spite of receiving threatening hate letters, he played a leading role in the sustained struggle for pay equity.[9] King's firm insistence that the Christian church should participate in civil rights activities set him apart from politically conservative scriptural fundamentalists. In 1940, he revealed his commitment to social gospel Christianity in an address on "the true mission of the Church" delivered to the Atlanta Missionary Baptist Association:

> Quite often we say the church has no place in politics, forgetting the words of the Lord, "The spirit of the Lord is upon me, because he hath [anointed] me to preach the Gospel to the poor; he hath sent me to heal the broken-hearted, to preach deliverance to the captives, and the recovering of sight to the blind, to set at liberty them that are bruised."
> . . . God hasten the time when every minister will become a registered voter and a part of every movement for the betterment of our people. Again and again has it been said we cannot lead where we do not go, and we cannot teach what we do not know.

As ministers a great responsibility rests upon us as leaders. We can not expect our people to register and become citizens until we as leaders set the standard.[10]

In addition to seeing his father as both a social activist and a scriptural conservative, King, Jr., was also aware of many other models of politically engaged religious leadership. He admired the Reverend William Holmes Borders, who had built Wheat Street Baptist Church into Atlanta's largest black church and who possessed the academic credentials that King's own father lacked. Although both ministers had struggled from poverty to graduate from Morehouse College, Borders had also obtained a divinity degree from Garrett Theological Seminary and a master's degree from Northwestern before returning to Atlanta, where he taught religion at Morehouse and became an outspoken preacher at Wheat Street. According to biographer Taylor Branch, King and his friends studied "Borders' mannerisms, his organizational style, and above all the high-toned sermons in which he aroused his congregation without merely repeating the homilies of eternal life."[11]

After entering Morehouse College at the age of fifteen, King was profoundly influenced by the example of the college's president, Dr. Benjamin Elijah Mays, a family friend who was the kind of dedicated, intellectually sophisticated religious leader that King wished to emulate. Selected in 1940 to succeed John Hope as head of Morehouse, Mays was the first Morehouse president with a Ph.D. Although not a "Morehouse man" himself, Mays had internalized the Morehouse tradition calling for students to use their skills on behalf of the black community. An outstanding debater during his own undergraduate years, Mays often used his Tuesday morning talks to the student body as occasions to express his commitment to the social gospel and to challenge Morehouse students to struggle against segregation rather than accommodate to it. By the time King entered college, Mays had returned from a trip to India as one of a growing number of African-American disciples of Mahatma Gandhi. King later described Mays as one of the "great influences" in his life.[12]

At Morehouse, King received his initial exposure to modern critical theology when he took a course on the Bible taught by another family acquaintance, Professor George D. Kelsey, a Morehouse graduate who had recently received his doctorate from Yale. In 1945 Kelsey had initiated an Annual Institute for the Training and Improvement of Baptist Ministers and had thereby gained the admiration of King, Sr., who described Kelsey as a teacher who "saw the pulpit as a place both for drama, in the old-fashioned, country Baptist sense, and for the articulation of philosophies that address the problems of society." Kelsey later remembered King, Jr., as an earnest student who took the subject matter of the course seriously. "I made it my business to present lectures on the most strenuous teaching of Jesus," Kelsey recalled. "It was precisely at this time that Martin's eyes lit up most and his face was graced with a smile."[13] Shortly after teaching King, Kelsey published an article arguing that "the problem of race is indeed America's greatest moral dilemma," giving King a phrase that he would use in his first book, *Stride toward Freedom* (1958).

In addition to Mays and Kelsey, King was also undoubtedly aware of many black religious leaders who combined academic erudition with a thorough grounding in African-American religious traditions. While at Crozer Seminary, King often debated theological and political issues with J. Pius Barbour, a family friend and Morehouse graduate, who had graduated from the seminary a decade before King's arrival. King was also familiar with the progressive ideas of Howard University president Mordecai Johnson, whose 1949 speech in Philadelphia recounting a trip to India stirred King's interest in Gandhian ideas. Howard Thurman, whose influential social gospel statement *Jesus and the Disinherited* appeared in 1949, was also a family friend of the Kings: he had attended Morehouse with King, Sr. When Thurman became Boston University's dean of the chapel, he developed a personal acquaintance with King, Jr., who was then attending the university.

Benefiting from this extensive exposure to proponents of African-American social gospel, King was able to perceive theological training as a means of reconciling his inclination to follow his father's calling with his desire for intellectual respectability. King's descriptions of his decision to enter the ministry reveal that he had accepted the social mission of the church even though he had not yet resolved his theological doubts. He realized that the Baptist religion he had absorbed during his youth had derived mainly from daily contact with church life rather than from theological reflection. Growing up in the church provided a substitute for orthodox theological convictions; born a Baptist, he never felt the need to affirm all the tenets of the denomination. In his "Autobiography of Religious Development," he explained: "Conversion for me was never an abrupt something. I have never experienced the so called 'crisis moment.' Religion has just been something that I grew up in. Conversion for me has been the gradual intaking of the noble ideals set forth in my family and my environment, and I must admit that this intaking has been largely unconscious."[14]

The consistency of King's basic religious and political convictions throughout his life suggest that his collegiate training was not a transformative experience but was rather a refinement of preexisting religious attitudes. Recognizing that a Ph.D. degree from a northern university would set him apart from most other Baptist ministers, he approached his graduate education with skepticism and perhaps even a touch of cynicism, self-consciously acquiring academic credentials that would add intellectual respectability to ingrained beliefs rooted in early religious experiences. King's rejection of scriptural literalism did not lead him away from the Baptist church but toward an increasing interest in liberal theology. His understanding that religious belief could be rooted in reason also enabled him to think more seriously about an idea he had previously rejected: becoming a minister.

The elder King had always wanted both of his sons to follow his career choice and eventually, perhaps, serve as pastors for the Ebenezer congregation. He listened to his wife's entreaties on the need for the children to make their own career choices, while hoping that his sons would make use of his connections among Baptists: "family ties, school and fraternal relationships, the so-called hometown connections that kept phones ringing and letters moving in consideration of help requested and granted, favors offered and accepted."[15] Despite being aware of their father's wishes, however, King, Jr., and his younger brother, A. D., were reluctant to conform to paternal expectations. The latter dropped out of Morehouse before finally deciding on a ministerial career, and the former spent his first three undergraduate years determined to become first a physician and then a lawyer—but not a minister like his father. Determined to assert his independence from his father and continuing to question aspects of his father's religious beliefs, King, Jr., nevertheless received a strong impetus toward becoming a preacher from his father's ever-present example.

A crucial period in King's deliberations about his career came during the summer of 1947, when he led religious services for his fellow student workers at a tobacco farm in Simsbury, Connecticut. Even before leaving Atlanta he had received his preaching license, and—more than he had during his 1944 stay in Simsbury—welcomed the opportunity to lead the weekly religious gatherings at the farm. After several weeks of deliberation, he telephoned his mother from Simsbury to tell her of his intention to become a minister. By the time he returned to Morehouse for his final year, he had pushed doubt out of his mind. His initial inclination to become a doctor or lawyer was overwhelmed by an "undying urge to serve God and humanity through the ministry." The decision was the culmination of his experiences. "My call to the ministry was neither dramatic nor spectacular," he later wrote in his application to seminary.

> It came neither by some miraculous vision nor by some blinding light experience on the road of life. Moreover, it was a response to an inner urge that gradually came upon me. This urge expressed itself in a desire to serve God and humanity, and the feeling that my talent and my commit-

ment could best be expressed through the ministry. . . . During my senior
year in college I finally decided to accept the challenge to enter the ministry. I came to see that God had placed a responsibility upon my shoulders
and the more I tried to escape it the more frustrated I would become.[16]

Once the decision was made, King's friends recognized its inevitability, given his experiences, contacts, and abilities. Even at this early stage
in his development as a preacher, his abilities as a pulpit orator were
evident to those who heard him. Samuel DuBois Cook recalled that King
delivered a "Senior Sermon" in the Morehouse Chapel a week before
graduation. "He knew almost intuitively how to move an audience,"
Cook remembered. "He asserted that there are moral laws in the universe that we cannot violate with impunity, anymore than we can violate
the physical laws of the university with impunity."[17] King resolved to
become a minister, but he continued to reject the anti-intellectualism
that he associated with fundamentalism. His subsequent critical study of
biblical texts and religious practices was driven by a desire to strengthen
the rationale for a decision he had already made. He applied to several
seminaries known to be academically rigorous and hospitable to liberal
religious views, including Andover Newton in Massachusetts, Union in
New York, and Crozer in Pennsylvania.

King's graduate school education should be viewed within the context
of his struggle to synthesize his father's Christian practices and his own
theological skepticism. Seen from this perspective, King's experiences at
Crozer and Boston constituted neither a pilgrimage toward the social
gospel views of his Crozer professors nor a movement toward the personalism of those at Boston. Instead, King eclectically drew upon the
writings of academic theologians as he moved away from Christian liberalism toward a theological synthesis closer to aspects of his father's religious faith, particularly toward a conception of God as a source of support in times of personal need. Rather than becoming more liberal in
college, he became increasingly skeptical of intellectualized conceptions
of divinity. As King became increasingly aware of the limitations of liberal Christian thought, he acquired a renewed appreciation for his
southern Baptist roots. His Crozer papers occasionally referred to his
experiences in order to explain his theological preferences. He noted
that his initial attraction to liberalism stemmed from its willingness to
"answer new problems of cultural and social change," unlike its theological opponent, fundamentalism, which sought "to preserve the old faith
in a changing milieu."[18] As he continued his studies, however, King
found his initial attraction to liberal theology "going through a state of
transition." His personal experience with "a vicious race problem" had
made it "very difficult . . . to believe in the essential goodness of man";
on the other hand, he explained that "in noticing the gradual improve-

ments of this same race problem I came to see some noble possibilities in human nature." While remaining wary of his father's conventional religious beliefs, King was becoming, he acknowledged, "a victim of eclecticism," seeking to "synthesize the best in liberal theology with the best in neo-orthodox theology." [19]

At Crozer, King was introduced to personalism, a philosophical school of thought that had developed in the late nineteenth century at Boston University and other American universities. After reviewing a text by Boston professor Edgar S. Brightman, a leading personalist theologian, King reported, in an essay for one of his classes, that he was "amazed to find that the conception of God is so complex and one about which opinions differ so widely." King conceded that he was still "quite confused as to which definition [of God] was the most adequate," but thought that Brightman's personalist theology held the greatest appeal.[20] Its emphasis on the reality of personal religious experience validated King's own religious experiences. King reaffirmed his belief that "every man, from the ordinary simplehearted believer to the philosophical intellectual giant, may find God through religious experience."[21] His reading of Brightman led him to discover his own spirituality:

> How I long now for that religious experience which Dr. Brightman so cogently speaks of throughout his book. It seems to be an experience, the lack of which life becomes dull and meaningless. As I reflect on the matter, however, I do remember moments that I have been awe awakened; there have been times that I have been carried out of myself by something greater than myself and to that something I gave myself. Has this great something been God? Maybe after all I have been religious for a number of years, and am now only becoming aware of it.[22]

Brightman's explanation of religious experience convinced King that he could experience God's powerful presence in his own life without the benefit of a sudden religious conversion. Personalism validated the notion that experience rather than intellectual reflection should be the basis of religious belief. "It is through experience that we come to realize that some things are out of harmony with God's will," King wrote in another essay. "No theology is needed to tell us that love is the law of life and to disobey it means to suffer the consequences."[23] King's adoption of personalism as a theological orientation enabled him to reject abstract conceptions of God while continuing his search for cogency and intellectual sophistication.

By the time King entered Boston University, he was learning how to use his theological training to enrich his preaching and, in the process, return to his roots as a Baptist preacher. King's academic theological studies at Crozer had encouraged him to question many aspects of his religious heritage, but by his final year King had also become skeptical of many tenets of theological liberalism. The church of his parents and grandparents had imparted an understanding of God and of the purposes of Christian ministry that could not be displaced by theological sophistication. He later explained that his study of personalism at Crozer and Boston reinforced his beliefs rather than supplanted them. Personalism's "insistence that only personality—finite and infinite—is ultimately real strengthened me in two convictions: it gave me a metaphysical and philosophical grounding for the idea of a personal God, and it gave me a metaphysical basis for the dignity and worth of all human personality."[24]

At Boston, King expanded his criticism of theological liberalism by adopting many of the ideas of Reinhold Niebuhr. King applauded Niebuhr's rigorous analysis of "the fundamental weaknesses and inevitable sterility of the humanistic emphasis" of liberalism in the twentieth century.[25] He was also drawn to Niebuhr's economic and moral analysis of capitalism, such as the notion that modern industrial civilization was responsible for "appalling injustices," particularly the "concentration of power and resources in the hands of a relatively small wealthy class."[26] Injustices are inherent in human society, Niebuhr argued, because humans engaged in collective activity are essentially immoral, whereas individuals acting on their own possess a moral conscience. Niebuhr sought to resolve the tension between "moral man and immoral society" by reinterpreting the traditional Christian notion of *agape,* or divine love.[27] Agreeing with Niebuhr's analysis, King stated that *agape* may not be achievable in an immoral society but "remains a leaven in society, permeating the whole and giving texture and consistency to life."

King was particularly receptive to Niebuhr's criticism of love and justice as conceived in both liberal and orthodox theology. In orthodoxy, "individual perfection is too often made an end in itself," whereas liberalism "vainly seeks to overcome justice [through] purely moral and rational suasions." Liberalism, King wrote, "confuses the ideal itself with the realistic means which must be employed to coerce society into an approximation of that ideal." King agreed with Niebuhr's emphasis on making realistic moral choices and with his social analysis, but he believed that Niebuhr lacked an adequate explanation of how *agape* operates in human history: "He fails to see that the availability of the divine *Agape* is an essential [affirmation] of the Christian religion."[28]

Given the academic environment in which he attended graduate school, it is hardly surprising that King's theological writings did not explicitly draw upon the insights of African-American religion. Yet, although King's graduate school writings understated the degree to which his attitudes had been shaped by African-American religious writings, he was certainly aware of the publications of Kelsey and Mays and probably those of Thurman and Borders. Once accustomed to contrasting the religious emotionalism of his father's religion with the intellectual sophistication he saw in the writings of white academic theologians, King became aware during his graduate research that orthodox Christianity was not necessarily anti-intellectual.

Overall, King's theological development in seminary and graduate school reflected his lifelong tendency to incorporate the best elements of each alternative. As when choosing between capitalism and communism or between power politics and pacifism, King sought to synthesize alternative orientations: "An adequate understanding of man is found neither in the thesis of liberalism nor in the antithesis of neo-orthodoxy, but in a synthesis which reconciles the truths of both."[29] King described his graduate training as an attempt to bring together "the best in liberal theology with the best in neo-orthodox theology" in order to come to an understanding of man. His enormous respect for the writings of Reinhold Niebuhr derived from the pleasure he felt in finding a theological stance that synthesized faith and intellect. He probably heard echoes of his father's fundamentalism in Reinhold Niebuhr's neo-orthodoxy, which reaffirmed the limits of human perfectibility. Niebuhr provided an intellectual rationale for King's recognition of the limitations of liberal theology. As King wrote during these years, he had become "so enamored of the insights of liberalism that I almost fell into the trap of accepting uncritically everything it encompasses." After reading Niebuhr, King recalled becoming more aware of "the depths and strength of sin" and

> the complexity of man's social involvement and the glaring reality of collective evil. I realized that liberalism had been all too sentimental concerning human nature and that it leaned toward a false idealism. I also came to see that the superficial optimism of liberalism concerning human nature overlooked the fact that reason is darkened by sin. The more I thought about human nature, the more I saw how our tragic inclination for sin encourages us to rationalize our actions. Liberalism failed to show that reason by itself is little more than an instrument to justify man's defensive ways of thinking. Reason, devoid of the purifying power of faith, can never free itself from distortions and rationalizations.[30]

By the time he finished his course work, King had come to affirm some of the enduring values of his religious heritage, particularly conceptions of a divine goodness capable of acting in history. In one qualifying examination King declared that, despite modern society's moral relativism, God's judgment was final and eternal. "God has planted in the fiber of the universe certain eternal laws which forever confront every man. They are absolute and not relative. There is an eternal and absolute distinction between right and wrong." One indispensable answer to the theodicy question, King argued, was contained in the concept of the suffering servant, one of the "most noble" teachings of the Old Testament. "His suffering is not due to something that he has done, but it is *vicarious* and *redemptive*. Through his suffering knowledge of God is [spread] to the unbelieving Gentiles and those unbelievers seeing that this suffering servant is innocent will become conscious of their sins and repent and thereby be redeemed. The nation would be healed by his [wounds]." The death of Jesus Christ on the cross was the fulfillment of the prophecy of the suffering servant, but King argued that humanity should not wait on His saving grace. An individual's "faith and fellowship with God," King wrote, was the "ultimate solution to the problem of suffering."[31]

King's choice of a dissertation topic reflected an interest in the nature of God that derived both from his academic studies and from his preaching. In addition to writing several term papers on the topic, King wove the theme of theodicy into several sermons while at Boston, including one entitled "What Does It Mean to Believe in God?"[32] In his introduction to the dissertation King explained that the conception of God should be examined because of "the central place which it occupies in any religion" and because of "the ever present need to interpret and clarify the God-concept."[33]

By early 1953, when King enrolled in a course on dissertation writing at the beginning of his research, he was fairly certain about the conclusions he would reach in his dissertation. King recognized the limitations in the thinking of theologians Paul Tillich and Henry Nelson Wieman. "Both overstress one side of the divine life," he wrote, "while [minimizing] another basic aspect. Wieman [stresses] the goodness of God while minimizing his power. Tillich stresses the power of God while [minimizing] his goodness."[34] With his own beliefs still rooted in an African-American religious tradition that perceived God as a personal force interceding in history, King found Tillich's and Wieman's conceptions of divinity unworthy of worship. In the evaluative chapter, King expressed belief in a "living" God, not Tillich's "being-itself" or Wieman's "source of human good." "In God there is feeling and will, responsive to the deepest yearnings of the human heart; this God both evokes and answers prayer." Conceiving of such a God as a person was preferable to Tillich's and Wieman's use of abstract philosophical terms. "It would be better by far to admit that there are difficulties with an idea we know— such as personality—than to employ a term which is practically unknown to us in our experience." King concluded that Tillich and Wieman both set forth a God who is less than personal, despite their comments to the contrary suggesting that God was more than personal, unable to be defined by the concept of personality. "Both Tillich and Wieman reject the conception of a personal God, and with this goes a rejection of the rationality, goodness and love of God in the full sense of the words."[35]

Despite his disagreement with certain aspects of both men's conceptions of divinity, King appreciated their criticism of humanism. King approvingly noted that Tillich and Wieman both emphasized God's immanence, or "the primacy of God over everything else in the universe." "Such an emphasis," he argued, "sounds a much needed note in the face of a supernaturalism that finds nature so irrational that the order of creation can no longer be discerned in it, and history so meaningless that it all bears the 'minus sign' of alienation from God." In a characteristic effort to reconcile two positions that were in dialectical tension, King extracted what he considered positive aspects of their thought to create an eclectic synthesis. Echoing his preliminary analysis of their positions, King asserted that "both Tillich and Wieman are partially correct in what they affirm and partially wrong in what they deny. Wieman is right in emphasizing the goodness of God, but wrong in minimizing his power. Likewise Tillich is right in emphasizing the power of God, but wrong in minimizing his goodness."[36]

In the sermons King delivered while writing his dissertation, he expressed his conception of God using more vivid language than his stilted, derivative academic diction. He skillfully incorporated into his sermons those aspects of his theological training that affirmed his ties to the religion of his parents and grandparents. His father later affirmed that his son's roots in the African-American preaching tradition remained strong even after years of graduate study. "M. L. was still a son of the Baptist South, there'd never be any doubt about that."[37]

King's ability to blend these elements can be seen in his earliest known recorded sermon, "Rediscovering Lost Values."[38] King delivered the sermon to a large Baptist church in Detroit in late February 1954, just days after finishing his final comprehensive examination and a few weeks before the graduate school approved his dissertation outline. In the Detroit sermon, King told the familiar biblical story of Joseph and Mary, who realized, while walking to Nazareth, that they had left Jesus behind in Jerusalem. Just as Joseph and Mary had returned to rejoin Jesus, King advised, society should rediscover the precious values that had become lost in the rationalizations that guided behavior in the modern world. "If we are to go forward," he said, "if we are to make this a better world in which to live, we've got to go back. We've got to rediscover these precious values that we've left behind." Despite the many technological advances and material comforts of American society, King argued, humanity had lost the spiritual compass provided by a deep and abiding faith in God. "The real problem is that through our scientific genius we've made of the world a neighborhood, but through our moral and spiritual genius we've failed to make of it a brotherhood." King insisted that "*all* reality hinges on moral foundations," that "this is a moral universe, and . . . there are moral laws of the universe, just as abiding as the physical laws." Decrying ethical relativism—"Now, I'm not trying to use a big word here"—King expressed a belief in moral absolutes that evoked enthusiastic responses from the congregation.

> I'm here to say to you this morning that some things are right and some things are wrong. *(Yes)* Eternally so, absolutely so. It's *wrong* to hate. *(Yes, That's right)* It always has been wrong and it always will be wrong! *(Amen)* It's wrong in America, it's wrong in Germany, it's wrong in Russia, it's wrong in China! *(Lord help him)* It was wrong in two thousand B.C., and it's wrong in nineteen-fifty-four A.D.! It always has been wrong, *(That's right)* and it always will be wrong! . . . Some things in this universe are absolute. The God of the universe has made it so.[39]

In King's view contemporary society had lost sight of this "mighty precious value," adopting instead "a pragmatic test for right and wrong." In the modern world, he asserted, most people believed that "it's all right to disobey the Ten Commandments, but just don't disobey the Eleventh, Thou shall not get caught." The moral decay that King identified in modern culture could be recovered only by ethical living. "The thing that we need in the world today, is a group of men and women who will stand up for right and be opposed to wrong, wherever it is."[40]

King argued that making ethical decisions was impossible without rediscovering the precious value of faith in God. King charged that many people, including those who attended church every Sunday, had lost their faith in God. "We must remember that it's possible to affirm the existence of God with your lips and deny his existence with your life." Returning to the biblical parable, King asserted that "we had gone a whole day's journey, and then we came to see that we had unconsciously ushered God out of the universe." The materialism of American consumer culture had caused some to lose sight of God, and King cautioned that "automobiles and subways, televisions and radios, dollars and cents, can *never* be substitutes for God."[41]

King's sermon drew upon traditional African-American religious ideas, particularly the notion of God acting in human history. Alluding to a verse in Psalm 23 and to a familiar hymn, King concluded by affirming faith in the God "who walks with us through the valley of the shadow of death, and causes us to fear no evil," in the God "who has been our help in ages past, and our hope for years to come, and our shelter in the time of storm, and our eternal home."[42] King concluded with a rousing affirmation of God as an integral part of his life. "As a young man with most of my life ahead of me, I decided early to give my life to something eternal and absolute. Not to these little gods that are here today and gone tomorrow. But to God who is the same yesterday, today, and forever."[43]

Seen in the context of his preadult experiences, King's graduate school years enabled him to acquire academic credentials while retaining his basic religious beliefs. When he applied to Boston University's doctoral program, King had stressed his desire to enter the world of theological scholarship, stating that he was "desirous of teaching in a college or a school of religion."[44] At Crozer, King had initially been estranged from his roots, but by the time he entered Boston University he had rediscovered the liberating potential of his African-American Baptist heritage. Although he clearly wanted to base his religious beliefs on solid theological foundations, he left Boston as a preacher rather than as a scholar. Forging an eclectic synthesis from such diverse sources as personalism, theological liberalism, neo-orthodox theology, and the activist, Bible-centered religion of his heritage, King affirmed his abiding faith in a God who was both a comforting personal presence and a powerful spiritual force acting in history for righteousness. This faith would sustain him as the civil rights movement irreversibly transformed his life.

King's rapid rise to prominence resulted from his ability to combine the insights of European-American theological scholarship with those of African-American homiletics. Although his published descriptions of his "pilgrimage to non-violence" generally emphasized the impact of his academic training,[45] in more personal statements he acknowledged his black Baptist roots. "I am many things to many people," King acknowledged in 1965, "but in the quiet recesses of my heart, I am fundamentally a clergyman, a Baptist preacher. This is my being and my heritage for I am also the son of a Baptist preacher, the grandson of a Baptist preacher and the great-grandson of a Baptist preacher."[46] Rather than being torn between mutually exclusive cultural traditions, King's public, transracial ministry marked a convergence of theological scholarship and social gospel practice. Drawing upon a variety of intellectual and religious traditions to arouse and enlighten his listeners, King was profoundly affected by his experiences both as a preacher's son at Ebenezer and as a diligent student at Crozer Seminary and Boston University. King's theological education distinguished him from all but a few African-American preachers and temporarily separated him from his childhood environment, but theological studies ultimately led King to a deeper appreciation of traditional African-American conceptions of God as a source of support, especially in times of personal crisis. Later in his career as a movement leader, King would reflect that when he had "been battered by the storms of persecution," he had gained strength and determination from

> the reality of a personal God. True, I have always believe[d] in the personality of God. But in the past the idea of a personal God was little more than a metaphysical category that I found theologically and philosophically satisfying. Now it is a living reality that has been validated in the experience of everyday life. God has been profoundly real to me in recent years.[47]

NOTES

1. See, for example, Martin Luther King, Jr., *Stride toward Freedom: The Montgomery Story* (New York: Harper & Row, 1958), chapter 6; Kenneth L. Smith and Ira G. Zepp, Jr., *Search for the Beloved Community: The Thinking of Martin Luther King, Jr.* (Valley Forge, Pa.: Judson Press, 1974); and John J. Ansbro, *Martin Luther King, Jr.: The Making of a Mind* (Maryknoll, N.Y.: Orbis, 1982).

2. See, for example, James H. Cone, "Martin Luther King, Jr.: Black Theology—Black Church," *Theology Today* 40 (January 1984): 409–12; Lewis V. Baldwin, *There Is a Balm in Gilead: The Cultural Roots of Martin Luther King, Jr.* (Minneapolis: Fortress Press, 1991).

3. Clayborne Carson, Ralph E. Luker, and Penny A. Russell, eds., *The Papers of Martin Luther King, Jr.*, vol. 1, *Called to Serve, January 1929–June 1951* (Berkeley and Los Angeles: University of California Press, 1992).

4. See Clayborne Carson et al., "Martin Luther King, Jr., as Scholar: A Reexamination of His Theological Writings," *Journal of American History* 78 (June 1991): 93–105.

5. Martin Luther King, Jr., "Autobiography of Religious Development," in Carson et al., eds., *Papers of Martin Luther King, Jr.*, 1: 361. According to King's application to Crozer Theological Seminar, the date of his joining the church was May 1, 1936.

6. Martin Luther King, Sr., with Clayton Riley, *Daddy King: An Autobiography* (New York: William Morrow, 1980), 127.

7. See Carson et al., *Papers*, 1: 102–7.

8. Ibid., 89.

9. Ibid., 104.

10. Martin Luther King, Sr., "Moderator's Annual Address—1940," quoted in Carson et al., *Papers*, 1: 34. On the eve of the Montgomery bus boycott of 1955–56, King would use similar arguments in a speech to the Birmingham branch of the NAACP criticizing the apathy of church leaders on political issues. " 'You must do more than pray and read the Bible,' to destroy segregation and second-class citizenship," the local newspaper reported him saying, " 'you must do something about it.' " See "Apathy among Church Leaders Hit in Talk by Rev. M. L. King," *Birmingham World*, January 25, 1955. King would later deliver the speech, entitled "A Realistic Approach to Progress in Race Relations," on many occasions.

11. Taylor Branch, *Parting the Waters: America in the King Years, 1954–63* (New York: Simon and Schuster, 1988), 54, 64. See also James W. English, *The Prophet of Wheat Street* (Elgin, Ill.: David C. Cook, 1967).

12. King, Jr., *Stride toward Freedom*, 145.

13. Renee D. Turner, "Remembering the Young King," *Ebony*, January 1988. In this article Kelsey recalled that King took Kelsey's course "The Teachings of Jesus" in his sophomore year.

14. King, Jr., "Autobiography of Religious Development," *Papers*, 1: 361.

15. King, Sr., and Riley, *Daddy King*, 128.

16. Statement of Martin Luther King, Jr., August 7, 1959, written in response to a request by Joan Thatcher, publicity director of the Board of Education and Publication of the American Baptist Convention, Division of Christian Higher Education, July 30, 1959, Martin Luther King Collection, Mugar Library, Boston University; quoted in Mervyn Alonza Warren, "A Rhetorical Study of the Preaching of Dr. Martin Luther King, Jr., Pastor and Pulpit Orator" (Ph.D. dissertation, Michigan State University, 1966), 35–36. While at Crozer, King wrote: "My call to the ministry was not a miraculous or supernatural something, on the contrary it was an inner urge calling me to serve humanity. I guess the influence of my father also had a great deal to do with my going in the ministry. This is not to say that he ever spoke to me in terms of being a minister, but that my admiration for him was the great moving factor; he set forth a noble example that I didn't min[d] following. Today I differ a great deal with my father theologically, but that admiration for a real father still remains." King, Jr., "Autobiography of Religious Development," *Papers*, 1: 363.

17. Samuel DuBois Cook, quoted in Turner, "Remembering the Young King," 42.

18. Martin Luther King, Jr., "The Sources of Fundamentalism and Liberalism Considered Historically and Psychologically," in Carson et al., *Papers of Martin Luther King, Jr.*, 1: 240

19. Martin Luther King, Jr., "How Modern Christians Should Think of Man," in Carson et al., *Papers of Martin Luther King, Jr.*, 1: 274.

20. Martin Luther King, Jr., "A Conception and Impression of Religion Drawn from Dr. Brightman's Book Entitled *A Philosophy of Religion*," in Carson et al., *Papers of Martin Luther King, Jr.*, 1: 410–11.

21. Martin Luther King, Jr., "The Place of Reason and Experience in Finding God," in Carson et al., *Papers of Martin Luther King, Jr.*, 1: 234.

22. King, Jr., "Conception and Impression of Religion," *Papers*, 1: 415–16.

23. King, Jr., "Place of Reason and Experience," *Papers*, 1: 234.

24. King, Jr., *Stride toward Freedom*, 100.

25. Martin Luther King, Jr., "Reinhold Niebuhr," April 2, 1952, in Carson et al., *Papers of Martin Luther King, Jr.*, vol. 2 (forthcoming).

26. Martin Luther King, Jr., "Reinhold Niebuhr's Ethical Dualism," May 9, 1952, in Carson et al., *Papers of Martin Luther King, Jr.*, vol. 2 (forthcoming).

27. Reinhold Niebuhr, *Moral Man and Immoral Society* (New York: Scribner, 1933).

28. King, Jr., "Niebuhr's Ethical Dualism," *Papers*, vol. 2 (forthcoming).

29. Martin Luther King, Jr., *Strength to Love* (Philadelphia: Fortress Press, 1963), 149. In resolving the conflict between capitalism and Marxism, he wrote,

"The Kingdom of God is neither the thesis of individual enterprise nor the antithesis of collective enterprise, but a synthesis which reconciles the truths of both."

30. King, Jr., "How Modern Christians," *Papers*, 1: 274. King later asserted that "Niebuhr's great contribution to contemporary theology is that he has refuted the false optimism characteristic of a great segment of Protestant liberalism, without falling into the anti-rationalism of the continental theologian Karl Barth, or the semi-fundamentalism of other dialectical theologians. Moreover, Niebuhr has extraordinary insight into human nature, especially the behavior of nations and social groups. He is keenly aware of the complexity of human motives and of the relations between morality and power. His theology is a persistent reminder of the reality of sin on every level of man's existence. These elements of Niebuhr's thinking helped me to recognize the illusions of a superficial optimism concerning human nature and the dangers of a false idealism. While I still believed in man's potential for good, Niebuhr made me realize his potential for evil as well. Moreover, Niebuhr helped me to recognize the complexity of man's social involvement and the glaring reality of collective evil." King, Jr., *Stride toward Freedom*, 99.

31. Martin Luther King, Jr., Qualifying Examination Answers, Theology of the Bible, November 2, 1953, in Carson et al., *Papers of Martin Luther King, Jr.*, vol. 2 (forthcoming).

32. King gave this sermon at First United Baptist Church in Lowell, Massachusetts, on April 12, 1953.

33. Martin Luther King, Jr., "A Comparison of the Conceptions of God in the Thinking of Paul Tillich and Henry Nelson Wieman" (Ph.D. dissertation, Boston University, 1955), in Carson et al., *Papers of Martin Luther King, Jr.*, vol. 2 (forthcoming).

34. King, Notes for "A Comparison of the Conceptions of God and the Thinking of Paul Tillich and Henry Nelson Wieman," February 4–May 22, 1953, Martin Luther King Papers, Mugar Library, Boston University, Box 107, Folder 28.

35. Martin Luther King, Jr., "A Comparison of the Conceptions," in Carson et al., *Papers of Martin Luther King, Jr.*, vol. 2 (forthcoming).

36. Ibid.

37. King, Sr., and Riley, *Daddy King*, 147.

38. A tape recording of the sermon at Detroit's Second Baptist Church on February 28, 1954, was preserved by the church's historical committee. The tape recording served as the basis for the transcription of "Rediscovering Lost Values" that appears in Carson et al., *Papers of Martin Luther King, Jr.*, vol. 2 (forthcoming).

39. King, "Rediscovering Lost Values," *Papers*, vol. 2 (forthcoming). The congregation's responses, which are indicated in italics and parentheses, have been retained in this lengthy quotation, but omitted in other quotations from this sermon. They are preserved in the complete transcription.

40. Ibid.

41. Ibid.

42. King alluded to the hymn "Oh God, Our Help in Ages Past."

43. King, "Rediscovering Lost Values," in Carson et al., *Papers of Martin Luther King, Jr.,* vol. 2 (forthcoming).

44. Martin Luther King, Jr., "Fragment of Application to Boston University," in Carson et al., *Papers of Martin Luther King, Jr.,* 1: 390.

45. See, for example, King, Jr., *Stride toward Freedom,* chapter 6, and Martin Luther King, Jr., *Strength to Love* (Philadelphia: Fortress Press), chapter 15.

46. Martin Luther King, Jr., "The Un-Christian Christian," *Ebony* 20 (August 1965), 76.

47. King, Jr., *Strength to Love* (Philadelphia: Fortress Press, 1963), 155.

NOTES ON CONTRIBUTORS

William L. Andrews is the Joyce and Elizabeth Hall Distinguished Professor of American Literature at the University of Kansas. He is the author of *To Tell a Free Story: The First Century of Afro-American Autobiography, 1760–1865* (1986) and the editor and co-editor of numerous scholarly books and anthologies on African-American literature and religion.

Randall K. Burkett is Associate Director of the W. E. B. Du Bois Institute for Afro-American Research at Harvard University. He is the author of *Garveyism as a Religious Movement* (1978) and the editor of *Black Redemption: Churchmen Speak for the Garvey Movement* (1978). Most recently, he has coedited, with Nancy H. Burkett and Henry Louis Gates, Jr., *Black Biography, 1790–1950: A Cumulative Index* (3 vols., 1991) and *Black Biographical Dictionaries, 1790–1950* (1991).

Clayborne Carson is Professor of History at Stanford University and the Editor and Director of the Martin Luther King, Jr., Papers Project. His first book, *In Struggle: SNCC and the Black Awakening of the 1960s*, won the Frederick Jackson Turner Prize of the Organization of American Historians in 1981.

Cheryl Townsend Gilkes is Associate Professor of African-American Studies and Sociology at Colby College and an ordained Baptist minister. Her articles on religion and African-American women have appeared in numerous anthologies and scholarly journals.

Vincent G. Harding, a scholar, teacher, and longtime justice and peace activist, is Professor of Religion and Social Transformation at the Iliff School of Theology in Denver. He was the first director of the Martin

Luther King, Jr., Memorial Center and a founder of the Institute of the Black World. He also served as senior academic advisor to the prize-winning PBS series "Eyes on the Prize." Two of his books are *There is a River* (1981) and *Hope and History* (1990).

Charles Joyner is a historian and folklorist whose book *Down by the Riverside: A South Carolina Slave Community* won the National University Press Book Award in 1987. He is presently Burroughs Distinguished Professor of Southern History and Culture at Coastal Carolina University.

Albert J. Raboteau was Henry W. Putnam Professor of Religion and chair of the Religion Department at Princeton University from 1987 through 1991, when he became Dean of the Graduate School at Princeton. His *Slave Religion: The 'Invisible Institution' in the Antebellum South* (1978) won the National Religious Book Award and the African Roots Award of the International African Institute.

Margaret Washington is Associate Professor of History at Cornell University. She is the author of *'A Peculiar People': Slave Religion and Community Culture among the Gullahs* (1988), which won the Sierra Prize of the Western Association of Women Historians. She is also editor of *The Narrative of Sojourner Truth, A Bondswoman of Olden Time* (1993) and the author of a forthcoming biography of Sojourner Truth.

INDEX

Adams, C. C., 148

Africa: Austin and, 137, 148–49; emigration to, 14; ethnic distinctions, 18–19; European colonialism, 88, 89; missions, 86–87, 148, 154n14; patriarchy, viii, 83, 87, 89; religion, 3, 4, 19, 20, 25–39 passim, 46n44, 66–72, 83, 86–87; secret societies, 66–72; women's roles in, 83. *See also individual tribes and places*

African Exports and Imports N.B.C., U.S.A., 149

African Methodist Episcopal (A.M.E.) Church, 7–8, 86, 116, 136; and biblical feminism, 99; missionaries of, 112; and slave revolts, 49–50; women leaders, 90, 92, 93, 94, 95, 103

African Methodist Episcopal Zion (A.M.E. Zion) Church, 100, 111, 125, 128

African roots and continuities, vii, ix; and African-European cultural confrontation, 80–89; cognitive ("grammatical") orientations, 37; community based on, viii, 58, 66–68, 71–72; creativity and, vii–viii, 36–37, 73–74; ethnic distinctions, 18–19; religious, 3, 4, 19, 20, 25–39 passim, 46n44, 66–72, 83, 86–87; and secret societies, 58, 66–72; and shouting, 70; slaves and, 3, 4, 5, 18–19, 20, 25–38 passim; and women's place, viii, 81, 83, 85–91

Afro-American Council, 124

Alexander, Lucretia, 8

Allen, Richard, 7–8, 99, 151

Allston, Robert F. W., 22, 25

A.M.E. church. *See* African Methodist Episcopal (A.M.E.) Church

American Freedman's Inquiry Commission, 57

American Missionary Association, 58

American National Baptist Convention (A.N.B.C.), 90, 100–101, 155n29

Ames, Mary, 60

Ancestor beliefs, 48, 86

Andrew, James, 50

Andrews, William L., viii–ix, 111–33, 179

Angolas, as slaves, 19

Anthony, Susan B., 101

Ashanti, religion, 30, 46n44

Association for the Study of Negro Life and History, 144, 146

Associations: Austin and, 135, 137, 143–53, 157n46; black societies, 55–58, 64–71; missionary, 2–3, 57, 58; NAACP, 125, 137, 146–48, 161, 174n10; praise houses, 55–56, 61–74; secret societies, 58, 67–72, 86, 88; Walters and, 124–25; women's, 94, 95, 138–39. *See also* Church conventions

Augustine, Saint, 132–33

Austin, Junius Caesar, ix, 134, 136–58; and associations, 135, 137, 143–53, 157n46; and economics, 138, 141, 143–44, 153n12; and politics, 137, 140, 143–46, 149, 150–51

Compositor: Maple-Vail Book Mfg. Group
Text: 10/12 Baskerville
Display: Baskerville
Printer: Maple-Vail Book Mfg. Group
Binder: Maple-Vail Book Mfg. Group